ISACQ

A NOVEL

Peter Dreyer

Hardware River Press
Charlottesville, Virginia

Many characters in this novel were real people, but it is in every sense a work of fiction. Very little is actually known about the protagonist Johannes Augustinus Dreyer, alias Isacq d'Algué, before his arrival in South Africa. No resemblance whatsoever is intended here to anyone living—and only the most highly notional resemblance to the many other actual early modern characters portrayed.

Cover background: Hugo Schnars-Alquist (d. 1939), *Marinestück* (1906), cyanotype photographic seascape print, in the public domain in the United States and other jurisdictions; cover inset: Johann Georg Puschner (d. 1749), copperplate engraving, *Der Rauffende Student* (1725), in the public domain in the United States and other jurisdictions. Cover inset and title page ornament: Spanish baroque cupido head, artist unknown, property of Mary Dreyer, used by her kind permission.

Author photo on rear cover: Peter Dreyer at the Monument aux morts in the Salle des pas perdus at the Gare Saint-Lazare, Paris, April 2016. Photo by M.-R. Hendrikse, used by her kind permission.

Also by Peter Dreyer

A Beast in View. London: André Deutsch, 1969. A novel.

The Future of Treason. New York: Ballantine Books, 1973.

A Gardener Touched with Genius: The Life of Luther Burbank. New York: Coward, McCann & Geoghegan, 1975. Revised edition, Berkeley: University of California Press, 1985. New, expanded edition, Santa Rosa, CA: Luther Burbank Home & Gardens, 1993.

Martyrs and Fanatics: South Africa and Human Destiny. New York: Simon & Schuster; London: Secker & Warburg, 1980.

Trinity Sunday 1738

STROLLING on the mountainside through the May sunshine in a breeze cold as charity, I spotted my boy Olly Kromboom shamelessly pissing up a wall newly erected by the Illustrious Company. I'd only myself to blame. Olly must have been emboldened to it by the pair of tie-front Cassimeer breeches I'd given him just that morning.

Though *passé* in Europe, such garb is still reckoned "shanty"—*gentil*, that is to say—in Batavia, not to speak of here at its humble outlier, the Cape of Good Hope—and Storms. Sadly faded though they were from their long-ago yellow splendiferousness adorning TF's runnagado rump, Olly thought they made him look a bit of a *baas*. In days gone by, I'd worn those pantaloons myself, but I always felt foolish in them. They were ripped in the rear now, too: I was reminded of a beggar's butt I'd seen dissected by Magister Quellinus in the theater of anatomy at Rostock.

Treenigheds søndag . . . The Danish slipped into my head in Mutti's familiar voice, an echo of my raising up in that other, distant world. I wondered if she still lived and felt a solitary tear trickle down my cheek: it's a sad dog, after all, that does not weep at least a little for his widowed old mother, so many of her babies dead, and himself now lost to her too forever.

But had I got the date of *Trinitatis* right? With a moveable feast, one is easily confused, and the Reformed, who order everything here, figure such calendrifications differently from us Lutherans. Did it matter? It was a Sunday—and almost June. Another winter was nigh upon us.

One thick wedge of hand the color of Indian teak—missing the index finger, lopped off years ago in a fight with a band of Gorachouquas—propped Noll against the wall, while the other directed his prick at the brick. His stream splashed at close range back onto his naked toes, from which the nails curled out and down, thick as the claws of a *tierboskat* I'd seen hung up for sale at a Castle market stall that morning.

You wonder, perhaps: Did he buy the critter?

No. The meat of such libbards is far too wild for my liking. I was not tempted, though many Afrikaanders and even some Sooterkins (who have been here perhaps too long) say it's as good as mutton when roasted or boiled.

But such folk will eat lion too. Not me. The sea's my pantry: give me rather a nice bit of galjoen or snoek with some *stamppot* and a platter of well-browned onions.

"Hey!" Philander Witbooij teased. "Don'! *Meneer* Adriaan don' wan' it!" Philander is a free Baster oddjobber I employ. He was supposed to be whitewashing the goat pen.

"The Governor don' wan' it and I don' wan' it—so why don' you yus' take it for you!" Noll said, twisting his mug into a squint.

The two of them laughed like hyenas, showing the blackened stubs of their teeth.

"Confound it," said Joop Juinbol, who walked by my side. "His excellency deserves more respect from the likes of this scum!"

The fellow reeked nastily of *jenever* and was trying again to sell me a bit of land he claimed to own in the Gunjeman area, although I'd told him a hundred times I didn't want it, infested as it is with baboons (and the water there is *brak* too).

"Let 'em have their laugh," says I. "It don't do the Illustrious Company no harm, after all."

"You always stand up for the damned slaves, *Monsou* d'Algué," he gabbled.

Well, perhaps because I was once one myself, and all too well remember the feel of the lash on my shoulders, which yet show the marks!

But I responded simply: "As I think you well know I'm no *monsieur!*"

"But you've a French name, and you speak French! I heard you spouting it just the other day to Japie Marais."

My Ostsee accent in French would fool no one but an idiot. Matt Prior and Peter Motteux mocked it, calling me *peutit koquin.* Unable to vent my fury on those prodigious good friends, whose love I valued above . . . above . . . well, above whatever you please, I raged within. (In those days I did a lot of raging within.) Later in France, to dissimulate, I acted the Savoyard—not my idea, but TF's, who himself did likewise. It was easier for him, of course; he'd been a hussar in Victor Amadeus's cavalry and could speak the *lenga d'òc.*

"It may seem so to you," I said, "but my name is in fact not French at all."

Noll, who had noticed us standing there, came over.

"Baas Isacq," he said. "There's a boy drinking in the *kroeg,* name of Asahel van Malabaar. He belongs to Baas Laubscher."

"So?"

"I think he's doing a bolt."

"Then he's not bolted very far!"

"I mean, he is *planning* to."

"Let's go have a shufti at him then, Oliver Protector, my boy," I said.

We strolled over to the Red Gate. "That's him," said Noll, pointing at a man who didn't carry himself much like a slave.

"Ask him something," I said. "Ask him, like, who he is, where he's from."

And I made a small signal with my hand to Philander—who had tracked along with us, anything to avoid work—to get the ladder.

"Where you come from, Hodmadod?" Noll said in a conversational tone.

"I'm a Nasrani Jacobite," the bloke said conversationally, looking up aslant. He added in an undertone: "Satan fuck you!"

To my surprise, he delivered this malediction in Greek. Even more astonishing, I saw that he was the spitting image of the Prince-Elector George forty years ago. His mug was dark as a varnished old portrait, but he had the same starting arrogant eyes, which had once peered so angrily my way as I stood aside on the path through the Orangerie in Hannover. For a moment I could almost fancy myself back at the great palace of Herrenhausen.

"So what's a Nasrani Jacobite?" Juinbol said, stepping forward.

I stepped forward too, to catch a better look.

"It means" I said, "from Nazareth. Christ's twin—the one they call Doubting Thomas—preached in India. The Nazranis are descendants of his converts."

"Converts!" Juinbol sneered foolishly.

"He speaks Greek," I said. "Where could he have learned it? Do they teach the κοινή in Coromandel?"

Juinbol, of course, had no notion of what I was talking about.

Noll said: "Headed for the Hangklip caves to join those devils there, is it?"

Philander had already fetched the ladder from its place in the corner, and Pompey had stepped forward to play his part in their sport. For when a drunken sailor gets rambunctious at the Red Gate we "ladder" the bugger, trapping him between the two middle rungs of a set of steps before he knows what's happening, then double-timing him out the door and flipping him headfirst into the Fresh River horse pond. At Taki's in Algiers, where I learned this *truc*, it was into the pool of the inner harbor—right where the town's main sewer lets out.

Philander and Pompey were very adroit and comical in this play, which they loved to perform. Folk would come out to watch 'em trotting downslope with their victim, laughing and cheering, yelling good riddance to bad rubbish. I confess I always enjoyed it myself, and I must admit I have once or twice dealt with someone that way just for the fun of it.

"They are not devils who seek their freedom from the Company that enslaved them," Asahel said with some dignity. "Freedom!"

Juinbol leapt on the Nasrani, his face contorted with rage—the idiot had been working himself into a lather, as is the way with blowhards of that ilk.

Asahel must have panicked—no doubt it was indeed his plan to escape to the maroons who hide out in the False Bay caves. Philander later said that he had already drawn his little dag, but I did not see that myself. The whole thing happened very quickly, as such things so often do. The two hugged, brown and pink skins in a tangle. Juinbol yelled and staggered. Philander leapt onto Asahel's back and knocked the blade from his hand. A pair of observant boozers grabbed the Nasrani's arms and pinned him against a hogshead.

Noll knelt by Juinbol, from whose coat blood now gushed.

"Troppo baddo!" I muttered to myself—which is to say, "Very bad!" in the Lingua Franca familiarly spoken among runnagadoes and *yoldaşlar* in Algiers and the Levant.

"Are you stupid?" I said to the Nazrani.

"Yes," he said, civilly enough. "I'm stupid. Very stupid."

A long minute or two passed.

"The caffers are coming now," someone said.

And the slave gendarmes in their gray uniforms stalked in: tall Guinea blokes with scarred cheeks, but also a pair of Javanese and a pigtailed Chinaman from Macao. Kochoqua Kooitjie, the *meid* who keeps the kitchen and has been with me longer than almost anyone, must have sent for 'em. Their knopkieries and iron-hilted swords crowded the modest taproom.

I knew their provost—a Lübecker, Schuback by name, formerly of An der Trave No. 309, not that far from our family's old pile that had to be sold up in what they called a *Zwangsverkauf*—or forced sale—when I was just a babe in arms.

He said: "What's up, Old Isacq?"

"'s name's Asahel van Malabar. One of Niklaas Laubscher's boys at Oranjezicht—a Christian! He stuck Juinbol with his knife by accident from what I saw."

"Well, the *landrost* must decide that, not us," Schuback said, petting Bijou, the pub cat, the latest of a long succession of creatures of that name, cats and girls both. The critter rolled on the counter, flaunting her brindled belly.

Juinbol's agony lasted half a week; I could hears his screams in my garden, sixty stangs (poles or rods) from where he lay dying. And when Asahel was brought before the *landrost*, the outcome could scarcely be in doubt: he would die too, on Gallows Hill. Had he but done for one of his own kind, he might have been *sus per coll*, as the London lawyers put it—which is to say, *suspendu per collam*, hanged by the neck; but a slave who kills a master is ever broke alive, be it on the wheel or the cross.

Shortly after the trial—but before the breaking—Philander told me that a *tovenaar* named Mar Bartolomeo had come to see me. Since *tovenaar* means "sorcerer," I looked forward to being entertained with some magic, or at least conjuror's tricks. But Philander said, "He's just an old beggar man, Baas."

Dignified Mar Bartolomeo was, though, and plump. He was very short too—almost a midget. Was he a slave? If so, whose? No, his feet were shod; so not a slave. There are some free blacks here. They tend to live by themselves, away from the whites. Often they have slaves. Even some Hodmadods have slaves—the famous Goringhaicona Krotoa who was baptized "Eva" and married Peder Havgaard (a Dane, whose name the tin-eared Sooterkins changed to "Pieter van Meerhof" for some reason best known to themselves) had slaves, for example. My great good friend *Mãe* Ansiela, a slave herself before she was manumitted and became a rich widow, had slaves too—there were nine of them in Ma's *boedel* when it was sold off after she died—and to judge by their names, some of them had been plucked from the banks of the river Ganges like her too. Perhaps they were even her relatives! But it didn't seem to bother Ma.

The tiny *tovenaar*—what was it about him that reminded me of my father? they were nothing alike!—addressed me first in Portuguese, but though reputed a Linguist, I have never given tongue to that most sibilant of Rome's daughters. When he saw me stumped, the Mar switched to the Tiburtine, showing himself no slouch in it. Introducing himself as the *catholicos* of Kottarakara in Hind, he begged me to intercede with the magistrate on behalf of Asahel, who was, he said, his parishioner.

Not that he might be spared, of course, we both knew that was impossible, given his offense, but that on Gallows Hill he might be given the heart blow to shorten his suffering. The Mar felt responsible, he said—for it was he who had in fact sold Asahel to the Laubschers.

"Troppo baddo!" I said.

Only Acting Governor van den Henghel could order the stroke of grace: and since Daniël did not like or approve of me, or indeed give a damn what I thought about anything, he would scarcely grant any request I might make to that effect.

After cajoling a little in vain, Mar Bartolomeo went off, short and stately, looking like one of the Magi who came to adore the baby Jesus. One of the Three Kings—Caspar, wasn't it?—was from India, after all!

"Why did Asahel say he was a Jacobite?" I yelled after him as he trotted down the slope. "How the devil could there be a Pretenderist in a place like this? What would even be the point of it?"

The Mar made no answer, no doubt already too far away to know I was talking to him.

Later, Seigneur Blanckenberg—that is to say, Johannes Hendricus (not his dad, who had died fifteen years before), a man of great learning, secretary of the Orphan Chamber and a member of the Council of Justice, one of the few people with whom one can talk natural philosophy here—explained to me, that this was an entirely different sort of Jacobite from those I had known in Europe: for the Nazranis believe, not in the divine right of the Stuart monarchs of England and Scotland, but in the creed of Jacobus Baradaeus, a bishop of Edessa in Mesopotamia, who was what they call a Miaphysite, contending that God is one, not three—which makes sense to me, for why, after all, would God need to be three?

In my Dad's time, though, a grocer in Lübeck was burned alive lashed to a post in the Koberg for doubting the Trinity. They condemned him for an Atheist. All he had to do to save himself was keep his mouth shut, the poor fool! But he couldn't.

In the end, Asahel got his heart blow: Mar Bartolomeo must have found the influence he needed in higher places. Either that or the *Henker* just decided to deliver the mercy stroke himself on the spur of the moment. He has a certain liberty of action in these matters, being a pro, that handy Bavarian, trained at Nuremberg under a master executioner of the old school who could cut your head off before you even noticed it had happened.

It was never explained to me how Asahel came to be a slave, if a Christian he was, as he claimed. The court didn't believe it—though having spoken to Mar Bartolomeo, I do myself. Anyhow, I did not attend the execution. I had all too much of that sort of thing when I was tipstaff to the Stellenbosch *landrost*'s court and obliged to flaunt my thorn-tree-wood wand with its ferrule of filigreed silver, *ex officio*, at such doings.

I've seen enough men die to last me many a lifetime. I've watched cannonballs sewn into the pockets of a pair of *pœderastes* (mollies they call 'em in England) on board a

Company warship, one, a boy, weeping, the other, older, stone-faced, roped together, back to back, in a reverse wedding, to be slid overboard from a plank and drowned like puppies in the scrotum-tightening Benguela Current for their supposed offense against Great Creating Nature. For that is the law of the directors of the Illustrious Company, known to themselves and all the world as the Lords XVII, being as there are seventeen of them and all Gentlemen—and the law of God too, for does not Leviticus 20:13 tell us: "If a man also lie with mankind, as he lieth with a woman, both of them have committed an abomination: they shall surely be put to death; their blood shall be upon them." But I looked away as they were going under the wave. Truth is, I often look away at the last minute when someone is about to be turned off. I'm not what you'd call a tough guy!

Uncanny that, but for his blackness, Asahel should have looked so like the late king of England, long gone to meet his Maker. Or not so strange perhaps: as Godfrey William remarked once, men are born again all the time, that is the true meaning of the saying of Our Lord, "I am the resurrection and the life." You have only to look at the children everywhere springing up, their eyes so full of the very same hope we once hoped—exactly the same, you can see yourself in there—to know that this is true.

Uncanny that Asahel the Miaphysite should have done what he did on *Trinitatis*? It's all the sort of thing that makes you think there is some kind of jokey pattern, a secret rhyme to our lives. But you don't know what the meaning of it is! Godfrey William would have had some thoughts on the subject!

I am old now and it's too late for me to speculate about meanings, high or low. I can't get my head around them any more. And to think I used to be a gentleman and fancy myself a philosopher! I fear this Eden at the end of nowhere has coarsened me. I just take things as they come these days, like any other clodhopper.

For what it's worth on Judgment Day, though, I've promised myself to free Noll and his mother and a few of the others when I come to die. They don't know it, of course, because that's not the sort of thing a sensible man would tell even his most trusted slave: that he will be manumitted when Lucifer kicks the bucket over for you.

Who was it said, there's nothing happy or unhappy but thinking made it so? And they say the old are happier than the young because life's great battles are behind them, and they have their "experience" to fall back on; but I have come to realize that the happiness of the old is of an entirely different *kind* to the happiness of the young: there may be *more* of it, but it's not nearly as *tasty*. It's like wine grapes to crabapples; good though they be in scrumpy, neither port nor claret is to be had from crabs.

I am resolved anyhow to be happy in the days that remain to me.

I walked up the slope, skirting the Illustrious Company's Garden, to commiserate with young Laubscher and his *vrouw* on the loss of their man. It seemed the decent thing to do, and *Mevrouw* Laubscher is a cute thing, always worth a reconnoiter.

Their place was a chaos of squalling babies, some crawling about the floor in soiled breechclouts, a couple being nursed at the tit by Hodmadod maids, one infant even up on the sideboard slurping down a dish of thin water gruel without benefit of spoon.

One day, I thought, these Laubschers will make a mighty tribe! But then, so may our lot. My grandkids are already many.

"I knew your grandpa, as you know," I said. "'When I was young in Fräschels,' he always used to say to me, 'It was the old people's day. Now, it's the young people's day. What I want to know, Isacq, is when does my damn day come!' But he did very well for himself all the same."

"Where is Fräschels?" said Lizzie Laubscher to make conversation: she knew perfectly well, everyone knows everything about everybody here, there are so few palefaces here. We talk over the same old stuff again and again. I could say new things, of course, things new to them, that is, but then they wouldn't understand.

"You know. It's a village in the Üechtland," her husband said. "In what they call the Grosses Moos—the Grand Marais. Where my people came from."

"It's in Fribourg, in the Jura mountains," I said. "Well, now I'm an old man too, of course. It's you youngsters' day now, Jan. Sorry about that Asahel! He must have been worth . . . what, two hundred daalders?"

As I was leaving, I heard Jan saying to her: "He always tells that dumb story about grandpa! Can't the old fart come up with something new for a change?"

They don't realize how sharp my hearing still is sometimes.

Scraps of the old silver tree forest glittered scraggily on the mountainside. Too bad it was mostly cut down for firewood. But that was back in van Riebeeck's time and by men now dead, so who's to blame?

I booted a pinecone out of my path, which bounced merrily into the underbrush and made itself scarce. Those pines were foreign. They'd been brought here from Portugal. Now they were quickly replacing the lovely shimmering silver trees, which existed nowhere else on earth.

And so was I also a foreign thing here. An *Unkraut*, an alien weed! Ask me if I care!

Well, since you ask: Yes, I do.

But no one else does, certainly not the Afrikaanders springing up all round (just a touch browner than their Dutch fathers) who will surely take charge of things here one of these days. "I'm an Afrikaander. Even if you kill me, I won't go, I won't shut up," I heard a half-breed teenager yell at a Sooterkin *landrost* just the other day.

"Why," said Sarie, "do you always say 'Hodmadod,' my treasure, when all the world knows that 'Hottentots' is what they are called and Noll must surely have said 'Hotnot,' because that's what he always calls them? He has hated them ever since those bad Gorachouquas cut off his finger."

She was raised by Hodmadod maids and speaks their language perfectly, even to the clicks.

"*Some people* used to say 'Hodmadod' when I was young," I replied, "or 'Odmadod,' and I still prefer that name for those poor folk. True, nine in ten of them died of the pox just before I got here myself, as you know, so that I saw only their pitiful remnants, but 'Hodmadod' has a better ring to me than 'Hotnot' and seems to do 'em more honor. In any case, no one seems sure what they call themselves, aside, of course, from the names of the various clans, such as Gunjemans, Kochoquas, Odiquas, Churigriquas, Namaquas . . . and so on."

At least they can't be enslaved—the Gents XVII themselves have so decreed. Which is more than has been done in America, where those unhappy Redskins are only too likely to be shipped off to labor on some sugar island in the Caribbean among the Negroes on the slightest pretext.

It was cold, winter, and Sarah and I had pulled more than one old *kaross* on top of us and snuggled up together under the sheepskins.

"Well, in 1713, four in ten Honquequas, as they call us, also died of the pox. So it was hardly a good year for Honkies either!"

"And why do you call the Hollanders 'Sooterkins,' Isacq? You know they don't like it!"

"Why it's perfectly innocent. I can't see why they object! *Soetekijn* just means 'sweetie,' after all." But it is for some reason the choicest insult a Briton can apply to a Netherlander. And I am after all a denizened Briton.

"I still don't understand either why you want to change our family's name to a common vulgar name like D——, which sounds so much less well! I'd rather go on as Madame d'Algué! Besides, the children won't never agree!"

"They'll do what I tell 'em! D—— was the moniker I was born with and I hope to die with it, even though I suppose I might be entitled to a much grander one!"

"So," she sighed. "Anyhow, go on with your story about the old days in your Fatherland, my darling."

"Well, we were a respectable family, you see, living in Lemgo and Münster and thereabouts in Westphalia. One of our forefathers was a defrocked Augustinian, a pal of the Pope of Württemberg's, as they called Luther in those days, until our guy went too far, as we D——s tend to do, you know, it's in the blood, we are *weerbarstig*, which is to say, obstreperous, and became what they called a libertine—but that's another story.

"So our lot were on friendly terms with an Osnabrück family called Immelman, one of whose girls got herself knocked up by Count Johan Axelsson Oxenstierna, who represented the Swedes at the great peace conference that ended the war that in 1645 had gone on almost forever in the German lands, doing in half of everyone, and two-thirds of everyone in Bohemia— nowadays they call it 'the Thirty Years' War.'"

"So, well, this Johan Oxenstierna was a handsome young man, but a useless sot, always drunk by lunchtime, and so vainglorious he had himself sounded to the dinner table and to bed by his trumpeters. He was the son of the Lord High Chancellor of Sweden, Axel Gustafsson Oxenstierna af Södermöre and had himself previously been governor of Swedish Pomerania, where they used to scare the children to sleep in those times singing:

Bet', Kindlein, bet!
Morgen kommt der Schwed'!
Morgen kommt der *Oxenstern,*
der wird die Kindlein beten lehrn!

Which means, since you don't know the German tongue: 'Pray, infant, pray! Tomorrow comes the Swede! Tomorrow comes *Oxenstierna,* who will teach you kids how to pray!' For in those days the Swedes were the terror of the north lands, not that they're all that peace-loving now."

I modestly forbore to mention that Axel Oxenstierna *père,* the lullaby's bogeyman, had gone to Rostock University, just like me—but the name of our alma mater wouldn't have impressed Sarie in any case; she'd never heard of it—nor of Oxford and Cambridge or the Sorbonne or any such famous college for that matter.

"And it was this Johan Oxenstierna, son of the great Oxenstierna, who made pregnant Elseke. Of course he couldn't marry her, because he was married already and loved his wife too, the darling, who was there in Osnabrück with him, though she died the following year. Would you believe it, Axel Oxenstierna would not even allow his son to accompany her body home—and he really wanted to get out of Osnabrück too, a terrible dump he thought it. So the two families got together and arranged for poor Elseke to marry a man they called Johansen, who was himself a *Findelkind,* or foundling, given into the care of Hinrich Tornarius, guild master of the woolen-drapers, who was almost certainly himself the actual father of the alleged foundling and so was no doubt simply taking his own son into his house but not admitting it. And this Johansen, the *Findelkind,* was my great-great grandfather. So you see, we are also descended from that great Swedish noble family of Oxenstierna, the heirs of Bengt Jönsson, who was regent of Sweden long time ago. By rights I should put ox horns on my *wapen,* don't you think?"

And I couldn't resist teasing the poor old girl: "Or would that make people suppose me to be a cuckold?"

"But what if the *Findelkind* really *was* a foundling?"

"In that case we are descended from an unknown nobody, the son of nobody. What a good joke that would be!"

"And what happened to the baby Oxenstierna got on Elseke?"

"Oh, it died in its crib of a strangulation—what the French call a *diphtérite*," I said [*but Pierre Bretonneau will actually only name it that in 1826, a spirit backstage observes*].

"And if it died in its crib, how are you descended from the Oxenstiernas? It doesn't make sense!"

"We are descended from them, my darling," I said pettishly, because it was not the first time I had explained this to her, "by what is called 'infection of the germ.' Aristotle explains it so clearly. The imprint of a previous sire remains on the womb of the female and is transferred to the *poupons* of his successor. It's a well-known fact, often observed in animals. It's even in the Bible. Don't believe me? Here, I'll show you."

I grabbed the tinderbox and lit the candle that stood on the bedside table. Taking down the great Bible I had bought at an auction, almost new, from its little stand, I paged to Genesis 38:8 and read in the flickering yellow light:

"And Er, Judah's firstborn, was wicked in the sight of the Lord; and the Lord slew him.

"And Judah said unto Onan, Go in unto thy brother's wife, and marry her, and raise up seed to thy brother.

"And Onan knew that the seed should not be his; and it came to pass, when he went in unto his brother's wife, that he spilled it on the ground, lest that he should give seed to his brother.

"And the thing which he did displeased the Lord, wherefore he slew him also."

I impressed even myself by coming up with this so quickly.

"And as Mr Hume observes—not the Scotch Socinian David Hume, but Bill Hume, the vicar of Tavistock and Milton

Abbot in Devon, a man I once knew, but that's another story, which I won't tell you now—by parity of reason, many similar cases may be derived. We are, in a nutshell, the relatives of the Swedish Oxenstiernas by *telegony* as natural philosophers put it," I said [*but Weismann only coined that term in 1892 the ghost backstage gibbers*].

"Anyway," I went on, "I was told the whole tale by Thomas Frederik when we were traveling through France that time. He said he heard it from my second cousin Johann Heinrich D——, who later became mayor of Lübeck: I've got a medal with his portrait on it someplace."

"And we all know what a great truth-teller Thomas Frederik was!" she said.

She had never met TF, of course, but she had heard my yarns many times. When you have been married for so many years, there's never anything new to relate to the other under the *kaross*. But she liked to have them served up on a cold winter's night.

I remembered TF saying: "The Lord slew Onan for being a selfish sod and not doing right by his ancestors. Old women of both sexes may suppose that it was for gaspillating his *Säuglingsosze*, something all men do, of course, even kings and cardinals. But that had nothing whatsoever to do with God offing him. God would surely never waste a guy for something like that, or we'd all be dead, the Pope of Rome included, who undoubtedly does it in his great gilded bed in the Vatican! Sure he does!"

"That," I said, "is what the French call *obscénité*: indecent lewdness. What would our uncle say if he heard you go on in such fashion!"

"The French may call it what they like, and old Augie may say what he wishes. I am an honest *Landsknecht* and I say what I like—and what everyone knows too, call it ruvid. The fact is, the Lord realized—because He realizes *everything*, of course—and had always realized, that Onan was holding out for a virgin. Because if he jumped Er's widow, like his dad had told him to do, the *poupons* would be Er's, not his, and Onan, lad that he was, wanted kids he could call his own. But the Almighty had plans for the tribe of Judah, had had 'em since the beginning of time (if time ever began), and He wasn't going to have some self-centered little lordling like Onan get in the way of His creating the Hebrew Nation!"

"But perhaps it would be better if that bad nation had never been created," Sara opined, after I had exposed TF's argument to her in politer terms than he used, though he had a way with words that Shakespeare or Grimmelshausen would not have despised. "Or so *Dominee* Wessels says."

"Wessels knows that he is a *dominee*, sweetie, but that's about all he knows! And in any case, he's a Calvinist. Your own dear husband lying here beside you in this bed (and with his tarse getting stiff again too as a result of the present conversation) is a thousand times the theologian that Wessels is, being a graduate of the University of Rostock, one of the oldest universities in the world! Why, some of my best friends have been Jews, and I should have been sorry indeed if they had never existed. I remember one bloke . . . But see now, you've distracted me from my story about our family history with all this talk about the *onanitischer Sünde*! Let's get this straight: Onan's sin wasn't tossing off, which is perfectly natural: you can see baboons doing it on the mountain, and I've heard that elephants jerk themselves off with their trunks, too, although I admit I've never actually witnessed that myself. No, the *onanitischer Sünde* was much, much worse than that: it was disobeying Levirate law and not doing what Jehovah wanted him to do, and which would have spoiled the Lord's plans for this best of all possible worlds, which is far beyond the ability of any human creature to understand. Godfrey William explains in his book *Theodicy*—I have it in my chest over there [*and have been meaning all these years to finish reading, I thought, but naturally did not say—but I'll get round to it before I pop my clogs]."*

I minced no words with Sarie, nor she with me. We spoke freely, *à la bonne franquette*, in the old Frankish manner, as La Fontaine puts it, such as was customary among the German peoples for almost thirteen centuries after the Romans packed it in. In those days (I mean in what professors of history would one day call the *Frühe Neuzeit*, or "early new era"), it was still the rule to call a spade a spade. The glutinous mutation in human conversation that was to spread like treacle over the long century after Waterloo had scarcely begun to make itself felt.

"But how can this possibly be the best of all possible worlds," said Sarie. "Go tell that to your Hodmadods—I mean Hottentots—dying of the pox and the measles in their hutments in the bush, or to the slave women that fester in that nasty barracoon that the Illustrious Company maintains downtown!"

"My darling, Godfrey William does not mean that *this* is the best of all possible worlds for *everyone*. After all, the Hodmadods in the bush and the slaves in the Company's brothel—to name it for what it is, and very needful it is too, alas—live in quite *different* worlds. No, it is simply that *this* is the best of all possible worlds for *us*, fortunate creatures that we are, you and I. What you must realize is that there are only a limited number of human monads that are mutually real at any given time and actually inhabit the same world simultaneously—probably just a few hundred. All the rest are mere figments, no matter how many billions (to use Mr Locke's new term for a million of millions) of them there may be. They don't really exist for *us*, that is, in the same supersensible sense that you exist for me, and I for you, my dear, though they may perfectly well exist in *other* worlds, perfectly good worlds in their own way, that are indeed the best for them, they being whatever they are."

"And what if, conversely, as I suppose it's fair to presume," she said saucily, "we are in turn mere figments to them, our figments?"

"No doubt we are! No doubt we are! But why should we begrudge 'em that? They need their figments just as we need ours."

We at this point by unspoken mutual consent let staunch this flow of crap—for both she and I knew full well that we were talking metaphysical *Dudeldidel*. Godfrey William himself would have made short work of such argument, although I have often heard self-styled philosophers in London coffeehouses rambling on in similar fashion, without making a scrap of what an honest *adelborst* would consider sense.

The fact is, we had better things to do. How can I put it? The Word became flesh and made his dwelling among us (John 1:14). The nature of the monad is both mechanical and spiritual! Ain't that the truth! To put it philosophically, it's all a matter of your *conatus*—your endeavor.

"I'm sorry, my treasure," Sarie said afterwards, as we lay back sighing. "I really didn't mean to interrupt your story."

I rolled over and began caressing her lovely breasts, taking pleasure in the thought that their large roundness ran quite counter to my youthful tastes.

"Hodmadod females often give suck to their chits on their backs," she murmured scantly apropos. "Many's the time I've seen them do it on the farm."

[*"Her Breasts are so long, that she can toss the Nipples to the Child over her Shoulders," disquisits Peter Kolb. "When it cries on her Back, she gives one of 'em a Toss, and over it goes: The Child catches it in its Mouth, and sucks, without once losing Hold, till 'tis fill'd. . . . She is generally smoking Dacha while she has the Child at her Back. . . .'Tis very diverting to see the Child, when 'tis Caseharden'd, envelop'd in a Cloud of Smoak."*]

"But a modish girl can't do that, now can she?" says Sarie. "Not even if she wanted to, which she wouldn't, would she? Or at any rate, not if she was wearing a nice mantua!"

Laia's and Zippie's were small and perky, and make no mistake, I adored them and thought I could like no other style—had felt that way long as I could remember. When I first came here I gaped with lust at the half-grown Hodmadod girls that walked about showing them off. But such is the power of love—don't ever underestimate it!—my dear little country wife had now plumb converted me to her own fashion—and like converts everywhere, I was wild about it and wanted nothing better. Needless to say, Novalis—wasn't it him who did it?—hadn't invented romanticism yet, but I was already head over heels *fleur bleue:* a born romantic.

"I get them from the Helm side of the family," she said. "You should have seen Auntie Hendrina's!"

"So to get on with my tale," I said, still stroking, but now a little mechanically, "my father became *designatus pastor primarius* in the village of Grube in Holstein, as you know, and my mother was the daughter of his predecessor, a Dane. There was a great shortage of clergyman at that time. For some reason, a lot of them had died—fully almost half of the pastors in Denmark— and also in Holstein and Schleswig—dropped off the twig in my Daddy's time, so he said. I suppose he must have found a place for himself more easily given the general dearth of 'em."

"What did all the poor *dominees* die of?"

"Well, you don't realize, my darling, because you are an Afrikaander born and you've never been there, but Europe is very unhealthy, not like the *Kaapse Vlek* here. There's always sickness of one kind or other in those countries. They don't have the Cape Doctor, you know, the wind that blows in from the False Bay, to sweep away the evil humors. I suppose many of those holy men died of the plague and the small pox—and some even of venereal Syphilis, the great English pox (though the English call it 'the French disease'), pastors though they were—and of the sweating sickness and bloody flux, that's a nasty one! Or their lungs were rotted by the White Plague. That probably did in many a black-robed, white-banded pastor."

How could I say that when my dear, infuriating old Dad, who had me down on my knees praying before I could walk or properly talk, and would never forgive me for not being ordained, like him, a black-robed, white-banded pastor of the Evangelical Lutheran Church, had fallen to just that White Plague, or Consumption, younger than I was now when he was stricken with it? He had never got nearly as old as me but perished in Grube in 1708. It was during the coldest winter anyone could remember. Fish froze to death in their streams. Farm animals froze to death in their barns. Birds dropped stone dead from the heavens. The firewood was frozen so hard it would not burn; and bread had to be cut with an axe.

And I, his youngest living son, was on the run, and not only from the Rostocker *Stadtpolizei*—the *Boren*, as they call them, though where in the world they get that word I don't know—but from the *Polizei* of many jurisdictions. The king of Prussia was even then trying to get an agreement among his royal cousins to repatriate the likes of me to face justice. For kings detest duelists—and you can see why if you think about it.

Since that time things have gone pretty well with me, in fact—but somewhat badly too on the other hand. Resemblances are lame, and do not run upon all four feet, as the saying goes: *Similitudo non currit quatuor pedibus.* I have assembled these reflections, not only for my own amusement, but—if I may borrow a phrase from Fulbecke in his *Pandects*—to purge with a clyster of ink the black jaundice that besets my innards.

A Whale of a Time

"WHAT'S that then?" Johann Augustinus asked his brother. It was November 28, 1708: *Mittwoch*, as we Germans call it, the middle of the week—*videlicet*, Wednesday.

"They call it the Wasserkunst, Hänschen," Berendt Jacob said. "It's the city waterworks. They're very proud of it, see. It's, like, a dodecahedron, got twelve corners. Centuries old it is."

"It's the most famous twelve-cornered thing in Wismar—when the great *dodécagone* himself isn't in town," their cousin Thomas Frederik said.

"Be careful how you speak of the king of Sweden, Tommi," Berendt said. "You're not in a *Reichsstadt* now; this here is part of the empire of the Swedes. His Majesty might take offense at your mockery."

"A pox on his polygonal empire!" said TF.

Showing off my Rostock learning, I wisecracked: "What does it matter to us whether it be square, triangular, or twelve-cornered!" And thinking myself very witty, I as usual took the joke a tad too far: "Or of whatever geometric shape—a cubical empire would be a fine thing indeed, would it not?"

"It'd be poxy bad for you lads if one of those *drabanters* over there were to hear you," said Berendt, nodding in the direction of a pair of Swedish guardsmen strolling through the square. "They'd cut you to ribbons in a minute just for the hell of it. For they are trained to butcher fellows like you with cold steel. *Blanka vapen!* Such is the Swedish taste for it, I hear that King Carel even makes his dragoons hand in their pistols before a battle: he wants 'em to use their sabers to cut the enemy to bits, not take pot shots at 'em."

"Speak of the Vasa!" said Thomas Frederik.

Behind the pair of guardsmen through a gateway came an array of massively bewigged gentry, five or six of them, flanking a tallish, slim, wigless figure in a blue velvet coat and buff vest, suede deerskin breeches, and black cravat; his reddish brown hair, cut *en brosse*, sticking up every which way above the broad cupola of his brow. The light fell so that even at a distance it seemed one could catch the deep blue flash of his eyes. He limped a bit.

It was the famous king of Sweden himself, Carel XII, the boy wonder.

Or, I wonder now, was it *really?* Perhaps we were mistaken. What, after all, could Carel have been doing there in Wismar in the fall of 1708? He was supposed to be at Minsk or somewhere on the Borysthenes (the "Dnieper" they call it now) with his army. Was I was remembering some other occasion?

Hovering in a *dwaal* (as we say at the Cabo) past an establishment that called itself the "Alte Schwede" in the Wismarer Marktplatz, I gazed bemusedly at the neighboring "Euroshop" and "Commerzbank" . . . elsewhere in this dream, huge, nightmarish Swedish officers' heads thrust up from the very ground.

TF was jabbing at my shoulder with his knuckle, saying, "Wakey, wakey, kid!"

"Schwedenköpfe!" I stammered. "Aaagh, the Swede heads!"

But could I not have seen Carel sometime in Lübeck perhaps? The past gets so mixed up with the future when you're old, and I won't deny that I've lately taken a *sacré coup de vieux*, as the French say: an unholy smack of old age. No, probably Carel had come to Wismar to meet Haersolte van Cranenberg, the envoy of the Sea Powers, Great Britain and the Dutch. They'd wanted Carel to make peace with the Muscovites and help them beat the French.

But no, no, I think I actually saw him in 1706 at midsummer in Karlskrona when my father took me there on some Church business of his.

"Look," said Berendt. "Look and remember. Carel's a great man—a hero, like Caesar or Alexander. No one else like him. You won't set eyes on his like again!"

In which he was wrong, for I would one day see Marlborough, who never fought a battle he didn't win and never besieged a fortress he did not take, as they used to say, *and* Prince Eugène of Savoy sitting together in the same room shoulder to shoulder, arms around each other.

"He wears no wig," I said.

"Never wears one," said TF. "Stifles the brain, he reckons. He prefers to ravage his tsarish Majesty's domains bare-domed. He's right too—filthy habit, wig-wearing. Bloody French fashion. Louis the Just started it."

"Louis the Just?"

"Louis XIII. Father of Louis XIV. Drove out the Calvinists at La Rochelle, which is why half Berlin speaks French now and we have Huguenots even in Pomerania. A soldier king, true, but a lot less sharp than that flat-faced fellow over there when it comes to tactics."

"You do run on, Thomas!" Berendt said, exasperated. "What do you know about tactics?"

"Can't help it. I've got the gift of the gab. And I've been in enough battles to know something of war."

"I need a drink," Berendt said. "I can't stomach your Nedersaksisch *baragouin* sober, not with those Rostock rolled *r*'s. Why can't you talk like the rest of us, for Judas's sake!"

In a tavern called Zur Vorhölle (which means "Purgatory") on Alter Holzhafen Street, we settled in a pleasant corner and beer and sausage was served us by an azure-eyed Polabian maiden with amazing bright red lips—she must have recently smeared beetroot juice on them.

"God, I adore these Abotrite girls!" said TF, before she was out of earshot. "I really think they are the most beautiful in the world."

"More beautiful even than French ones?"

"Yes, more. Besides, the Abos know German."

Stanislaus, a Pole who had slipped in among us uninvited, interjected: "But it's Kashubian they speak."

"The language of love!"

The pub door creaked behind them and a pair of blue-coated corporals shouldered in.

"Speak of the Devil," Berendt muttered. "Here are some of his Kunglig Majestät's *drabanter*. All we needed! *Possunt, nec posse videntur.*"

"Excuse me?"

"They do the impossible. Their motto."

The *drabanter* had noticed them too.

"Greetings, *Schinkenfresser!*" one said, pivoting elegantly on a gleaming scabbard of chased bronze.

"Well, don't you eat gammon too, you Swedes?"

"Indeed, *they* eat it. But *we* are Muslims, sent here by our master Sultan Ahmed to learn the Swedish art of war from His Majesty King Carel's *Livgardet*. Turks and Swedes together we'll make a fine bonfire of the filthy Rus. Allahu Akbar!"

"Nasty smell it would make, indeed, what with all that hair the Russians sprout, *Knoblauchfresser!* Want some sausage, garlic gobbler?"

"We eat our own, but not those you are munching, made of pig flesh, which is repugnant to us," said the Turk.

"And where have you been living? It's been at least ten years since Tsar Peter made pilgarlics of his boyars," said his mate. "Bald as coots they are now in Moscow!"

"They shave their beards and their heads too, it's the law, and wear wigs just like all you other pig-eaters," said the first.

"Well, then, to change the subject," said Berendt, who obviously thought it best changed, "Do you drink beer, noble Turks?"

"We do. And wine and spirits as well. It is not approved by the Mufti, but what else is one to drink in Europe? The water tastes weird here in Wismar, and we fear the bloody flux, which kills more men than bullets can."

"Funny, you don't look a bit like your common-or-garden Turks," TF said. True, both of them were blond as butter and gray-eyed. Their stark features looked to be carved out with an adze. And on their caps they wore silver badges bearing a death's head and crossbones.

"I am Attila and he is Ali. We are twin brothers, born in Üsküp on the bank of the Vardar. You have heard of it?" He chanted singsong:

> *Vardar akar lüle lüle*
> *Sesi de benzer bülbüle*

> Vardar's waters' purling
> Like the nightingale trilling

"So, then, Illyrians," Berendt said.

"Macedonians rather. The world-conquering Megalexandros himself, Alexander the Great, gave rise to our race. Our parents were Christians. Perhaps still are. But we had the good fortune to be taken up as boys in the *devşirme*, when the blood tax was collected, and thus we became janissaries," Attila said.

"Good fortune?"

"Indeed. Had it not been so, we should have spent out lives mucking out pigpens and gleaning stubble. As it is, in Adrianople, we are gentlemen, and here, seconded to the Swedish service by our master the Sultan, we live like lords. You know, of course, that a *drabant* private is the equal of an officer in any other Swedish regiment, and as corporals, we are like captains! And we get a captain's pay too."

"We have told you who we are," Ali interjected. "Who are you?"

"I'm on business—I'm with the Lübeck Schonenfahrer Guild," Berendt said. "And this is my little brother Hans, who swots up on theology at Rostock—that is, when he's not hanging about in bars or annoying the *Stadtpolizei*. And this is our cousin Thomas Frederik, a *Landsknecht* of renown currently seeking employment."

"If he is a veteran, he will have no trouble finding it here!" said Attila. "Carel is hiring for the war on the Rus. They'll take anyone except a Dane." And he quoted the common saying: "A Swede will not trust a Dane till hair grow in the palm of his hand."

"Ça fait branleur," I said. "They say hair on the palm means you're a wanker."

"Aren't we all!" said TF, laughing. "But we don't have hair on our palms."

"It seems uncertain whether it is the Swede or the Dane who is to have hairy palms to complete the prediction," Berendt said.

He and I thought it wiser not to mention that our mother (née Jensen) was Danish.

"So you Turks don't trust Danes either?" Thomas said.

"And by the way, Berendt Jacob, I don't annoy the *Boren* if I can help it," I said.

"Just funning, my boy. Just funning!" Berendt said. "But I know very well you students go around all duded up in the latest style, swords slung over your shoulders, even though it's not permitted, blowing tobacco smoke all over the place, *herbae nicotineae trahentes*—in short, getting up your elders' noses as youngsters have loved to do since Cain."

He cited Milton: "And when night/Darkens the streets, then wander forth the sons/Of Belial, flown with insolence and wine."

But in fact Berendt never knew a word of English. I was just recalling something Matt Prior liked to quote.

"Others may do so, not me."

"A *lutherscher Pastörchen* born to be," said TF. "A little Lutheran pastor. I swear he still has his maidenhead!"

The beetroot-lipped Abo came by with another lot of drinks. We were knocking back home-made Kashubian aquavit, fierce stuff distilled in the Hinter Pomeranian woods, with beer chasers. And there was a flagon of Burgundy on the table that somebody had ordered.

How many rounds was it now?

"O glorious Magdalene!" Thomas orated. "I can scarcely wait to taste your nectar."

I was embarrassed to see that my cousin was flirting with the creature—and she was flirting back too with her smiling eyes.

"Thomas, don't call her that! The *Magdalene* was present at both the Crucifixion and the Resurrection of Our Lord! What would Great-Uncle Francke say?" I whispered.

"Let the old bugger say what he likes." And he mockingly mimicked the voice of our uncle August Hermann Francke, professor of Greek and Oriental languages (*videlicet*, Hebrew and Syriac) at Halle: "Avoid unnecessary mirth. If others laugh at foolish jests and improper expressions, do not join with them." He laughed. "Did Our Lord laugh? No! Did He dance? No! Can one even imagine such a thing? No! So don't you go commit such abominations either."

"You should always remember, Thomas, that women have souls," Berendt said. "Our Lord suffered and died for them too, you know. They are not simply put here on earth to service the likes of wicked types like you."

Stanislaus cackled rudely: "Face it, cunt, this cunt's on a cunt hunt!"

"Adam, we may surely believe, was not risible before the Fall," said I, quoting Professor Quistorpius pretty much verbatim. "Laughter is a result of Original Sin."

"Crap!" said TF. "If that's the kind of rot the schoolmen teach you, they'd be better off spending their money on 'ores an' 'arquebuses, as my old horse sergeant used to remark."

As you may very well know, getting drunk on aquavit hits you suddenly. One moment you are sober; the next, as they say, shitfaced. I had had little real experience of it. I lived in the home of my docent at Rostock, Professor Quistorpius, who would have thundered down ("de Donner up den Kop fohren," as he put it in his quaint Mecklenburgish) like a yard of salted herring on such behavior. Besides, I couldn't afford it. Our father paid for my lodging and *Studium* and gave me only a pittance above that. So today, being a greenhorn, I was pissed before I knew it.

I was not so drunk, though, as to miss the fact that my relatives and the two Macedonian corporals were drunk too, and that Thomas and Attila were getting into a huff over the rights to the bright-lipped Abo and glaring daggers at each other.

There are two kinds of men in the world: the peaceful kind and killers. Luckily, the ratio is about 10:1 in favor of the innocent or there'd be nothing human left alive under heaven. To quote old Agur son of Jakeh: "There is a generation, whose teeth are as swords, and their jaw teeth as knives" (Proverbs 30:14).

Our Uncle Jacob (Berendt Jacob was named for him and for his brother, Uncle Berndt), who had been a *Landsknecht* in his day, once told me: "I never knew this, or which I was, until I served under the *gottorfischer* flag. Imagine my surprise when I found out that I was a killer myself! But I was a lovely lad in those days. To look at me, you would have thought the schmaltz wouldn't melt in my gob."

"What would have happened if you had been the other kind?"

"I would have done what so many did and aimed my musket to miss. In a cavalry action they waved their sabers about, you know, and rode around any old which way trying to avoid the enemy. Happily for them, the enemy dragoons were mostly trying to avoid them too."

"And you?"

"I slaughtered those holy innocents like geese, my boy. Chop! Chop! Slash! Although with the *arme blanche* the thrust has always defeated the slash. We had a great victory that day.

The duke himself spoke to me kindly afterwards and gave me a purse full of gold coin, which I handed over to your grandma, because she ran the family finances. The which she used to pay for my brother Berndt's *Licentia*. So he became a lawyer. I never got any part of his fees either—and I could have used some spare change from time to time."

Attila and Ali, I thought, were killers. You could tell. They had the same kind of cruel insouciance Uncle Jacob had had. Even as an old man, he'd smacked a sturdy beggar on the head in the middle of the Fischegrube and rammed his walking stick up the man's ragged arsehole until he screamed for mercy, causing old ladies out shopping for cod for their suppers to shudder and make themselves scarce.

I wonder which I am, I wondered. I think perhaps I'm a killer. I'd never aim to miss! But everyone probably thinks that about themselves. You can't know until you've been tested, can you? And if you are never tested, you'll never ever know. It'll be a mystery all your life.

"Let's get out of here before Thomas and this Turk murder each other," Berendt Jacob said, sotto voce.

"To your mother," TF said, looking at Attila. "Qu'elle a fait un pet à vingt ongles!" He tipped the last droplet of red wine in his glass onto his thumbnail and licked it off.

"What's he say?" Berendt Jacob asked.

"That the Turk's mom gave birth to a fart with twenty fingernails," I explained. "In French, you see, fingernails and toenails are all just *ongles*. They don't have separate words for the two."

"God Almighty help us!"

Attila pushed back his chair, stood up, and wacked TF across the chops hard with his fawn pigskin gauntlet. TF's nose trickled a thread of red.

TF stood up too and wiped his nose with the back of his hand.

"Tomorrow at dawn then on the Whale," Attila said briskly.

Ali stood up:

"Pistols or swords?"

"Oh, for fuck's sake!" Berendt Jacob said. "Is this really necessary?"

"What's the Whale?" TF said.

"The Walfisch island out in the Bucht. There's no garrison there now, so it's nice and quiet. A good place for you to die," Attila said. "Just ask one of the boatmen to take you over. Won't cost you more than a half groschen. You won't need the money when you're buried anyhow."

"Or *you* won't," said TF, suddenly seeming very sober. But still crazy, I thought—TF was a killer too.

"I never knew Turks fought duels," I said.

"You forget I am also captain in his Kunglig Majestät's Livgardet," Attila said. "You should be honored indeed to be fighting me—or whichever of us you draw."

"Me?"

"Well, of course, we'll fight you all three. The more the merrier! We'll bring along our pal Axel. He's always spoiling for a fight. We'll tell him you insulted King Carel. So, what's it to be, pistols or swords? On foot or on horseback?"

The Pole Stanislaus had disappeared.

"How about both?" said TF.

"Pistols, I think" said Berendt Jacob. "Pistols. On foot."

"Good," Ali said. "Axel's a crack shot. Of course, he is also good with a sabre, that goes without saying. But the sergeant has just got in some new Husqvarna flintlocks—virgins!—that we can borrow."

He meant us to be the depucelators of these infernal maidens, I realized with a shudder. A hemicrane migraine announced itself on the right side of my skull, and I was wracked with embarrassing borborigmi.

"How much more honorable it is to die upon a sword's point than to perish of a megrim," says Don Francisco de Quevedo, who, though bespectacled like me, fought a duel with the king of Spain's own fencing master and lived to write a parody of it. Was it he who said that life is a dream? No, it was not— although he wrote about dreams too. That author was Don Pedro Calderón de la Barca. It is quite possible, even likely, however, that before he was himself inexplicably imprisoned, Quevedo saw Calderón's play *La vida es sueño*, about a man in prison whose only crime is to have been born, and whose father tells him he is dreaming. I learned these things in conversation with Don Felix Pacheco, a philosopher I met in Valladolid some years later. "No, no," said Don Felix, "Life is not a dream, life is struggle. ¡La vida es esfuerzo!"

The unanswerable questions, of course, always remain: Is life a dream? And, if so, who exactly is doing the dreaming? An *esfuerzo*? But then who is exerting himself? And can there not be effort in a dream? Or maybe dreamy efforts?

The night was long, but it was only too suddenly morning. A boatman had rowed us across through the fog, and we stood now on the Walfisch, all with hangovers, except for Berendt Jacob.

"What a sad excuse for an island," said Berendt Jacob.

Axel turned out to be a burly ash-blond Swede with a nose like an enormous cucumber. I recalled Slawkenbergius's disquisition on such organs and their meaning with respect to character.

An oboist from the Life Guards' band named Jacob Bach had also come along—to play something suitably solemn for us to murder one another by. It was the fashion in the Swedish Life Guards to have some music at duels, Attila explained.

Bach had brought along his instrument in a little black case. He was at the battle of Poltava the following year and, after the Swedes were thrashed there by Tsar Peter, he escaped with King Carel to Bender in Bessarabia. I believe he ended up a music master in Constantinople.

"We must all be mad," said Berendt Jacob. And to Axel: "What's this got to do with you anyway?"

"I act for my king. Honor of the *Livgardet!*" the tall Swede said with a grin. "Sorry to tell you, Attila—Sergeant Björnstjerna only had four pistols he could lend me. But luckily I myself have a pair of doglocks that belonged to my gramps, who apparently got them off a Bavarian he slew in the Thirty Years' War. How shall we arrange it."

"Load the weapons," said TF. "I and Johann and Berendt Jacob walk back twelve paces on our side. You and Ali and Attila walk back twelve paces on your side. We all turn when Bach begins to tootle and then fire at will. One shot only apiece, though, and honor is satisfied. Fair enough?"

"Fair enough," said Attila. He looked a bit pale despite his bravado. Or perhaps I was imagining it.

Each man faced his opposite. I faced Axel. Thomas faced Ali. Berendt Jacob faced Attila.

"Reculez!" Bach yelled softly.

We each turned and walked back twelve steps.

"My little brother Johann Sebastian composed this piece," Bach said. "It's an arrangement of the fugue from his Capriccio in B-flat major *sopra la lontananza del suo fratello dilettissimo*—which *fratello*, believe it or not, guys, was me myself! So, here goes and good luck to *tutti quanti*."

"I believe I heard that Johann Sebastian play it on the organ once," I said. "It was at an *Abendmusik* in the Marienkirche."

There was a long moment of silence. Then the *fuga all'imitazione della cornetta di postiglione* began with a terrible abruptness. I thought it a bit lugubrious.

I swiveled. I'd drawn for my gun one of the heavy old doglocks, which I now clutched clumsily before me. The fog swirled around me and my eyes had somehow filled with tears. Everything was a blur. I could hardly see the three figures in front of us. I wouldn't shoot, I decided. No doubt, I'd soon be dead. In a minute or so. I'd miss that Greek oral next week. Magister Quistorpius would be mightily pissed off, too, after all his coaching.

What would it be like to be dead? No doubt I'd be consigned first to the Purgatory from which yesternight's Zur Vorhölle tavern borrowed its name—if not to Hell proper! Could I already have earned a place in Hell? Me, Johannes Augustinus, baked meat for the devil!? Really? Hell, I was only eighteen. Or was it nineteen?

I heard the discharges of the others' weapons, each amazingly distinct. Bach's oboe continued to sound. Something sharp had struck my left ear, like a needle going in, and I staggered and half fell, involuntarily jerking at the trigger of the doglock as I did so.

Through the fog I saw Axel's tall figure crumple slowly, first to its knees, then face down in the loam.

I lunged forward, tripped and fell. Blood streamed warmly down my cheek from my ear and dripped into the turf. My spectacles had flown off and lay smashed in pieces on the shingle before me—though you would have thought that they'd be behind. My mother said they made me look distinguished.

"Hänschen, Hänschen," I heard TF shout. "You got him! You nailed Axel!" And then: "Oh, God! Fuck it! Berendt!"

I had, it seemed, shot Axel, although without meaning to do so. Attila meanwhile had murdered my brother Berendt. TF and Ali were by some miracle unscathed—Satan's spawn like them were not so easily killed off.

Leaned against a tree, I puked up my breakfast of beer and sausage.

"So. We'd better get the hell out of here," TF said.

[*How absolutely awful! So that's how you lost your earlobe, Sarie said, sitting upright in bed. So what did you do, Isacq, my love? I've never seen you wear spectacles! She'd heard the story many times before, of course. But she always liked to hear me tell these things—or pretended she did, the darling!*]

There lay poor Berendt Jacob shot clean through his brain. There lay Axel expiring in agony, with Attila saying heathenish prayers over him. I had hit the lad in the breast, a deadly shot, no fault of my own—that bullet must have had his name on it, as the *Landsknechten* say. At the same time, a kind of miracle had occurred, for from that moment on I found my eyesight so improved that to this day I can read even the smallest printed bookstaves and perceive distant objects with no difficulty. I have never replaced those spectacles broke on Whale Island.

"Quite the little sharpshooter, you are!" Ali said. "Plugged plumb in the heart! You and your cousin here would have done well indeed in the *Livgardet*. But I fear King Carel will want your bollocks on his *brännvinsbord*, my lad! You've just offed one of his favorite equerries!"

"*Coquin de sort!* What shitty luck!" said TF, shaking his head. "We need to get out of Wismar pronto!" But he loved this sort of thing really. I knew he did, the shit. He lived for drama, the richer the better.

And it was TF, as always, too, who knew what to do. A cog headed for Kiel with a load of Livonian pitch took us off from Wismar that very noon (stopping only at the Walfisch to collect poor Berendt Jacob's corpse) and carried us straight across the sea to Dahme—from where, of course, it's but a hop, skip, and jump to Grube.

Sea ice was already starting to form along the shore. It was as cold as . . . well, let's just say that winter bunnies froze to death in their burrows, and by February you could skate clear across the Kattegat from the Scaw to Sweden.

TF didn't want to go to Grube, though. "I'd just as soon go straight on to Kiel," he said. "I've got a whore there I really want to look in on. I'll catch you later in Lübeck though. Look for me at the Schokoladenhaus on the Koberg next Saturday."

"You bloody fucking bastard!" I said. "You don't really even care that Berendt's dead, do you?"

"Look, Hänschen. I know it's tough. But what can I say to your parents that you can't? And they wouldn't be pleased to see me. Your Dad never liked me, you know."

Realistically, that was true—my Dad detested him. And as it happened, it was just as well he didn't come back with me to my birthplace among the linden trees by the Jürgen-Kirche.

Pietas Hallensis

THERE was no carriage at Dahme for me to hire, but I borrowed a handcart from the son of the *Pächter* of the Meierhof, Nico Gribbohm, and trundled Berendt Jacob back in that by way of the country lanes, a melancholy homecoming; as indeed all our final homecomings must be, I thought.

[*"Don't talk like that, Jannie. It's bad luck!" Sarie said, snuggling up.*]

I got home in the late afternoon, with the winter sun setting redly over the Mare Balticum, and paused by the old *Pfarrhaus*, the former vicarage, built in 1569, which was used as a farm shed in my day. The Schleswig-Holsteinische Freilichtmuseum has it now; you can find it online, looking pretty spiffy—much better in fact than it did back then in 1708!

There I stood numbly gazing down at the shrouded body of my brother in that rough cart, bits of straw still sticking in the cracks. Tears came to my eyes, I'm not ashamed to say, though as you well know, Sarie, I'm not much of a one for tears. I didn't even cry when Baby Utricia died.

What could I tell my father and mother?

I put the cart with Berendt in the barn, where the chickens were already getting up on their roosts for the night, and walked over to the kitchen door, my boots crunching the gravel and a little breeze ruffling me, just like at the end of any other day.

I went in.

"My dear boy!" Great-Uncle Augie said, advancing toward me across the room with his arms extended in greeting, always a huge presence, though not a big man. "I'm so very sorry. Of course, you came at once. But how could the news have reached Rostock so quickly?"

"News?" I said stupidly. "What news, *Großonkel?*"

"One who dies as your father died, so full of sanctity, dies well," he said. "Wer so stirbt, der stirbt wohl. He is with Christ now. Although he had not attained his three score and ten, he was a good ripe old age—sixty-two, you know. Death comes to us all."

Dad, who had through carnal generation traduced to me, not only my physical body, but, as Tertullian tells us, my very soul and ψυχολογία, or "psychology," in Goclenius's coinage—was no more! "Has Thomas Hinrich been told yet?" I muttered stupidly.

"Word has been sent to him at Grömitz."

Our eldest brother, so different from me, or even from Berendt Jacob, was consistorial assessor and pastor there.

[*So your father was dead and could not help you in your trouble, Sarie said. Perhaps your mother could help? My poor mother was quite overcome, I said.*]

There was nothing for it. I had to tell Great-Uncle Augie about the duel and how I had killed a man.

"It was God's will," he said.

"Tell that to the Swedes! King Carel wants my ὄρχεις on his schnapps table, they say," I said, not without vainglory, alas.

"I'm sure his majesty wants no such thing! Notwithstanding his terrible reputation, he's no cannibal. But we must send you away, I fear. They will have put out a warrant on you, of course. Even my influence at the Prussian court wouldn't stop Carel from extraditing you if he chooses to. But where to send you? You could go to Gottfried at Hannover. But he's probably traveling in search of material for his Guelf *Scriptores*—the first volume of the *Historia Domus* appeared last year. Duke George Ludwig is so importunate about it and gives the poor dear man such a hard time! Pity! Gottfried could then have recommended you to Duke Anton Ulrich at Wolfenbüttel, who is his great friend. (Gottfried helps him with his novel writing.) And Anton Ulrich might then have sent you to his daughter Elisabeth Christine, of course, who has just married Archduke Karl, so she is queen of Spain— always provided the Austrians win this war they're having, of course. So in that way you could perhaps have entered the service of Archduke Karl—or rather, as he would be, if they won, His Most Catholic Majesty Carlos III! Why not! There's great need of German pastors in Catalonia to provide Guido von Starhemberg's brave lads with guidance. You've studied theology at Rostock. So you could perfectly well become a regimental chaplain."

"But no," he said, "it won't work, alas! Gottfried is in fact most unlikely to be in Hannover. He's probably in Munich or Vienna researching the history of George Ludwig's ancestors. Or pretending to. What a pity!"

"Perhaps I could seek him out in Munich? Or Vienna" I said hopefully, having always wanted to visit both cities.

"No, no. Won't do, won't do. Here's a good plan, though. We'll ship you off to London instead. I'll send you to Anton Böhme, a former student of mine at Halle who is now chaplain to Prince George of Denmark at the Lutheran Royal Chapel in St. James's Palace. The prince died in October of a consumption, of course—much mourned by his lady wife the Queen, they say—he was half a Dane, like you, don't you know, his mother was Duke George Ludwig's aunt. But never mind all that. Böhme'll take good care of you."

[*And thus it was, Sarie, that I went to England.*]

"Böhme translated my *Fußstapfen*, you know," said Uncle Augie. "The Society for Promoting Christian Knowledge published it in London. Perhaps he can find you work with them. Wait, I think I gave your father a copy of the SPCK translation. Pastor Johannes said he could read English." He gazed at the narrow bookshelf and plucked out a volume. "Here. Why don't you take it? It's no use to your poor old *Vati* now. And no one else will ever read it in this house."

Thus I got my very first English book, a book originally composed and written by my famous great-uncle himself: *Pietas Hallensis: Or, A Publick Demonstration of the Foot-steps of a Divine Being Yet in the World.*

"You are troubled, I think, my boy?"

"Uncle, my mind dwells on Axel, the poor Swedish trooper I killed. I saw him last night in my dreams, with such a nice smile on his face. We could have been friends, I think. There was an oboist at the duel playing Hannes Bach's *Capriccio on the Departure of the Beloved Brother.* Actually, the musician was the self-same brother himself, Jacob Bach, who is now in the Swedish service."

"When you mourn him, poor fellow, always remember the words of Matthew at the twenty-ninth verse in chapter eleven, where Our Lord says: 'Take my yoke upon you, and learn of me; for I am meek and lowly in heart: and ye shall find rest unto your souls.' It is there that you will find the cure for what ails you, Hänschen. It's pride and vainglory that makes us lament the dead, you know. And they don't thank us for it, the dead ones! So be humble. The Swede passed on by God's will. You were merely the instrument. One might almost say you had nothing to do with it! That Axel was taken up by God, if he was a good fellow, as you say he was, and he is with God now. Reflect on that. You'll feel the better for it, I assure you."

"And is that what I must teach Starhemberg's soldiers in Spain, Uncle?"

"It is—exactly!" Uncle Augie said. "Exactly that. Chapter and verse."

I did not, of course, reveal to my uncle that I had then for some months been an adherent of the Pythagorean doctrine of metempsychosis, or reincarnation, believing with Virgil that after drinking of the waters of Lethe, the virtuous dead are translated to a higher earthly estate and the wicked to a lower one, perhaps being reborn even as lice or other vermin. So I thought at least until Godfrey William corrected me afterwards at Herrenhausen: "Of what good would it be to you, Hans, to be reborn as a king in Arabia, if in the process everything that the Johannes Tornator *ici présent* represents must inevitably be obnubliated? . . . as though God created an Arabian king and in the same instant destroyed you, my *liebe* Hänschen!"

"I must go find mother," I said. "I've got to tell her about Berendt Jacob."

"No, no. You leave that to me," said Uncle Augie. "But do go into the village and roust up young Deacon Wincke. And tell Kuntz the gravedigger that his services are needed while you're about it. We must get poor Berendt in the ground before it freezes hard."

Media vita in morte sumus. In the midst of life we are in death. *Mytten wir ym leben synd mit dem todt umbfangen.*

Nothing at all, dear fellow future cadavers, that we can do about it, is there?

So I was placed on board of an English vessel at Hamburg, ticketed as Herr Abelard Oberhuber, a trader in woolens, but known speciously to the ship's captain as Hans Tornarius, my name having for safety's sake been plebianized and latinized after the style of our Westphalian ancestors. I was cabined in some discomfort since I was not a paying passenger but conveyed *gratis* as a favor to Pietas Hallensis (*videlicet*, my uncle).

Mr Böhme, a small plump man with nothing Bohemian in his looks, met me at the dockside in Gravesend after a nasty crossing. He lost no time, as we walked away from the wharf, in telling me of his charitable work with "Palatines," German refugees, numerous of whom had appeared in London on their way to the New World in consequence, not only of French ravaging of their native soil, but of the pyrrhic triumphs of the Allies under Marlborough and Prince Eugène. Meanwhile, they subsisted on Queen Anne's charity. "The worst of it is," said the court preacher, "that the poor folk fail to grasp that we live in a time of providential Judgment, which must be met, not with emigration, but with the uprooting of our inner sinfulness."

I knew how to answer that sort of thing. "Weeding out the wickedness from our souls is surely the sole purpose of our being born into this vale of lamentation," I replied.

"In any case," said Böhme, "these refugees are not *really* that persecuted in the Palatinate, you know. What they in truth want is to better themselves materially—they expect to find a land of milk and honey—but they don't understand their own impulses."

"So will they go to America?"

"The Trustees have a plan to resettle some of them at New Providence in the Bahamas, others in New York or Virginia, which evidently has almost limitless room for them—no one even seems to know how big that country actually is! It just goes on and on. I suppose, alas, they will contribute to the sum of worldly sinfulness by growing sugar and tobacco there. Meanwhile, I supply them with Bibles, New Testaments, Psalters, and devotional writings, the reward of which they will enjoy in glad eternity. Arndt's *True Christianity* seems the work likely to be most useful to them in the American wilderness— but your uncle's books are also very apt to the purpose."

"*Pietas Hallensis*," said I. "Surely that is just what is wanted by the Indians in the Bahamas and New York!"

"Quite, quite," said Böhme. "But the Indians are all dead now in the Bahamas. The pox killed 'em. It's black Negroes they've got there now. But to change the subject to more important things, might I ask, my son, since you have trained in theology, where you stand on the doctrine of the Ubiquity of Christ?"

A curious question, I supposed, to ask of a runaway duelist!

"I surely do not question the Christology of Luther! *Communicatio idiomatum* and all that. But then I have no theological ambitions," I said, a bit peevishly. "I wish to be a humanist, *artium studiosissimus investigator*, and make poetry of the universe. I've made some little progress in physics and hope one day to study that science at the feet of the greatest of mathematicians, Herr Leibniz, councilor to his Serene Highness at Hannover."

"Science! The Knowledge of Good and Evil, offspring of the 'Sacred, Wise, and Wisdom-giving' Tree that grew in Eden, as Mr Milton has it."

"Rather simply a matter admitting propositions proven by cause and effect, as Burgersdicius teaches."

"I don't know him well. A Dutch moral determinist, isn't he? Perhaps a bit Spinozaesque?"

"Rather the other way around: you might say that Spinoza was a Burgersdijckian," I said pettishly, and was immediately ashamed of myself.

"In any case, one may be both a natural philosopher *and* pious," Böhme said. "I must introduce you to my friend Mr Slare, who is not only a member of the Royal Society and the Royal College of Physicians but was a founder of both the Society for Promoting Christian Knowledge *and* the Society for the Propagation of the Gospel in Foreign Parts. Like your Uncle Augie and our Mr Addison, Mr Slare has also long been a correspondent of Mr Leibniz's, I believe, and is acquainted with both Sir Christopher Wren and Sir Isaac Newton. However, it is my own considered opinion that natural reason and wisdom stand in the way of salvation."

When we came to St. James's Palace after traveling a lengthy and arduous route through the streets of London, we entered by a back way through a very small door, and after passing through some grand rooms with tapestried walls, and then many stairs and passages, came to an attic containing a bed, table, and a chair and not much else: this was to be my domicile for the night.

"King Charles the First slept here in the palace just before he was decapitated, and the heart and bowels of Queen Mary—or 'Bloody Mary,' as she's called again nowadays—are interred in the Chapel Royal," Böhme said. "I must apologize for the bleakness of the apartment. But there might be a view of the park if one were to stand on that chair."

"Tomorrow," he added, "I'll take you to the German bookshop, where I think you might find employ. We may with luck find a more comfortable place for you to rest your head there too."

The German Bookshop, Cornhill, off Pope's Head Alley

IT was there we went on the morrow after breaking our fast on kippered Northumberland herrings and a cake of buttered pandemain, washed down each with a mug of small ale tapped from a little keg on a shelf by Mr Böhme's Irish manservant, the inevitable Paddy.

"Permit me to present Mr Johann Christian Jacobi, our bookseller and keeper of the Royal German Lutheran Chapel,"

Böhme said. "And here is his friend Mr Abraham Mackbeth, who supervises our *Englander* at Halle. And here is our friend Mr Steele, who was gentleman-waiter to *feu* Prince George. Well, I must go and speak with Mrs Rippchen about finding a bed for you. Mr Jacobi will show you the ropes here, so to speak." And off he bumbled.

The bookshop was a narrow space in Cornhill, off Pope's Head Alley, wedged between a goldsmith's and a stationer's; it had but few books, and fewer bookshelves. Not knowing what to say, I took down and examined a copy of Arndt's *True Christianity* in a Latin edition.

"There you have it, in the words of the excellent Arndt, *Wahres Christentum*: 'The whole economy of God towards man, and the whole duty of man towards God,'" Jacobi commented. He was a man about forty with a snaggletoothed henge of a smile. "But for a true Christian who understands such economy and duty, we need look no further than that saintly man Mr Böhme himself."

"So I understand you have just arrived from Hamburg," said Mackbeth. "I myself must once again face the German Ocean soon. I return to Halle tomorrow."

"I have," I said. "The crossing was a calm one, God be praised!"

"And do you stay?"

"Great-Uncle Francke suggested I might continue my studies at Morton's Academy here, but I haven't been there yet."

"Ah, yes, Morton's in Newington Green. Our dear hymnist Isaac Watts was matriculated there. And Sam Wesley. And Dan'l, of course, learned to chop the logic there at which he is so clever. We must certainly arrange for you to meet Dan'l. No way you could avoid him really. He's always dropping in to see Rippchen when he isn't on one of his 'journeys.'"

"The first thing I must do," I said, "is learn to speak English better. However, I have a talent for languages, I'm told, and I already know some Frisian, so it should not be that difficult for me."

"Don't ever tell that to an Englishman! He'll take it to mean that you think he's a Sooterkin, and you'll have another duel on your hands. They hate the Dutch worse than the French, I sometimes think. 'Froglanders' they call them."

"Or 'Hogen Mogens'!" said Mackbeth.

"Please?"

"'High Mightinesses.' In Dutch, you see, the Lords States-General claim the title of Haar Hoog Mogende d'Heeren Staeten-Generael, *videlicit*, Their High Mightinesses the Lords States-General."

"And what's a Sooterkin then?"

"Why that comes from the old Flemish word *soetekijn*, which is to say *Süßigkeit*, sweet thing, with the meaning of *dulcis amica*," Jacobi explained. "But ever since Admiral de Ruyter sailed up the Medway and burned their warships during the Second Anglo-Dutch War forty years ago, the English have chosen to confuse it with 'soot'—*das Sott*—and now they think it means some kind of dirty, filthy thing, like a rat—or a Dutchman. The Devil shits Dutchmen, they say."

"Especially when they fuddle their noses!" Mackbeth added.

"Please?"

"Get drunk and fall with their noses into their tankards—*se piquer du nez dans sa chope*. For they like more than anything to bowze—there's another British word for you to remember—their beer and claret! More even than playing at hazard and whoring, and those they certainly adore."

Learning English might be more difficult than I had thought.

"And the trouble is, you know, these islanders sometimes take *us* for Dutch."

"Good grief! But we're so totally different. Can't they tell a Calvinist from a Lutheran?"

"Their own 'Anglican' religion is more Calvinist than otherwise. Or so the professors say at Halle."

"Really? I always thought it was more Lutheran."

"Well, perhaps in the sense that as Luther wrote to Melanchthon, 'Be a sinner, and let your sins be strong—for there is no grace without abundant sin of which to repent.' The

English undoubtedly sin more boldly than any other nation! But Böhme teaches that it doesn't matter—or shouldn't. As long as a man is a Christian, and *acts* Christianly, why should we quibble over the particulars of his belief? Everyone has a different idea of these things."

"Come now," said Böhme when he returned. "On my recommendation, Mrs Rippchen has found room for you in her house, I am pleased to say."

Given her surname, I was astonished to find that Mrs Rippchen was an Englishwoman. We came upon her in her kitchen surrounded by her children (Maria, Hannah, Benjamin, and Daniel, the baby). She seemed to me quite simply the most beautiful creature I had ever seen, with the loveliest complexion imaginable—though she was doubtless middle-aged, about thirty or so, I guessed. But I was no judge of women's years!

Since I could not manage much English yet, we all three spoke in French, and the older children also joined in the conversation in that language.

"I was baptized Jane Melmoth," she explained. "People call me Jenny. My father Sir Menelaus Melmoth is a barrister at Lincoln's Inn. He is of the High Church party and busy in the Society . . . for Promoting Christian Knowledge, you know? He regards the theater as impious, utterly wicked, and so he does not accommodate well, alas, with my dear Rippchen, who when we were married against his wishes performed in the Queen's Theatre at Dorset Garden. I first saw him there in Mr Purcell's opera *The Fairy-Queen*. He was a falsettist, and he sang 'O let me weep'—do you know it? *Habillé en femme* as he was, I was most taken with him! He plays little part in the theatrical world now, because his voice changed. But my father still does not like him. They simply cannot agree about play-acting. My father is a perfect fanatic, I fear. For him the theater is part and parcel of the abominable heresies of the Church of Rome, as perpetrated by the 'bloody and wicked' house of Stuart."

"Mr Cutlett is engaged in diplomatic business these days," said Böhme. "He is a colleague of Mr Foe's."

"Mr Cutlett? Mr Foe?"

"Ah," said the lovely Jenny. "English people have much difficulty pronouncing the funny name 'Rippchen,' so it was simply translated by someone at Dorset Garden, I'm not sure how accurately. The tradespeople all call me 'Mrs Cutlett' now, you know," she said with a smile. "Indeed, everyone does!"

"And we are the little Cutletts," said Maria. "Nous sommes les petites Côtelettes."

Hannah and Benjamin chanted: "Cutletts! Cutletts! Cutletts!" They all danced about the table, while I gazed on amazed at this mysterious new wilderness of domesticity, to which I felt both very near and strange. It seemed to me I must have known that square-shaped, blue-figure teapot with the gilt handle all my life. I trembled with pleasant confusion, into which fragments of conversation filtered.

"And Mr Foe is the great Dan'l after whom little Dan'l here is named. He is our *genius*. You'll meet later, I have no doubt," said Böhme. "But where is Mr Cutlett?" he asked Jane.

"On the Continent, I think, but I don't know exactly where at this moment," Jenny said. "Perhaps at Hannover, watching over the Successor."

"Does the electress Sophia need watching, then? She must be very old—almost eighty, I think."

"That's right. No, she's impeccable! But perhaps just because she *is* so old, her son Prince-Elector George Ludwig needs to be kept in close view. Or at least Lord Godolphin thinks so, it seems."

"Well, if the High Treasurer of England thinks so, it must be so."

"Mr Leibniz, who is the dowager electress's special friend— she adores natural philosophy, you know—greatly admires

Mr Cutlett as a musician. And Cutlett is a Hessian, of course, and it seems that the Landgrave of Hesse-Kassel takes a great interest in Mr Leibniz's calculating machine. Why, you poor boy! You look about to swoon!"

I was completely at sea in all this. I simply gazed at the beautiful Mrs Cutlett, watching the movements of her lovely lips. In them, and in the incomprehensible, magical words that spilled from them, I seemed to glimpse, what was it? Divinity? The word seemed inadequate. Providence perhaps? I could not look away from her face—I tried. A powerful current of feeling moved restlessly up and down my body.

"I am enslaved," I thought. "How wonderful! I've always wanted to be and didn't know it until now. What joy to be her child! This is my fate, my wonderful fate. How fortunate I am." It was like suddenly, unexpectedly, being able to see the far side of the moon—impossible, of course, but it's nonetheless *there*, waiting for us.

I had fallen into an infatuation, it would appear. It happens, though whether for better or worse *je n'en sais rien*: I know nothing about it.

What could be better than to inhabit a small, clean sunny room in the home of the woman one loves? I could think of nothing—unless it was also to be married to that woman.

I was not that, and two days later, after looming at it for a moment, a very short man, shorter than has wife, but broad of shoulder and huge handed, pushed open a windowed door and abruptly entered the comfy *parlatorium* in which a young man was being given an English lesson by Jenny. It was, I immediately perceived, Ranulphus Rippchen, the legendary former Dorset Garden falsettist, alias Mr Cutlett.

Where had this accursed *Husband* been all this while? Not on the Continent by all accounts.

"I've been touring Norfolk with Master Bubb to sound out the fens for Jacobites," Cutlett explained. "And then I had to attend a tedious affair of Lady Middlesex's in behalf of Mr Inchiquin. All in all I've beem bery busy. Very busy. *Le tout pour la tripe.* All for the gut! I must put bread and cheese upon the table for you and my little ones. What else can I do now that my voice is buggered, God curse it?"

"Say no more thus, Rippchen! And I don't care for that sly Master Bubb," said Jenny. "No, I don't. Not one bit!"

"Dan'l thinks Bubb shows great promise. He knows the important thing in politics, which is to steer one's little barqie 'with the tide, but near the shore,' as Dan'l puts it so well, and will sit in the Commons one day." [*About eighteen years old at this time, Bubb would eventually rise as George Bubb Dodington to be first baron Melcombe Regis and the favorite of Frederick, Prince of Wales, whose life I once saved, too, you know, Sarie, though he never survived to be king.*] "And who is *this?*" he said, turning to me. "Pray introduce us, my dear."

"This is Mr Tornarius, a young protégé of Mr Böhme's, sent to us from Lübeck by his great-uncle. We are teaching him to speak English."

Rising, I greeted Mr Cutlett in German.

"None of that, please," said Jenny. "I don't speak a word of it, you know. Or at least very few words that I care to say in polite company."

"And I should for that matter have difficulty with your Lübsch," said Cutlett, much to my irritation.

I'm sure I don't come across in the least bit Lübsch, I thought, frowning inwardly, if one can suppose such a thing. But I probably did sound Lübschish, I see it now—as a *terrae filius* it's hard to escape the speech, and even more so the habit of mind, of one's native plot.

"You speak very good English," I said slowly in that tongue to Cutlett.

"And so shall you too, depend on it. You *must* do so. For there's nothing an Englishman likes less than a Dutchman or a

German, unless it be a Frenchman, Spaniard, Italian, Scotsman, or Paddy. It don't do to be a foreigner in England—Londoners drink perdition to the lot of 'em at every meal—and for that matter they consider all those to be foreigners who do not live in the City. So you had better learn to speak like a Cockney." He spread his chops in a pleasant grin and traced an elaborate bow to his wife. "My charming Jenny is an excellent teacher—indeed, she taught me. We may rely on her to have you up and chattering like one born within the sound of Bow-bell in no time at all."

"It's the accent that's difficult," his lady said. "So it was with you, my dear Rippchen."

"And when you speak it well enough, Tornarius, you must come into the country with Master Bubb and myself. There is much work to be done out there."

"But what is a 'Cockney'?" I begged to know.

"A Cockney, some say," said a melodious voice behind me, "is an eater of buttered toasts who believes that Christendom ends at Greenwich, a cockered dandiprat hopthumb ignorant of honest country matters; the term being a back-canting inversion of 'incock,' which is to say, *incoctus*, raw or unripe, scarce out of the egg. But others say that it comes from the French *coquin*, meaning an infamous creature *qui fait des bassesses indignes d'un homme de cœur*. The word is also used in France of dogs that fawn on their masters, thus, one might say, 'Ce chien est fort coquin.' And does that not perfectly describe the London *mobile vulgus*?"

"But there are cockneys of all climes," said Rippchen. "I have seen Scotch cockneys and many a Dutch one for sure. Your Sooterkin Dutchman is a natural kind of cockney. Indeed, they say there are even American cockneys to be found these days—Bubb claims that the entire population of Boston consists of cockneys! But what does that puppy know of it?"

"Look! Here is Mr Motteux!" said Jenny. "Cutlett sang in his opera *Love's Triumph* at the Queen's, you know, Mr Tornarius. We shall have Bohee tea! And Madeira cake from the beaufet!"

Barren Mountains!
Lonely Groves and weeping Fountains
Feed my Anguish,
While I languish!

Rippchen declaimed mockingly in a wailing falsetto. "Pietro Ottoboni could not have done worse himself. It ran for all of eight nights."

"Come, come, Cutlett!" exclaimed the newcomer, twitching off a scarlet cloak that seemed of dazzling newness. "Do you mock me?"

"Cod's body, Peter, I do not! If anyone is teased, it is Ottoboni, who wrote the sad thing in the first place. But your original certainly knows whereof to languish. He sires poupons by the dozen *en cachette* and has his whores painted as saints hung up in his bedchamber, they say. All that and Heaven's benison besides—a cardinal's hat he gets from his pontifical nuncle for his twenty-first birthday. Love's triumph left and right, I'd say! Still, Ottoboni patronizes Corelli and Vivaldi. We must do him honor for that." And he resumed singing:

Fly, fond Lovers! Fly to Pleasure!
Seize the Treasure,
And enjoy.

"Ah ha, sauceboxes!" the newcomer said to Hannah and Benjamin, running his fingers through their hair. "Smoke what I have in my pockets for you!"

"Indeed, but I have smoked it!" said Benjamin. "It's sugar-plums."

"Mr Motteux is too kind," said Jenny as he delicately dusted comfit crumbs from his fingers into the fire after distributing his gift to the small ones. And I could see at once from the look on his face that he was in love with her too.

"Let me then introduce you," she said. "Mr Hannes Tornarius, lately of Holstein in Germany: Mr Peter-Anthony Le Motteux, of Rouen in France, *jadis*."

"I came here in 1683, when I was just twenty-one," Motteux said. "I've been an English subject since '86—denizened by royal letters patent."

"And now you are a Briton," Rippchen said, smilingly yellowly. "For want of company, welcome trumpery."

"Pray don't call it Britain," Jenny Cutlett said. "I never will call it Britain. For the common Scotch never wanted Union. It was forced on them. Dan'l was there when it was done, he can tell you."

"Alas, m'dear," said Motteux. "It was *in*evitable. The Scotch and the Irish must be *made* English, just as the Bretons and Béarnaise are being *converted* into Frenchies. That's what they call 'Progress,' which you, Madame Whigissima, must surely approve."

I marveled that this handsome, outspoke man was over a quarter of a century my senior. You would not have thought it—he seemed so young.

"That a Huguenot such as I should have been so favored by the former King James—no loyal friend of the R.P.R., as they call our faith—is no doubt a wonder," Motteux said to me. "Well, I never could quite smoke the reason myself!"

"The R.P.R.?"

"The *religion prétendue reformée*—the 'so-called Reformed Religion.'"

"But wasn't King James a Protestant himself?"

"No, not even a *prétendu* one! That's why he was deposed and exiled, and why today his Anglican daughter, Queen Anne, sits on the throne and not his Catholic son, Jamie Blackbird."

"Forgive me. I am very ignorant of these matters. Why 'Blackbird'?"

"Well, he's a dark man, you know, dark hair, dark eyes, like his grandfather—the proudest, peremptoriest prick alive, as Lord Rochester puts it:

> Restless he rolls about from whore to whore,
> A merry monarch . . ."

"Who never said a foolish thing, and never did a wise one," Rippchen interjected. "But that was the grandpa."

"To further explain it, it was the late King Charles," said Motteux, "Furthermore, I have heard it said that the name Stuart comes, not from 'steward,' meaning 'guardian of the pigsties,' as Whigs uncivilly like to bandy about, but from *svartr*, which means black in the old Norse language, from which the Scotch tongue long ago took many vocables. Thus, for instance, the Scandiwegian marauders who settled in Scotland and Ireland called evil spirits *svartr alfr*, which is to say 'black elves.'"

This erudite discourse delighted me. Like me, Motteux was clearly a lover of old things and strange words.

"The papist Irish *mobile*," he went on, "are reported to call the striking together of weapons in battle 'blackbird music,' or 'blackbird speech,' and by some supposed correspondence of qualities, the Pretender is thus known in Jacobite cant as 'the Blackbird.' The Whigs took the name up—using it makes one seem 'political,' they fancy—and were imitated, of course, by hoi polloi. Now everyone and his brother says it."

"No reason for *us* to do what the mob does," said Cutlett.

"What puppies are mankind!" said Jenny. "The Pretender is the Queen's own half-brother, after all, not some Scythian tsar."

I was struck by how very British—I mean English!—this Huguenot Motteux and this Hessian Rippchen had become. They seemed as natural as life in their casual Londonish chat (albeit it was mostly in French), but I reckon their own mothers would scarcely have recognized them. Would my own mother, though, have recognized me? I imagined she was by now living at Grömitz, on the Bay of Lübeck, with the family of my respectable eldest brother, Thomas Heinrich, pastor and consistorial assessor of the town. Uncle Augie would have seen to it that she got there. He could always be relied on to take care of things. Or could she have gone to her cousin my aunt Grete in Ærøskøbing in Denmark, whom I never saw in my life, but was said to be rich as Etzel?

I stood there, vainglorious in my new English clothes, staring foolishly, no doubt. Was I perhaps even smiling? I could not tell and thus can't recall, but since Jenny was there, I must have been happy—and my mind caressed and toyed with the world of possibilities that seemed to open up to me.

Presently, I found myself walking down Leadenhall Street with Mr Motteux, and he invited me to lunch with him.

Miracles do happen, don't let anyone tell you otherwise. How fortunate I was to meet with such a band of fellow spirits as Peter Motteux and his pals! I do believe they were the greatest Conversationists the world ever saw since old Socrates and his symposiums.

[*And somehow they accepted me into their company, Sarie. I regularly dined at one house or other with poets and painters in those days. I even met Jos. Addison—Mr Spectator himself! But you won't know who he was. Qoth she a bit crossly: Oh, yes, I do too!*]

Having been denizened under King James in '86, Peter Motteux had been in England when the Glorious Revolution took place in '88 with the coming in of King William and Queen Mary. He told us about it one evening:

"Indeed, I had that privilege," he said. "I had gone to Dover on some business, and I watched from Dover Castle the mighty Dutch fleet—fifty men of war, twenty frigates, as many fire ships, and full four hundred transports, with thirteen thousand troops—sailing in square formation, twenty-five ships deep, the warships on the right and left simultaneously saluting Dover and Calais. The soldiers were all lined up on deck, firing musket volleys, flags flying and bands playing. My friend Paul de Rapin, who was on board, having enlisted in a company of Huguenot volunteers, has written that it was the most splendid sight ever seen by human peepers."

The Dutch had come ashore at Torbay in Devon. "Je maintiendrai," proclaimed William, and inscribed it on his banners: "I will maintain the liberties of England and the Protestant religion." James's chief commander, Marlborough, promptly went over to Billy with his army, and the game was up for Séamus *an chaca*—James the Shithead—as the Irish dubbed him after the famous battle of the Boyne.

"You were ungallant with the lovely Jenny this morning," Peter said to me as we took a postprandial stroll. "You scarce spoke a word to her." And he added: "I know of a first-rate bawdy house near here. Shall we drop in and visit the trulls?"

"I have never been with a whore, sir," I said.

"Well, there's a first time for everything."

"I'll not defend myself," I said.

"I must introduce you to my compatriot Falaiseau," he said. "He, like you, it seems, is indifferent to the ladies, though quite admirably mentulated [*by which he meant, of course, having a large Penis*]."

"It is rather that I like 'em too much, sir," I said. "Indeed, Jenny Rippchen seems to me the most wonderful being I ever saw. She's like a nymph out of Homer or . . . or Theocritus!"

"She Chloe, you Daphnis, eh? But she's merely a sensible Englishwoman, second only in that office perhaps to the divine Lady Mary Wortley Montagu, whom you must also meet! In a nutshell, the highest type of human creature to be found anyplace. The disgusting Rippchen is quite unworthy of her, of course, the brute."

"I shall become English then," I said. "And become worthy of her."

["*You talk too much about this Jenny, Jan,*" *said Sarie, to whom I had not even told the last few lines. Remember, I am your wife and the mother of your children.*]

"It takes money to play the gentleman in England," said Motteux. "You'll have to get some. But if all else fails—as observes Mr Prior, to whom I shall introduce you shortly—an ounce of arsenic can be had for ninepence—and should that be still too dear, a rope costs but three halfpence."

So saying, gaily enough, he led the way to Matthew Prior's house in Duke Street, Westminster, where the back door stood open to receive us. There I met that long-faced poet and diplomatist, of whose admirable conversation on this occasion I recall chiefly, alas, him complaining that the Kit-Catters had grown highly saucy again of late.

"Indeed, they have passed a resolution, I hear," said Peter, "that Matt Prior's travelling wig, having grown musty and cornigerous since his late visits to Paris, be demolished and burned by the public hangman."

"They resolved something similar of Harry Boyle before me," said Matt. "Their jokes grow stale. In truth, I don't fash my thumb that the Kit-Cat toasters mock me! They have hated me ever since I quit their club."

Matt was a Tory, needless to say, and the members of the Kit-Cat Club were a rabidly Whiggish clan. I did not understand these insular politics, but passions ran high, as passions of that sort will. He had not so much quit the club as been expelled from it.

"I fear there is nothing but roguery and double dealing in this world," said he. "Everyone is so busy inventing secrets, or detecting them, or giving them away. London has become a city of spies. Meanwhile, puppies like that fool Gropecunt T——walk about and do damage. I hope I may soon get a good *sine-cure* and retire to the country to grow cabbages!"

"For all his quarters, Lord T——is a mere *figmentum*," said Motteux.

"Peter believes, you see, that there are only a limited number of real people in the world, say a hundred or two, for each of us, and that all the rest are figmental, arbitrarily framed notions concerning empirical phenomena about whose reality there can be no certainty—those shadows, don't you know, on the wall of Plato's cave," Prior explained.

"As we are doubtless to 'em, if they actually exist, as I suppose they must do in some sense that we cannot comprehend," said Motteux. "I don't choose to pass judgment on that issue."

"But how do we know who are real?"

"We *know* them when we see them! Admit that we know it. Two minutes after I met Tornarius here, I said to myself, 'Ah, hah, here's a fellow Troglodyte, or I'll be damned!'"

"And so he has proven to be!"

Thus was paid to me by Mr Swift, who had but lately arrived and had not previously intruded himself into the conversation, perhaps the greatest Compliment I ever received.

"I feel a similar thing about places," Motteux continued. "You have your spots and routes, tunnels of space that you inhabit, *façon de parler*, with the nodes being the places you visit, spend time, use; and all the rest of the city or space around you has a lesser reality."

"I have always felt some of those new-made streets in Mayfair to be only dubiously actual," said Prior. "They have a ghostly air about 'em despite their fresh plaster."

I must remember, I thought, when the occasion presents itself, to interpolate *façon de parler* like that. Prior was famous for speaking the best French of any Englishman, which enabled him later to negotiate the Treaty of Utrecht, called "Matt's Peace," face to face with the Sun King himself at Versailles.

I surprised myself with boldness, asking: "And is Louis Baboon a figment?"

"I could never tell!" said Prior. "Sometimes he seemed remarkably real. But come, bannisons la mélancholie! Let's have a bottle or two, gentlemen. And what say you to a small tub of oysters?"

There followed now a year or more in which nothing very memorable happened to me that you might be interested to have reported. Mr Jacobi kindly undertook to employ me in the German Bookshop, but there was little for me to do there. Evidently, such Germans as there might be in London did not buy many books. And surprisingly, too, that did not trouble Mr Jacobi, who scarce seemed to care whether he sold any. So after some months, in spirit sore fatigued—one can only read so many sermons without sinking into acedia and wondering how painful it could *really* be to cut one's throat if one did it adroitly and without hesitation—I quit that post.

Subsequently, I was employed by the Society for the Propagation of the Gospel in Foreign Parts to translate into German—High Dutch, they called it—an account of its charter and founding. This did not mention that my pious employers owned a plantation in Barbados where their black slaves were branded with the word "Society" on their chests to hinder their escaping—although almost half of the wretches nevertheless managed to do so by simple dint of dying within three years of being brought to the island from their homes in Africa.

I only heard tell of that much later.

Mr Böhme then got me a post as teacher in a charity school of another society, the Society for Promoting Christian Knowledge, at St. Sepulchre's, Snow Hill. I was under Mr Pilcrow, the "dead master," as the witty boys liked to call him (but not to his face, of course, although sometimes to mine). Our brief, he informed me, was drawn from Genesis 18:19: to whit, "they shall keep the way of the Lord, to do justice and judgment." With this in mind, the charity boys were taught reading and writing and casting of accounts, while the charity girls sewed and worked in the school kitchens. All of them learned the Catechism, needless to remark, in which they were publicly examined after the Sunday evening sermon. My particular role was to teach Latin to some boys thought exceptional; my colleague the longanimous Mr Leatherbarrow taught them Greek with even less success, prescinding many a fond parental hope. Is it not perhaps wrong to encourage such expectations? I think not, for if even one in a hundred boys is thereby infected with a love of Virgil and Homer, it would be well done. In that one, however imperfectly, would reside the memory of our race, which in the other ninety-nine is lacking.

Before I could take up this post at St. Sepulchre's, however, I had to be sent for a stay at Lincoln, where the dean, the Reverend Dr. Willis, welcomed me into the Church of England, had a prebend instruct me in its Thirty-Nine Articles, and presented me with a copy of the *Book of Common Prayer* bound in blue buckram. There seemed no harm in this provisional conversion, especially since it was all done, it seemed, with Uncle Augie's approval.

What he had in mind for me I'll never know since I never saw him again.

It was an English captain brought me news of Peter Motteux's end many years after. He had led, said this seaman, *une vie crapuleuse*, and he shewed me a clipping from the *Daily Courant*, Saturday, March 15, 1718, to wit:

... on Tuesday the 18th of February last, a Gentleman in a Scarlet Cloak, with a Sword, in Company with another Person, was carried to White's Chocolate-house, St. James's, where the Coach waited from about 9 a Clock to near 11, and then carried him and the other Person, and let them down at Star-Court, in the Butcher-row, behind

St. Clements Danes Church, and the Gentleman being found dead the next morning, in a house in that Court, and it being violently suspected that he was murdered there. The Coachman is earnestly desir'd forthwith to come to Mrs. Motteux, at the Two Fanns in Leadenhall-street . . .

"The whores strangled him," said my captain. "They forgot to cut the cord they had tied around his neck and attached to the bedposts to provoke more active venery."

Thus we are ruled, not by our stars, but by our stones: "Against the Charmes our Ballocks have,/How weak all humane skill is," as Lord Rochester so nicely expresses it in his poem "On Mrs Willis."

Peter was almost fifty-five years of age; it was a few days till his birthday. "Love begins by Fooling, till we Fool our selves; and what is worse, we know it, yet go on." So he wrote in his play *Love's a Jest*:

> Who can bear, and not be mad
> Wine so dear, and yet so bad?
> Such a noise, an Air so smoaky.
> That to stun yee, This to choak-yee,
> Men so selfish false and rude,
> Nymphs so young, and yet so lewd?

Dear Peter Motteux, rake and *homme de lettres*! I yet remember his scarlet cloak swirling about him and regret him to this day.

It was mostly by his example I learned how to be an Englishman, if such I am or ever was. And he it was who taught me to esteem Shakespeare, as he explained to me, not only the greatest dramatic poet who ever lived, but the genuine originator of our natural and empirical philosophy. "For," Peter said, "Lord Bacon, being a politician and a busy statesman, employed in the writing of his works a whole covey of secretaries, among these being Thomas Hobbes, Ben Jonson, Will Shakespeare, Francis Beaumont, and John Fletcher, and it was such men, first and foremost among 'em Shakespeare, and not the great Lord Chancellor himself, who originally writ many of the famous essays published under Bacon's name, including works such as *The Advancement of Learning* and *The Wisdom of the Ancients*. Shakespeare wrote Bacon!"

"Are you happy, Peter?" I once asked him.

"What is happiness? 'When thou do'st meet good hap,' Shakespeare says. Now what I myself desire most in the world is love, and loving is much ado about nothing, the matchless Bard considers, which, he says, 'goes by haps.' So yes, I am happy when I find that nothing, love, good hap; but no, I am unhappy when I don't, bad hap. Hap-hap-happy! Hap-hap-unhappy!"

At Star Court in Butcher Row that night in 1718, Peter Motteux's good hap had failed him, alas.

I Become a Briton

IN May of 1709, it seemed that the British and Dutch had resolved to confirm their Grand Alliance, and the armies were in motion in Spain and Flanders. Prince Eugène had gone to meet the duke of Marlborough at the Hague. The Prussians and Saxons who were to reinforce the army of the Allies had arrived near Brussels. A large amount of specie had been remitted to the Low Countries to pay the British troops before they took the field. And on May 4th, Captain-General Marlborough embarked at Margate for Holland, where he was expected with great impatience.

The French were getting nervous. The Dutch Post on Saturday, May 7th, informed us that the French king had notified the court of the Blackbird Pretender at Saint-Germain-en-Laye that he and his queen might be desired to withdraw out of his sunlit dominions; but saying that wherever he went, he could depend on the cash subsidies that Louis gave them, and they would even be increased.

The whole world, it seemed, was being turned upside down. The Muscovite resident at the Hague had informed the States General that Tsar Peter's army had in two battles, one of which lasted ten hours, defeated the Swedes, and that the king of Sweden, with some thousands of men who remained to him, was making his way toward Poland. Thus in passing perished countless of those fine Swedish soldiers who had traveled so far and fought so hard for Carel, attended, they liked to kid, by three illustrious physicians, to wit, Dr Garlic, Dr Akvavit, and Dr Death.

His tsarish majesty's officers then proceeded to deal with his rebellious Cossack subjects, hanging them up in their hundreds on gallows erected on log rafts, which were set floating down the country's rivers as a caution to the followers of Mazepa and the Zaporozhian Cossack Host tout court. And Peter's political police, the *sbires* of the Secret Office of the Preobrazhenskoe, were kept very busy snuffling out traitors and organizing their speedy "transfiguration" (which is, after all, what *preobrazhenskoe* means) into a world thought more to their taste.

Bills of exchange to the value of £150,000 had meanwhile been transmitted by the British government to pay the duke of Savoy and persuade him to invade France.

A fleet of some hundred vessels, with two regiments of foot, had set sail to reduce Newfoundland, and two vessels had left Plymouth for St Malo with eight thousand French prisoners to be exchanged.

On Wednesday, the Dutch Post advised that a squadron of English men of war had arrived at Gaeta and was loading on board the artillery and other wherewithal to reduce the kingdom of Sicily, in which, it was reported from Naples, the cardinals were endeavoring to constitute an Inquisition. The Pope had excommunicated Prince Eugène, and an Imperial regiment of horse under Colonel Patte was on the point of invading the Papal States to oblige him to declare Karl, the emperor's brother, King Carlos III of Spain. The Pope had therefore ordered that his fortresses be put in a state of defense.

But this was old news. The Austrians had in fact already occupied the Church's territories in January.

A confederate army of 137,000 men under Marlborough and Eugène was to be assembled at Courtrai, on the left branch of the river Scheld, to invade France. There was great dearth in that country, where the cheapest bread was now said to cost eight pence the pound.

All this, whether true or otherwise, we learned from the newsletters pasted to the walls of taverns and coffeehouses and furiously expounded on by all comers.

But there was for me a far, far more important happening than any of these even: on Friday, May 13, a mob of Germans and Huguenots crowded into Westminster Hall to be sworn in by the Court of Queen's Bench under the Foreign Protestants Naturalization Act, lately passed in Parliament, and be denizened as British subjects.

I was among them.

"Well," said Peter Motteux, who had kindly accompanied me as a witness. "Now you are become an Englishman—and all your descendants will be English too, every last one of 'em!"

"Let's have a bottle on it!" said Sidney (soon to be Lord Heneage) of the Moon Calves Club, who was my other witness.

Since I had accomplished this feat even before the prince-elector of Hannover himself, though his right of succession had been confirmed, I can justly claim to be of older English descent than the monarch of the United Kingdom. It is true that George Ludwig was descended from the House of Stuart—but the Stuarts were not English but Scotchmen, right? I owed this to Matt Prior and, I learned later, to Lord Oxford: for the premier had taken an interest in me. Uncle Augie had reached out again, and his reach was long—as I would discover, it stretched all the way from Massachusetts to Madras. With the Emperor's approval, but without the Pope's, his royal master the prince-elector Friedrich of Brandenburg had lately crowned himself king in Prussia, an up-and-coming power if ever there was one. Soon Prussian regiments all had Pietist chaplains, and Uncle Augie's *Pietas Hallensis* was to be found in the knapsacks and saddlebags of even the most ferocious Brandenburgers.

And so to dinner then at Butler's, where we had roast beef and a mince pie, neither very good. But we washed them down with as much claret as was required, and they slipped down awful grateful, as Peter liked to say.

At the Sign of the White Peruke

SHOES well rubbed, periwig powdered: I'm a jack-a-dandy in my sparkish toggery. My new high-collared blue velvet *justaucorps*, paid for by a recent remittance from Uncle Augie, who would surely not approve of it, has large matching buttons all down the front and smaller ones at the pleats of the *fente d'aisance* in the rear, is lined with jonquille yellow satin, finely striped in crimson. Its wide cuffs are trimmed with lace, and a cicisbeo of colored ribbons decorates my right shoulder. Peter Motteux has arranged a meeting for me with a gentleman called Claude at the Sign of the White Peruke in Maiden Lane, Covent Garden, who, he says, will tell me something to my advantage.

How shall I know this prospective interlocutor?

"Look for a spare, thin man, in middle age, of a complexion brown enough not to be womanish," Jenny said. "A high nose, a long chin, gray green eyes like your own. There's a mole alongside his mouth. But never trouble yourself about it—he'll know you."

And what will this Guilot see in me? An oval, fair-skinned good-natured face, likewise with the high and eminent nose of the Romans, rising above a shortish upper lip. My chin, I fear, is insufficiently salient (just as I am perhaps inadequately mentulated—or so I suppose, though none of the gentle sex who might have judged has ever been so ungracious as to confirm this for me, and I have never dared enquire of one).

I am told by that painter fellow, Varney, who made a sketch of me, that my visage is somewhat asymmetrical, that one ear sits higher than its counterpart—as, perhaps, does one eye. This is surely true, for it squares with my body as a whole: one of my legs is a bit shorter than the other, so that I tend to slope at an angle when I must stand for more than a minute or two.

"Shall I speak with him in what . . . French?"

"Your English is good enough, Smooth Boots, after all these months in London town! And conversing at bumble-puppy with the bucks in the Moon Calf Club until the cards are wore out."

"Cards are very dear; there is a duty in 'em of sixpence a pack. So my poor brother Moon Calves must make 'em last. And we play most often at five-card loo, you know, not bumble-puppy! But surely Monsieur Claude is French?"

"He speaks English as well as I do. Better in fact!"

The Sign of the White Peruke had seen better days. Once it was that the wit, the cit, and the man of pleasure had gathered there to sneer, laugh, sing, and drink perdition to foreigners all, have their boots liquored, their thirsts quenched, and their baser desires relieved. Now, its modish name did not well represent it, nor the shabby carousers that chammed rancid mutton chops and gulped bad hockamore at its crowded tables. I moved diffidently across a floor strewn with sawdust— someone had puked. The smell hung in the air, mingling with the acrid stink of unwashed bodies.

A thick-tongued man slurred aslant at me: "Hey, Frog! Sod off back to Versailles!" Pronouncing it to rhyme with "Wales." Others laughed and grinned nastily. "Tiens, voilà mon arsouille," some francophone muttered.

[*That's an anachronism, my darling, said Sarie. Didn't you say yesterday there was no such word in French until Bolingbroke taught Voltaire how properly to pronounce "arsehole"! No, dear heart, it was even later than that, I said—I think it may have been Julie Herbert who first told it to Flaubert . . . or perhaps it was Oscar Wilde who told it to André Gide.*]

Forgetful for the moment of my recent denizing, I explained: "I'm not French! I'm an ally, noble Englishmen—from the Imperial free German city of Lübeck."

"Come aside," says a voice, taking me by the elbow. "Pay 'em no heed. They're not worth the trouble" And to the roilers at the table: "Let him alone. He's a friend of mine just come from Germany on business."

"All the world's your friend, Goldsmith!" interjects a buttinski. "Unless it be your creditor! But you owe the Germans money too, no doubt."

"Well, I owe none to you, Sam Symons," said the man with the mole at his mouth. "So spare me your filthy circumquaques. If there's a lower place in hell than another, I believe it is reserved for you."

"Lord! What a horrid crowd is here! What devil has raked this rabble together!" said an enormously fat man at the next table. "Pray remove your elbow, honest fellow!"

"A plague confound you," said his cadaverous elbower. "Bring your own carcass to a reasonable compass and there'll be room enough for us all."

"You cannot be Mr Guilot," I said.

"I can indeed—I must be! But west of Fleet-ditch I am more generally known as Alexander Goldsmith. Let's get out of this wretched place. It's far too active for our business."

We strolled down Henrietta Street a bit.

"I think we'll just look in at Lady Devoe's," said Goldsmith. "Never mind the name. She's no relation."

I followed him, aware that I was doing so blindly.

A fat black footman with stockings sagging over enormous calves admitted us.

"Ah, Dan'l," said a lady of some indeterminate age, popping up all too abruptly, whose swaggy jowls drooped almost as much as her servant's stockings. Pinkish enrobements swayed unsteadily. She wore a great high head-dress, such as was in fashion fifteen years before. "How very good of you to come to my swarry!" she said. "And who, pray tell, is your young friend?" She put a hand to her bosom and genteelly adjusted her tucker (i.e., the little muslin ruffle that trimmed her stays).

"Your Ladyship, permit me to present Mr Tornarius, recently arrived from the Continent, where he has been interlocuting with the Swedes. He has decided to adopt the English form of his name. Which is Turner, you know"

"How do you do, Madam?" I said faintly, feeling overwhelmed by the heat of the place and the strong scent of patch-leaf that emanated from her.

"Charmed, I'm sure, Mr Turner. I once knew a man called Turner, but he was a barber and a wig maker who affected to be a portrait painter. And he painted a very bad portrait of *me*."

"Is His Lordship with us?"

"In the snuggery with his Tokee, Dan'l," said she.

"First Tokay?"

"First bottle, yes."

"Good."

"If any man was ever born under the necessity of being a knave, he was," Lord Chancellor Cowper said of Robert Harley.

Sitting so squarely and stiffly there, the Dragon, as they called him, looked like nothing so much as the *Ölgötze*, or oil-painted idol, of Luther's simile. But beneath a spanking new bob-wig, the idol was oblectating his palate with anchovy toast, washed down with claret—the old pundle had probably said he drank Tokay to impute to her shambles a bit of the *bon ton* that even my naïve eye could see it wanted badly.

It was the first time I was ever introduced to a lord. Dan'l did the honors, and since small talk is hardly to be avoided in England, we spoke first, in a desultory way about music and the wonders of Mr Ray's *Historia insectorum*. I knew little of the beetle tribe, but was pleased to be able to remark that at one of Herr Buxtehude's *Abendmusiken* in Lübeck I had met Johann Sebastian Bach, the younger brother of the *Livgardet* oboist who had serenaded us in Wismar. Johann Sebastian, who was just a few years my senior, had walked all the way to Lübeck—two hundred and fifty miles—to learn about toccatas and fugues from the great Buxtehude, who for his part had Bach in mind as a husband for his oldest daughter, Anna Margareta.

[*I think you misremember, said Sarie, for Mr Ray's book was not published until the following year. But did Bach marry the girl? He did not, I said—and neither did Herr Handel, who also went there in hope of inheriting Buxtehude's post.*]

"Dan'l tells me you have made astounding progress in learning our language," Harley said to me in Latin. "Forgive me if I don't speak to you in French. I never learned it at school."

"Have some wine," he continued. "Lady Devoe has just laid in a parcel of Lafitt, Margouze, and La Tour, don't you know."

And in an aside to a hovering server, he said: "Bring us another flask of your best Bordeaux, my man, and mugs for my friends."

"I see, My Lord, that you do not subscribe to the opinion that *port* is the patriotic drink, and French *claret* the tipple of Pretenderist traitors," said Dan'l.

"You surely do not suppose me to be a Whig, Dan'l? I was weaned on claret and I shall always prefer it."

He raised his glass and said: "The Queen—long may she reign over us!"

Having no tumblers as yet, we could not drink this loyal toast. However, Dan'l raised an invisible glass; and, not knowing what to do, I imitated him.

"Well, let's to business," Harley said.

First, he embarked on some generalities. The king of France (whom, much to his credit, Harley did not call "Lewis Baboon," as almost all Englishmen other than Jacobites commonly did in those days), he said, was a man so obsessed with what he saw as his glory that he sacrificed the lives of myriad other men in order to burnish it.

"And do you know, Mr Tornarius, our Lord Marlborough too makes many a hecatomb for the sake of his honour."

I muttered something in the way of agreement.

"Now what do you know, my boy, about His Most Serene Highness George Ludwig, Archbannerbearer of the Holy Roman Empire and Prince-Elector, Duke of Brunswick-Lüneburg?"

"Nothing at all, my lord."

"Well, you see, he is the eldest son and heir of Her Most Serene Highness Sophia, Dowager Electress of Hannover . . ."

"Um . . ."

". . . who is heir to the throne of Great Britain, should the Queen die, which Heaven forbid!"

"So His Most Serene Highness would be heir to it after her?"

"Precisely. And his mother is now eighty years of age, in excellent health, they say, but still, even Dowager Electresses are mortal."

"George Ludwig will then be king?"

"It is most likely, if the Protestant Succession is to be ensured and the Pretender is to be kept out."

"Um . . . Who is he, my lord?" I knew but feigned ignorance, although it might be thought risky so to impose on a man as astute as Harley.

"James Francis Edward Stuart, the Queen's half-brother, known in France as the Chevalier de St George; they also call him 'the King over the Water,' since he is recognized by his cousin as King James III of this realm and James VIII of Scotland."

I let Harley see that I was now quite lost.

"His cousin is King Louis of France, the Roi Soleil, as they style him." And he added in English: "The Sun King."

The very Lewis Baboon, I couldn't help but think, little to my credit as a gentleman though it were.

"The Pretender is just about your own age, a very active, plausible young man—but a fanatic, alas, taught by the Jesuits, who swarm in his train. If he were to set foot in Britain, it would mean a new Civil War, worse than the last one. French armies would command these isles—and all of Europe. We would end up a colony of Versailles—and, worse yet, the spiritual vassals of the Pope. Liberty of conscience would be abolished. It is quite likely, indeed, that the fires of martyrdom would burn once again in our British plazas."

"And might the Pretender come in, then?"

"Indeed, he attempted to come in only last year, proposing to land at the Firth of Forth with six thousand Frenchmen and raise up an army in Scotland. Fortunately, Admiral Byng was in the way, and the Blackbird had to return to Dunkirk, though they say he wept tears of rage and damned the French admiral's eyes for not going on."

I wonder why Harley wanted me to know all this.

"I tell you all this," he said, sipping his claret, "because I want you to understand the supreme importance I attach to the life of His Most Serene Highness George Louis—and, moreover, to the life of his son George Augustus, who has already been proclaimed duke of Cambridge and must be next in line after his father—another plausible young man, one who likes to fight the French and lives dangerously—he had his mount shot dead under him leading the Hannoverian cavalry charge at Oudenarde, you know."

Harley gazed at me, very sincerely, it seemed.

"I want you to go to Hannover, Mr Tornarius. There you will find that remarkable man Mr Leibniz, who is George Louis's counsellor and is writing the history of his noble line, the Guelphs, of whom you will have heard, an ancient breed stemming from Henry the Lion, who founded your native town of Lübeck. You will assist Leibniz in whatever he demands. He knows his business well enough, but there has not been sufficient pains taken. We cannot of course send anyone but a native German on this task, and Dan'l tells me he has confidence in you. And you are a good latinist too, I believe, which suits the nominal post we have in mind for you of secretary. I want you to note everything that may be relevant and report it to me by the means that shall be made available to you. At the same time you will take every opportunity to extol the probity of the present administration in particular and the British nation in general and to arouse suspicions as to the intentions of the French in general and King Lewis in particular. Your face is your highest qualification. No one will suspect a young man of so perfectly innocent a countenance of being what the Italians call an *intrigante*. You will be to them, as they say, *comme un petit enfant candide*."

Dan'l said, turning to me: "The wretched Cutlett was there before, but he committed an indiscretion in a woods and had to be recalled for fear he might be murdered in revenge by the child's relations. He has just come back, and we are in urgent need of a replacement."

And to Harley he said: "I propose to put Mr Tornarius on board a fast Dutch dogger now at Harwich, which will carry him over to Hellevoetsluis. Van Heijningen will meet him, bring him to Rotterdam, and arrange for his onward journey. Leibniz expects him and will take him into his service immediately in the guise of a pen pusher, archiver, and general amanuensis."

"You will be paid £10 a month from the Secret Service account, in addition to whatever the Hannoverian court may allow you as a secretary to Leibniz," Harley said.

My bowels borborygm'd by this generous offer, I nonetheless exulted: at last I would be playing a worthy role on the stage of the world, with a path that led upward. Matt Prior was much less well born than I, after all, and he had met with the great—with ministers and secretaries of state, yes, even with Lewis Baboon himself in private audiences.

What's he like? I asked Matt. His upper teeth are out, so he picks and shows his under teeth very affectedly, Matt said. But he's a likeable enough bloke for a Sun King.

"Well, Jack, my lad," Dan'l said. "You will be pleased, too, I think, by the sturdy collaborator I have found for you—you're a scholar and a gentleman, after all, not a ragamuffin. You'll need someone who knows how to rob a hen roost, so to speak, and to request of a rogue that he stand and deliver, or, if not, he'll blast his brains out. I'll just ask Lady Devoe to send him in."

He stepped out of the snuggery and shortly returned with a monstrous familiar figure looming at his back (Dan'l was only a short man, you see—about five and a half feet tall).

"*Grüß Gott*, Cousin Torney," said TF.

"What, are you now turned Imperialist?" I responded, half stupefied not only by this apparition but by its uncustomary idiom—to tell you the truth, I was almost knocked out of my seat by this turn of events, Thomas showing up at Covent Garden and jabbering Austrian. I'd have like expected Saint

Jerome—or was it Androclus?—and the kindly old Lion asking to have the thorn pulled from its paw!

"Why not? We'll soon enough be in the Imperial service, won't we?"

"In the Hannoverian service, Tommy. Not the same thing, not the same thing at all," said Dan'l (who had understood our exchange in German, yet another surprise in this always surprising man). "Or shall we say in the service of his future royal majesty King George I of England, Ireland, and Scotland—not to speak of France, as heir to Plantagenets."

"Hannover!" said TF. "Why, my Uncle Christoph Bernhard lives at Braunschweig, very near there!"

"Gentlemen, leave you I must, alas," said Harley, draining his tumbler. "For I have a supper appointment with Swift and Harry St John [*who was to be Viscount Bolingbroke, Sarie, and also played a part in my destiny*], impatient men both of them."

After he had departed, we left too. I went home to my attic room at the Cutletts and gave my *justaucorps* to Jenny to be dried by the fire against the morrow. As she bore it off, she sang in a soft voice Mr Blow's anthem "Stay, silly heart, and do not break."

Did she perhaps mean me?

A dogger is a bluff-bowed Netherlandish fishing smack, or ketch, of two masts, suchlike as troll for the cod and white herring on the Dogger Bank. [*It sounds nice, such a vessel, my treasure, she said.*] Our passage was arranged in a dogger called the *Charming Polly*, but Thomas Frederik and I never sailed in her . . . I'll tell you how that came about.

[*Let me get the girl to make some coffee first, she said, walking barefoot to the kitchen.*]

"The girl," Rosetta, had been with us since the summer of '23, when she was brought here from the great isle of Madagascar. For her I paid 180 rijksdaalders, a high price, but she was well worth it. She makes good ninny-broth, as the Moon Calves used to call coffee back in the day. Indeed, she does just about everything well! When I purchased her, I gave another 100 daalders or so for the baby she carried in a sling. He was then about one year old, and I dubbed him "Cromwell" in memento of the Scottish lute player Jack Cromwell, once my friend, whom he remarkably resembled in the phizz, even as an infant, and *not at all* as everyone wrongly surmises, because she had herself named him Oliver after God's Englishman and erstwhile Lord Protector. Cromwell always refused royal honors, of course, but he was venerated as a monarch by the Sakalava nation to which they had belonged (before, that is, they came to belong to me), Rosetta said, and he was closely allied by treaty with their King Andrtandahifotsy. The Sakalava, she told me, annually bring out and cleanse Andrtandahifotsy's teeth and bones, and those of their other kings, in a solemn ritual called, I believe, Fitampoha (meaning, to hazard a guess, something like "Fit-and-Proper") and would have been only too happy to wash Oliver Protector's too, as a diplomatic nicety, had those not been lost after Oliver was dug up and posthumously hanged at Tyburn by the Restorationists: Rosetta was totally aghast when I told her of this. I was not so unkind as to add that the Englishmen who had concluded the treaty with Andrtandahifotsy on Oliver Protector's behalf had almost certainly been pirates, and perhaps even Sooterkins having a joke.

This playful nickname Cromwell later morphed into "Kromboom," which is to say "Crooked Tree," after I heard Rosetta say to him one day, "Noll, you are as crooked as that thorn tree over there!" He grew up, though, to be a fine lad, and I would almost say our house depends on our Noll and his mother.

They are just like family to us.

So here is how it was, though, back that day in the long-ago year 1709:

"Harwich is a town of hurry; all business, not much gaiety; but its folk sleep warm in their nests and some of 'em are rich,"

Dan'l told us. "See you don't bother 'em." He smiled. "When you get there, just ask some old character at the port the shortest way to the Sooterkin Arms. That's not its real name, but anyone at the harbor'll direct you. They'll take you for Dutch loggerheads. At the pub, ask for Captain Neat. He also goes by the name of Netjes. *Net-ches.* Give him the password, which is *Oranje-Blanje-Bleu.*" He pronounced it carefully for us; his accent was quite good. "Neat is an owler. He will take you directly over the water to Hellevoetsluis. Machlou van Heijningen will meet you at the port when you arrive and bring you to the Hague. From there to Hannover, it's only a hop, skip, and jump. You can do it in a week or so."

"What," I said, "is an owler?"

Dan'l explained: "An owler is a traitor to the Queen's government, liable to be indicted for felony before the justices of oyer and terminer and hanged, his body to be displayed in chains—but a benefactor of British mankind in general. Owlers smuggle wool and Pretenderists to France and bring us back claret, lace, Geneva water, and cognac, among other desiderata." And he recited:

> To gibbets and gallows your Owlers advance,
> That, that's the sure way to mortify France:
> For Monsieur our Nation will always be gulling,
> While you take such care to supply him with woolen.

"I like it," I said. "How clever you are!"

"No, but it was writ by my late friend Tom Brown. A deedy man, dead now," he alliterated. "Very well, boys, now you have your instructions. Tell no one, mind, where you are going. Say rather you are pursuing a strumpet to Bath, or some such thing."

"Well then, you must give us a foy, Jack Turner!"

"And what's that then?" I said.

"Why, it's the parting peck and booze offered to their booty fellows by those that go on a journey," said Sir Jasper Charnock, drawing himself up to the height of his twenty-three years and five and a quarter feet of extension. "It's the oldest rule of our club! May such who fail to furnish friendly foy be rubbed forthwith to the Whit to serve out their liability to the society of Moon Calves!"

"He affects to mean hauled off to Newgate Prison for debt," said Henry Varley, a young barrister at Lincoln's Inn whose particular pleasure it was to offer me patronizing instruction in the *vernacula vocabula*. "It's rogues' canting, not proper English," he added. "Beyond the gutters of the City no one would even know what it signified."

"Well, boys, I cannot offer you much in the way of meat or of tipple, alas, for I have hardly any money at all," I said. "I have been hoping for a remittance from Halle, but it has not come yet. My uncle is probably in Potsdam tête-à-tête with the king of Prussia on the subject of regimental sweetness and light and so did not get my letter. In short, asking that I treat you is to beg britches of a bare-arsed man."

"No matter, *we'll* treat *you* then," said Lord Heneage. "There's no shame in it! Indeed, the contumely would be ours if we permitted a Moon Calf cheek to be rubrified by a mere insolvency! Bankrupt one, bankrupt all!"

> For De Foe and the Devil,
> At Leap-Frog do play;
> And huffing young Moon Calves,
> Are broke every day.

Which is not quite how the song goes, of course, and it made me think that Sidney—they all, no doubt—knew more about my business than was at all proper and sensible. I should never have introduced TF to them. But I was proud to have this loggerhead *Landsknecht* as my cousin, and I had wanted these friends of mine to meet him. It had pleased me to think of him beetling over them, his cobalt blue stare sending shivers up their spines—a man, after all, who had been one of Eugène's dragoons at Zenta when the Imperialists drove the Turkish janissaries into the river and slaughtered thirty thousand of them. By comparison, fond though I was of them, Jasper, Sidney, and Henry were mere schoolboys.

"Don't let it obvaricate you for a moment, Jack! When you return from across the Narrow Seas, you can reimburse the club," said Henry, who was the closest thing the Moon Calves had to a treasurer.

So I threw my foy at their several expense.

And a right crapulous one it was too. Harry's spaniel Evil (short, he said, for Evilmerodach king of Babylon in II Kings 25:27 who did lift up the head of Jehoiachin king of Judea out of prison) puked on my shoes.

Good times!

Bilious the next day, I greeted the dawn disgusted with myself. The remaining scraps of my faith in myself seemed to be ebbing away, leaving me washed up on the shores of a bleak, unwelcoming world.

"I fear I am becoming a Socinian against my will," I said.

"Crap! You are simply suffering from what they call a *crise de foi*, or is it *foie*, I can never remember unless I see it written down," said TF. "I recommend you quit drinking so much and tormenting yourself with theology. It's better to think soberly. Or so I have found who manage without such folderol."

From London to Harwich is about eighty miles. Dan'l had got us nags for the journey and next day we horsed away merrily enough, stopping to puke just past Chelmsford (both of us, for TF kept me company at it), he telling me of his doings in Kiel and how he was almost trapped into marriage there by someone called Angelika but escaped by claiming the sudden onset of a clerical vocation. And I gazing at the prettily flowering verge, now soiled with our spew, ravishing in spirit the fair Abotrite Magdalene with beet juice staining her lips who had waited on us in Wismar at the Purgatory tavern. Riding, of course, always tends to produce a cock-stand in a young man, even one badly hung over, and one thing leads to another, don't it?

"What a lovely springtime!" TF said after a while, changing the subject because he could see that I was tired of his boasting and paying no attention to his tales. "Where are we?"

"Somewhere in Essex," I said, proudly feeling myself a veteran *Englander* by comparison with my cousin, who usually came across so superior to me, although managing not to seem blatantly patronizing, so that I could never call him on it.

"Es-sex. What strange names they have here!"

"Not at all. It's just English for *Ostsachsen*. This was long ago the kingdom of the East Saxons, you see."

"How could they be *East* Saxons? We're way west of Saxony here."

"East in relation to the other Saxons in England, who lived in Middlesex, Sussex, and Wessex, and so on. They're all *en masse* called Anglo-Saxons these days. But as Mr Dooley says, an Anglo-Saxon is a German that's forgot who his parents were."

"Never heard of him!" Alas, TF was no scholar.

"Londoners think that the girls here are easy lays," I explained.

"The usual crap in other words. Other people's women are *always* easy lays in lads' imaginings—it's wishful thinking, you know."

So I told him an Essex trull joke (the one about the green mare), but it somehow didn't work in Lübsch, and he didn't smoke it until I'd translated it into French for him. Even then he didn't think it was funny. So to pass the time a bit more, changing animal and color, I recited the rhyme that has to be pronounced by an unfaithful widow who seeks to recover her husband's tenancy at a manorial court, where she must appear mounted backwards on a black ram holding its tail in her hand and say:

Here I am, riding on a black ram,
    Like the whore that I am;
And for my crincum-crancum
    Have lost my bincum-bancum,
And for my arse's game
    Am brought to worldly shame,
        To ask for my lands again.

"Then the steward is bound by custom to restore her to her 'bincum-bancum,' which is to say, in the language of the country clowns or hodges, the free bench—*francus bancus*—right of tenancy," I explained.

But he didn't think that was funny either!

Come near Maldon, where we were to get fresh horses, it seemed time for a drink. Only another forty miles or so to go. They could be there by nightfall.

[*It always seems time for a drink to you, Jannie, said Sarie.*]

We stopped at the Goose and Goblet, or perhaps it was the Swan and Bottle—who can remember when you've fuddled it at so many inns in a long life!—and called for ale.

"Tastes funny to me," said TF. "They put strange things in beer in this country! I prefer the honest Ingolstadt recipe—water, hops, and barley, nothing else."

"You boys aren't Netherlanders or Germans, I think" said a voice behind me in mangled Dutch. "I do believe by the sound of you, that you must be from somewhere more northerly."

"Indeed we are," said TF. "Danes and proud of it."

Why did he lie?

There were a couple of them. They weren't Netherlanders either, but Scotch Cameronians who had seen service, they

said, with King Billy in Flanders and so picked up the Dutch
language.

Prick-eared Puppies

I WON'T deny it. We were fools. There we sat dipping our
noses into our mugs, puppies that we were, gaming with
dice and cards until we had lost the little coin we carried,
chattering, grinning, mouthing, jabbering a mixture of tongues,
none of them nicely, but all blending together into the general,
comfortable vainglory and lubricity. We discoursed deeply on the
Whiggish notion of Progress, to which I subscribed (and not only
because I bore a torch for Jenny Rippchen) but Thomas did not,
honest *soldier* that he was, while our Scottish companions held
it open to dispute. I recall expounding on the subject of aerial
transportation that "in the next Age it will be as usual for a Man
to call for his Wings as it is now to call to call for one's Boots!"

"What rot!" said TF. "Men will never fly, take it from me."

"I'm cooked," I muttered and slipped beneath the table.

[*Now, Jannie, you know you didn't ought to, said Sarie. I knew
it. You know I know it.*]

"We know," said one of our Cameronian friends as he hauled
me to my feet, "of a better way to get to Harwich. Why, you can
sail there in the moonlight in an hour or three, and its much
easier on the *cul* than riding horseback along a stony ditchway
that likes to call itself a road. Spare your bums, my pals. We'll
fix you up!"

What an excellent idea it seemed.

But first, of course, we drank another sneaker of punch.

Soon, we were very drunk. I had never drunk so much punch
before in my life. We were led somewhere where there was

water; we were told the boat that was to carry us out to the ketch was ready; we tumbled into it, and away we went.

After some indefinite quantity of time, we were roused and told we were at the ship. "Here, boatswain," said a voice. "Take care of these gentlemen, for they are very weary."

And when we waked in the morning and peeped on deck, we found ourselves far out on *epi oinopa ponton*, the snotgreen sea, in blind Jimmy Homer's words, on a great ship, the land in sight yet, but at a distance.

Were we not almost come to Harwich? I asked a sailor.

"Harwich? Why should we come to Harwich?" he replied.

"Because that is where we are going, is it not?"

"Are you still drunk? Fools, you were sold by those Scotch friends of yours. Why, you were trapanned on board to be delivered to a plantation owner at Newport Newes in Virginia, where this ship is bound!"

"What does he say?" TF asked.

And when I translated to him what had been said, Thomas flew into a rage, raved like a madman in several languages, including Polish and Latvian, as far as I could tell, drew his sword and would lay about him, as I did too, but the sturdy seamen, who were many to our two, disarmed us, one thereafter kicking Thomas in the groin so hard that his stones pained him badly a long while.

In short order, the captain came up—Habbakuk Peddie was his name—and told us that we must be quiet and orderly aboard his ship or we would be shackled, carried down between the decks, and kept as prisoners there during the voyage along with some others lodged there. Servants were *always* put on board by their owners, the captain said, and it was no business of his to enquire about their entitlement. The boatswain added that we would soon be tied to a grate and the cat-a-nine-tails got out of the bag, which is to say, we'd be whipped and pickled, if we did not submit.

"And will you then carry us to Virginia?" "Yes," says Captain Peddie. "And shall we be sold when we come there?" "Yes," says Peddie. "And there you must stay, I fear. I carry papers saying that you are being transported for housebreaking and battery, and that you are to be hanged if you return to England"—but this was all lies, I later learned, because the importation to Virginia of jailbirds deserving of death for such notorious offenses had since been prohibited, the Virginians being sick of having such villains sent among 'em.

"Why then, sir, the devil will have you at the hinder end of this business."

"So you say," says Peddie.

The wind continued to blow hard, though very fair, till, as the seamen said, our ship (*Phansy* was her name) was past Orkney and began to steer away westerly. With no storms and a northerly wind, we should be in Virginia, said Captain Peddie, in two-and-thirty days.

Why did we go north to reach Virginia in the southwest? Because, said the mate, in that way we avoided those great rogues of French corsairs who swarmed in the lower parts of the Narrow Seas.

After we had been at sea for about two weeks, a furious storm broke over us, by which we were obliged to run away afore the wind, as the seamen call it, wheresoever it was our lot to go. After having beaten up again as well as he could against the weather, the captain resolved to try to touch the Carolinas. However, we overshot the latitude, or something nautical of that nature. Captain Peddie and the mate differed to an extremity about where we were, their reckonings being more than usually wide of one another, and argued over it until purple-faced. I was not seaman enough to understand their reasoning, but presently by the captain's order, we stood away NE and made good speed.

Behold! however, in the nasty-fingered dawn a French cruiser or privateer appeared and crowded after us at full sail—just what Peddie had been seeking to avoid by taking a northerly route.

We could not fight *l'Éclatante*—it would have been suicide to do so (her armament I was later told comprised 22 demi-cannon, 28 culverins, and 16 demi-culverins, among other engines of destruction). Did Captain Peddie therefore wisely strike his flag and surrender?

He did not. But fired a broadside at them; whereupon the Frenchman's guns promptly raked us.

We were quickly shot through and through—and between wind and water. "Master," says Peddie, "try the pump, bear up the helm. And sling a man overboard to stop the leaks." They trussed a poor bloke up in a bit of sail and suspended him on a rope with a mallet in one hand and plugs lapped in oakum, well-tarred, in a clout on his belt to fill up the holes the cannonballs had made.

"What cheer, mates!" says the master. "Is the kettle boiled?"

"Sound drum and trumpet. Saint George for the United Kingdom of Great Britain!" says our Peddie.

Truly, men are mad, and Scotchmen are madder than most.

After a fight, which lasted all night (for they fought in the dark too), we found ourselves with the *Phansy*'s mizen-mast and bowsprit shot away, and many dead, among them Captain Peddie himself. When the French boarded, the Scotch lunatic led his crew sword in hand until he was brained by a ball—I supposed fired from the Frenchman's crow's-nest—and his blood streamed out from his mouth through the scuppers with the rest.

[Come! I hear TF butting in. This is a fine invention! You should be a contriver of novels, my boy! Confess that no sooner had the Frenchman hung out his lily-white banner with the black skull and marrowbones than old Peddie meekly surrendered, who is himself at this moment likely swallowing his fish soup in that pittoresque little resto gazing upon the plage de l'Éventail!]

I had taken up an axe to join the defense, but soon saw it was hopeless and so threw up my hands in hope of quarter, crying, "Miséricorde!" TF (whom I had not seen much of during the fight, but appeared at my side after the surrender) and I presently found ourselves prisoners of the French, who stripped us of everything we possessed, even of the clothes on our backs. I was especially sad to lose my lovely boots, smooth as silk, which I had bought only a few weeks before in St Martin's-le-Grand by Cheapside.

Meanwhile, the surgeons of the two vessels looked to the wounded, and the dead were shrouded up, each with a cannonball at head and feet to make him sink. The pursuer wrote down their names and the French politely gave them three guns for their funeral. Swabbers swabbed, gunners spunged the cannon, the boatswain set men to repairing the sails, and carpenters went about their work putting things to rights as best they could.

When I disclosed to the French captain, whose name was Jacques Cassard, that we were prisoners of the English, wrongfully taken, and condemned by them to be sold into slavery in the Americas, although subjects of the duke of Schleswig-Holstein-Gottorp (luckily Cassard had no idea of where the latter stood in the War, and indeed Duke Karl Friedrich was then a small boy of about eight years old living in Stockholm with his mother, the Danes having occupied his ancestral lands and family castle), he very civilly ordered that we be given shirts, coats and hats, and obliged the seamen to return us our boots. For in France, it is not customary for convicts to be Barbados'd as the English practice is, and they think it very wicked and uncivilized; French prisoners are sent to His Most Christian Majesty's galleys to live out their remaining lives as oarsmen.

To cut a long story short, Cassard and I had many a pleasant conversation, mostly on philosophical subjects, he being an admirer of Mr Descartes, until we separated, he to go about his privateering, and we sent back aboard the *Phansy*, staffed by a prize crew, to the walled city of Saint-Malo, where these filibusters nested. Some years later, in 1713, when the *Nesserak* made a stop at Ribera Grande in the Cape Verde Islands, I learned that it had only lately been sacked by a French squadron under the gallant Cassard, who had been elevated to the rank of commander in *La Royale*, as the French call their navy. I was sorry to have missed him!

When the *Phansy* was brought into the harbor of St. Malo, I expressed to TF my fears as to how we should live; for we had no money or anything else.

"Do not trouble, yourself," he said. "We shall travel in style to Hannover about the business to which Lord Harley set us."

"How can that be, Thomas?"

He knew the whereabouts, he claimed, of 600 Spanish pesos that the late Captain Peddie had concealed in the orlop. "And I have a plan," he said, "for how to extract them to our benefit without these Frenchmen knowing."

Later, much later, I gave Dan'l an account of these happenings and wrote it all down for him to submit to Lord Harley, who wanted to know the reason for my disappearance and he himself after made use of the tale in a book he wrote called *Colonel Jack*, even to using my very own name and words.

"Waste not, want not," he said. "For Wicked Waste makes Woeful Want!"

This was after he had given up spying and had published *The Life of Robinson Crusoe*, the most famous book in the world that was not written by God Himself. Dan'l was celebrated then; and I reckon I should be famous with him, too, if *incognito*.

"We must above all things avoid being *embastillated*, which is to say lodged in the Bastille at His Most Christian Majesty's pleasure," said TF. "France is crawling with police seeking to discover *espions*, whom they look for particularly among foreign young vagabonds of exactly our description. Moreover, we have, of course, no *passeports*. Wait here for me!" And off he went, staying away for some hours.

When he returned it was with a chaise attached to a piebald horse, and he wore a brown capuchin habit. Tossing me another such in a bundle, he said: "Quick, don this!" And once I was thus travestied, he handed me a document signed, apparently, by the chancellor de Pontchartrain himself, in which I was identified as "père Albert de Sainte-Eugénie," authorized to pass, *allant et venant*, during a period of three months, through the territories of the Most Christian King.

Like gods in France, as the saying goes, we traveled, TF and I, through Brittany, Normandy, and Picardy, *de couvent en couvent*, which is to say, from monastery to monastery—"so many Retreats for the Speculative, the Melancholy, the Proud, the Silent, the Politick and the Morose," in Mr Swift's words. Sometimes, it is true, we had a cow or some hens for our bedfellows, but needs must when the devil scours the pot!

If we found no ecclesiastical accommodation, we cheerfully put up at a *cabaret*, as they call a tavern, where one had the advantage of being able to order a twelve-egg omelet, a sallet of asparagus or samphire, and a pitcher of cider or *poiré*. I was surprised that the *cabaretiers* seemed quite incurious that mendicant friars should command such nourishment—and pay for it in Spanish pesos too. As to our deficient French intonations, they were explained by the fact that we hailed, we told them, from the Franche-Comté, where we normally spoke either our native *patois* or Latin (as a quick "Pax vobiscum" and a dignified *signum crucis* or two served to establish).

As we clattered along the roads that led through their fields and down the narrow streets of their villages, where the sides of our coquettish *coupé* almost grazed the walls of their rustic dwelling places, the blue-bloused Gauls gazed at us with eyes blankly uninterested to know what we might be. Aside from their giant hats, so well adapted [*as Vigny would one day observe long after my death, Sarie*] to their pulverous climate and delving nature, they seemed little different from the Holsteiners among whom I had grown up (and whose speech I at least understood, unlike that of these French yokels), the pitiful Danish churls of my mother's country, or the English clunes who still spat into their cupped hands to ward off bad cess when they saw a foreigner—which is to say, a mug not of the parish, conceivably even that of a damnable Londoner.

"They are the same the world over, are they not, these country clowns?" said TF.

"But they are men," I said.

"Yes," he said, "men, but men very different from us, and who will never be like us either, but for the chances of the lad who enlists in the *archers de la garde*, adopts the military profession, and has the luck to live; yes, and the girl who makes bold to go a-whoring and may hope one day, if she survives clap and syph, to end up swanning around as mistress of a fine château structured in a whalebone corset and with some of that new perfume Johnny Farina's been concocting across from the Jülichs Platz in Köln—eau de Cologne, they're calling it. Lovely stuff, I hear—like orange blossoms and daffodils on a spring morning. I've been thinking we should drop by and get a few flasks. Köln's smack on our way, you know, and with some of this Kölnisch Wasser to gift them with, we should sure as shit be able to ingratiate ourselves into the affections of the Fair Sex at Herrenhausen."

In Godfrey William's apothecke in the Hannoverian Elector's great summer palace of Herrenhausen, *Kater* Bressler and *Katze* Bijou (the first feline of that name I was to know) even now inhabited a high tower room, their elevated location foiling unwanted lovers when Fraulein B was *rollig*, to use the German term, which is to say, hot to trot. The stately *Breslauer*—a gift to

Godfrey William from the Halle philosopher Christian Wolff—
had earlier in life suffered the grave indignity of being thrust
head first into a Polish dragoon's boot and untommed by a
jobbing barber. Finding the young gib disconsolately lapping
the green water of the Oder, and struck both by his marbled
beauty, and what the great *Aufklärer* determined to be the cat's
extraordinary ability to reason mathematically (attested to in a
paper in Wolff's *Kleine philosophische Schriften*), the perceptive
Wolfius concluded that he must be presented to the world's
highest mathematical intelligence—namely, of course, Godfrey
William himself, who else?

But TF and I were still in Flanders. Great military events
were taking place not far off in that autumn of 1709, such as
the siege of Tournai and the enormous battle of Malplaquet,
in which the Allied generals Marlborough and Eugène were
successfully able to exterminate some thirty thousand of
their fellow beings, two-thirds of them their own troops,
mostly Dutch and Austrian, although the English claimed the
victory was theirs. Whereafter the noble duc de Villars, the
French commander, who had come out of it with his knee
barely smashed by a musket ball, reported back to his king:
"Encore une défaite comme ça, sire, et nous avons gagné la
guerre!" Another defeat like that, sire, and we'll have won the
war. In reward for this providential disaster on the part of
his enemies, Lewis Baboon promptly made Villars a peer of
France.

We for our part took great care to be far from all such
happenings, moving in the opposite direction whenever we
heard the distant sound of fifes and drums, or even just chatter
on the part of the country folk that soldiers of any kind were in
the offing. With such precautions, we continued north by many
a byway and leafy sunken road betwixt and between fields and
hedgerows, meadow saffron and windflowers.

Though we were bound for Hannover, first we had to go to Braunschweig (the English call it "Brunswick"), TF said, to visit his uncle the painter Christoph Bernhard, who resided there with his wife, Agnesa Benedicta, in a little house near the church of Saint Giles, patron of cripples and of the city of Braunschweig, too, a holy man who had lived in the forest with a deer as his only companion and eaten no meat. The best way to get *there*, TF said, was to go to the Château of Saint-Germain-en-Laye first, which was quite near Paris. At which palace, he said, there was *someone* who could supply the further *passeports* we would need to cross the frontier.

I made no objection. For I had always wanted to see Paris and to do so would happily be reconciled to these amphibious circumstances.

"Versailles has it in for Paris right now," said TF. "A man may live seven years in France and still remain blind to all the things the police, blast their eyes, get away with here, Dan'l says. They must likewise be acquainted with nothing we do. We must, in short, perform our business surreptitiously—*subrepticement*. Isn't that a lovely word?" And he said it again lingering on each syllable: "*Sub-rep-tice-ment.* I don't know why, but I think it's my favorite French word. What's yours?"

"I don't know. Maybe *jadis.*"

"*Jadis!* In bygone days. It suits you, melancholy fellow. What does Boileau opine? 'Son rabat jadis blanc, et sa perruque antique.'" His cravat once white, and his ancient wig. He grabbed me by the neckband and gave it a tug. "Not white now but grubby, I'd say! And perukeless in Paris, what will people think!"

Saint-Germain-en-Laye was where the Pretender lived and plotted his plots, in a palace once inhabited by the kings of

France. We crept up on it as quietly as we could. "You just wait here under this tree," said TF when we got near. "I'll do some inquiring. Won't be long!"

It was pleasant under my lime tree, which was in an out-of-the-way-enough corner, and I was glad of the opportunity to think some thoughts of my own. The trouble with TF was that he always *knew everything* and seemed to have thought of everything before I did. His wits got in the way of mine, if I can put it that way. I liked him—well, of course, he was my cousin—but I also liked him *not to be there all the time*. It permitted me to laze my wits a little.

I thought a lot about God in my young days. I hardly ever do now that I'm old enough to expect a closer acquaintance. But I lay there under the tree that afternoon and allowed myself to drift into a pleasant reverie mixed with senses of divinity and wonderment, hardly thinking at all of what lay ahead when we had got our *passeports* and must cross the Rhine.

Returned whistling through the long grass, TF said: "It's a done deal. Tomorrow we shall be admitted to the Chevalier"—by which he meant the Pretender, I supposed—"and get his benediction."

"I don't understand," I said. "Isn't that treason? What if we are brought before those justices of oyer and terminer when we return to England and disemboweled and hanged as seditious? And how could you possibly have arranged to see HIM?"

"As to how," he said, "it was by the token of this." And he put into my hand a bronze medal on the obverse of which was the head of a distinguished man with a long nose and laurels in his locks, with the words "CVIVS EST,"—namely, "Whose is it?"—and on the reverse a finely chased outline of the British Islands, surrounded by little ships, all wonderfully done, with the single word: "REDDITE"; to wit, "Give it up."

"And as to being hanged, drawn, and quartered, we shall be *admitted* to him but not *see* him, so that if brought to trial we may honestly deny it."

I understood that we were playing jack o' both sides—a double game. But what I didn't understand was why.

"How can that be?"

"You'll see," he said.

"'I see' said Blind Joseph to Deaf Mary as he took up his hammer and saw."

"You have it, my lad. Just so."

At the Château-Vieux de Saint-Germain-en-Laye

"WHY do the great like to inhabit such vast houses, huge halls that even huge hearths cannot heat? Better to live small and lie snug, I say!"

"Why you must recall that the Pretender's Household embraces upward of seven score persons," said TF in explanation. "Think of all the bedchambers, privy chambers, guard chambers, chambers for receiving visits, antechambers, closets and cabinets, chapels and oratories that are wanted for his comptrollers, chamberlains, gentleman ushers, grooms, barbers, clerks, closet keepers, nurses, bankers, officers of the guard, equerries, almoners, preceptors, and pages. Then you have also the king's, er . . . the Blackbird's staircase, the Blackbird's back-stairs, etcetera, the *petite cour des cuisines*, the bakehouse, kitchens, and larders, not to speak of pantries, vestibules, and, of course, jakes—the excrementitiousness of such a quantity of people is considerable. There's everything you can imagine—even an admiral. It's quite as grand as Saint James's. Grander! But Séamus *an chaca* when he set up house in exile here found it too small for all that, since the Château-Vieux possesses only a single antechamber between the king's guardroom and his bedchamber."

"He needed more?"

"Ahh, my dear, a king in England is expected to have *plusieurs pièces de suite* setting him off from his protectors: a presence chamber, a privy chamber, a withdrawing room, and so on, don't you know? Babylonish though it may all seem to you, it was Castle Come-down for His Majesty."

The Old Château stood about ten miles to the west of Paris, quite near to Versailles, on an enormous esplanade of *jardins à la française* and *gazon*, or lawn, that gazed over the river Seine. We neared it by way of a road that ascended sharply upward from that famous *fleuve* through magnificently drafted landscapes, including M. La Nôtre's new *grand parterre* and the *boulingrin*—"le mot Anglais est bowling green; mais on prononce en Français *boulingrin*," I explained to TF—all marching in line across the terrace like so many detachments of Lewis Baboon's *Maison militaire*. A dun cow grazed across the *boulingrin*.

"And how are we to pass all these ushers, equerries, guards, and so on and penetrate the Pretended presence chamber?"

"Who would exclude a pair of humble disciples of Saint Francis bearing a note of introduction from Lord Bolingbroke—or is it Harley? One of those lordly traitors anyhow. The Blackbird, you see, must live by treason, as other men live by meat and manchet bread."

"*Primarius panis*," I said, unable to pass up the opportunity to exercise my pedantry. "If they are lucky enough to get bread, that is."

"Indeed, if they are lucky enough to get it. If not, they must live on cheat-loaf and bastard gravy. In any case, he has no hope of being restored king unless a number of British nabobs turn traitor, and he is always on the lookout for 'em, longs for 'em constantly as I do this very minute for a slut, drools at the very thought of 'em, is always glad, never sad, to see 'em. And they in turn—even the likes of General Marlborough—lust after him, though they won't admit it and put it about that he was an imposter brat conveyed into the birth chamber at Saint James's in a warming pan to make up for a stillbirth."

"You are excessively knowledgeable," I said.

"I *am* Thomas Frederik Francke," he explained.

"But I don't understand why these nabobs, as you call 'em, would *want* to turn traitor to their Queen."

"Because they are all always deep, deep in debt, since they live so luxuriously and wildly beyond their means, erecting palaces in the heart of nowhere in Northumbria and places like that and surrounding themselves with hordes of servants, who very naturally rob 'em blind. They anticipate that if they bring him in and set him up on the throne, the Blackbird must reward 'em, just as King William rewarded *his* supporters with half the arable land in Ireland and much elsewhere besides. They'd defenestrate Ann in a minute if they could be certain of not being drawn and quartered for it. But they never *can* be certain, you see, not unless Lewis really commits his fleets and armies to the Pretenderist cause, which he always threatens to do, because it suits him well enough to make the English squirm, but never actually does."

Thinking of the Queen so defenestrated by her ministers—it was a vivid image that sprang to mind—I learned also that the awful Pretender was just six months the elder of myself—which is to say, about twenty-one. His father the king had died some eight years before, leaving to him the whole family business. Just a boy, then, I thought. What a thing to come down on one at twelve years of age, as it had him! And so I felt a certain sympathy, later that morning, for the shadowy figure who sat with his back to us in the audience chamber with the blinds drawn and the shutters closed against the bright summer sun so that we might not treasonably "see" him.

Then the bloke [*I thought you'd swore off gypsy cant, said Sarie*] got up and raised a blind, let the sun stream in, and faced around to us,

I was dumb-found to see a man of perhaps fifty-five, with a square, solemn face and a long, unhappy lip. He had the phizz of one about to weep at any moment.

"Your Highness," said TF, clicking his heels and gazing upward with his nose in the air.

"His Majesty is in Flanders with the army, where he goes every summer to risk his life during this interminable war," our interlocutor said. "I am David Nairne, undersecretary of state and clerk of the King's Council. I shall attend to your business. But let's have a bottle, reverend fathers, what say you to that?"

To this amiable suggestion we happily agreed, quickly righting our ideas, and soon we sat at table drinking claret from silver cups. Nairne seemed to cheer up a good deal after a few sips. They were clearly not his first of the day either.

"So you are bound for Herrenhausen, another vast and wasteful court, no doubt," he said. "I wonder if the poor servants there are as ill done by as they are in this one."

TF and I looked at each other.

"I was heir to a small estate in Fife, you know, but the Dutchmen who ruled all in Scotland under blasted Billy confiscated it before ever I set my foot there. Now I have not even an apartment here in the Château but must live in rented lodgings in town. I applied for a post in the Household for my wife, but it was refused because she is French. My salary is £104 17s. 6d. per annum, and I have just recently got myself a new suit, with brass buttons, for the old one was wore out, and a new sword that together cost me £58 14s., but a man in my position must have a decent sword, you know—I may be made Secretary of the Closet any day now, handling the king's private letters and dispatches. And a wig, of course, may cost you sixty *livres* these days! So you may well wonder how I live! My chief joys are my flute, violin, and viol, of which I paid twenty-six 26 *livres* for my new one. I have played with Charpentier, *maître de musique* to the Sainte-Chapelle in Paris, and Couperin, who is employed here in the Chapel Royal as an organist and instructor in the harpsichord to His Majesty King James, who plays passably—very tolerably. I console myself too by translating Scripture once in a while."

And he chattered on and on in this vein—I can't possibly remember all he said—calling when needed for a fresh bottle, and scarcely leaving us room to speak. Presently he offered to play upon the viol for us.

But we wanted no more music. "Now about our *passeports* . . . ," TF said.

"My *huissier*, M. Arouet, will see to it," Nairne said, not untestily. "He attends to the legal side of things. Now at Herrenhausen you and Mr What-d'ye-call him here are to seek out a Scotsman named Rabbie Paisley, an alchemical sort of fellow with a nasty ginger beard on him. You can't miss him, I think. Shew him the medal in secret and he will direct you. And God be with you, yours is a cruel task, but it must be done, alas. Must be done. We can't let those Hannovers succeed, pox take 'em!"

He got carefully to his feet, steadying himself against the table—a quarter-decking landlubber in the chops of the Channel, I thought in my lately learned nauticalese. "Now," he said, "I think I'll just go and have a bit of a lie-down. Speak about your papers to Arouet as you go out. He's a cunning forger and very obliged to us. The queen mother kindly got the Jesuits to accept his child into Louis-le-Grand—the French Eton, you know. Nasty precocious little brat!"

And off he toddled.

So I never did see or be seen by the famous Blackbird, or, as he preferred to be called, King James III of England and VIII of Scotland.

Monsieur Arouet, who had a starveling look about him, was most helpful and outspoken. Her Britannic Majesty (Madame Blackbird, that is) had absolutely insisted on arranging a place at Louis-le-Grand for his little son, he vouchsafed, as if it were of interest to us. "But I am fearful that he may not become too wise for his own good," said the father. "He is already prattling at us in Latin and Greek about Aristotle and Euripides," he added vaingloriously.

The day was slowly advesperating as we walked back down the long road to the Seine. "What a lot of *basse cour* talk!" said TF. "For a gentleman such as Mr Nairne to put on the poor mouth like that, as our Irish friends say! Still, he's right about this being a cruel business. Do you know Lord Stair, the British ambassador in Paris, actually sent hired assassins last year to murder James on his way to Boulogne the other day? He had a narrow escape, too, Dan'l says."

Hungering at Herrenhausen

SO we got our *passeports* from Monsieur Arouet and after much tedious traveling came at last to Braunschweig and the house of the artist Christoph Bernhard Francke. We found TF's relative and his lady, whose name was Agnesa Benedicta, in a somber state. Their eldest child, Rosina Elisabeth, aged nine, was unwell, it seemed, as was their latest baby, baptized Christian August only that February. TF promptly came up with a show of diagnostic ability and offered to take a look—he had been assistant to a barber surgeon in Hungary as a lad, he averred.

While he checked the bantlings, I browsed in some copies of *The Review* that I found piled up there, which I knew to be written by Dan'l (he is in fact known to hoi polloi as "Mr Review"). In it, Dan'l mightily berated King Lewis, who, he said, had made "a private League with *Soliman* the Emperor of the *Turks*, and at the same time clap'd up a Truce with *Mezomorto* the Dey of *Algier*, in order to embarrass *Europe*," whereupon "the *Algerine* Pirates came into the Channel, took Prizes even in the Mouth of the *Thames*, and were admitted to carry them into the Ports of *France*, as they did three Ships bound from *London* to *Amsterdam* at one time—"

Yawning at this rant, I turned to the Advertisements:

The *Hatton Garden Clap-Preventer* that treats his Patients with *poysonous Mercury Sublimate*, is desir'd to take Notice that Mr *Joshua Stephens*, at N° 3. *Symmonds-Inn*, tells People that he is the author of the *Translation* of Dr. *Greenfield*'s Book, that is printed with the name of *John Martin* in its Title Page. This makes People suspect, that the said *John Martin* is an *imposing, cheating Quack*, and an *ignorant Pretender*, and that his *Letters, Stories of Cures, pretended Medicinal Secrets, &c.* are (like his Pretentions of being the Author of the said Translation) but so many *Shams* and *Impositions* on the *Publick*; as to which Particulars, the said *Martin* is desir'd to publish the *Truth of the Matter*, in some one of the *News-Papers* . . . not forgetting, if he pleases, to tell the World, whether he knows who is the Author of the *Quack Pamphlet* call'd the *Charitable Surgeon*, which is only a Bill of Directions for the Use of a *Pacquet* of *Hotch-Potch Mixtures* . . . Price between 3 and 4 *l.* which he advises you to use for 40 Days, (which will be about 20 *l.* Expence) and then, if not cur'd, to apply to a *Surgeon*! Whether this ought to be call'd *Charity*, or *Cheating*, Reader, judge you.

N.B. At the *Golden Bull* in the *dark Passage*, between the *Sun* and *Castle Taverns* in *Honey-Lane Market*, you may, by

the Author of the Book call'd *Quackery Unmask'd* be cur'd
of the *Venereal Disease* in a few Days Time, without running
the *Hazard* of being *poyson'd* with *Mercury Sublimate.*

I could not quite follow from this philosophical dissertation
who exactly might be the Hatton-Garden Clap Preventer, or
what his relation to Stephens and Martin was, but in subsequent
numbers of *The Review*, the battle of the Advertisements
continued, with Stephens denying authorship, another swearing
to the truth of this, and the authors of "the Book call'd *Quackery
Unmask'd*" (Sintelear and Spinke now revealed to be their
names) further taking Martin to task, both for his bad Latin—
"you can't distinguish the Parts of Speech, the Singular from the
Plural Number; nor what Cases Prepositions govern"—and for
claiming to possess "a Liquor to prevent the Venereal Disease"
that "will not fail once in 1000 times" even if one should "enter
the most infected Wh——s!" Martin had also absurdly asserted
too, Spinke jeered, that "the Word *Cunnus* signifies to conceive."

I took vague mental note of the whereabouts of the Golden
Bull "in the *dark Passage*, between the *Sun* and *Castle Taverns* in
Honey-Lane Market," and also of the purveyor of

The Famous LOZENGES, being effective in all Scorbutick
Cases; they ease Pains in the Head and Stomach, cause a
good Appetite, purifie the Blood, and give speedy Relief in
Rheumatisms, Dropsie, and Gout, and totally destroy the
very Seed of Worms,

They cure Agues and Fevers of all Sorts, give present
Ease in the Cholick, Stone and Gravel, cleanse the Body
after hard Drinking; as also after the Small-Pox, Measles
and Child-bearing, and are a more general Cathartick
Medicine than any yet known.

Prepared only by R. *Owner*, Apothecary, at the Pestle
and Mortar, in *East Smithfield*.

You never know, do you? And indeed I would soon wish to have had some of those *famous lozenges*—and, what's more, I'd get them too. But I don't recommend them—they didn't do me any good, and they taste horrid.

"Back in '02 when Hannover and Lüneburg invaded Wolfenbüttel, I served with the rank of *leutnant* in the Leibregiment zu Fuss under Captain von Henning, you know," said Bernhard Francke. "So you cannot say I lack courage. But now I am a *paterfamilias* with sick children and how can I not be afraid for them?"

"Well, *I* am certainly afraid," TF said later, after the poor father had gone to seek a physician for his babies. "You haven't had it, have you?"

"No."

I knew what he was talking about: the *petit vérole* raged in other parts of Westphalia, and now it was certainly here too. I felt an intense shiver and must have given a start.

"What's wrong?"

"Nothing." But as Mutti says, it was as though a demon had set its cloven hoof on the place where my tomb would be.

"I had a brush with the small pox when I was just a boy. I was serving under Balthasar von Klinkowström in the Morea. He loved me, you see, and he had a Griffin botanologer he had got as booty when Koroni fell to the Holy League to inoculate me as they do in the East, by implanting pock powder from one who survived, which he carried about him in a walnut shell, under my skin. So I got off lightly—as you see, my mug is quite unpocked. And they say for sure you don't get it twice, so I don't think I shall again. No, it's you that I fear for, kid. You are still so young, and *la petite vérole* loves a pretty face like the *bas clergé*. It's always worst with children. Not that it isn't terrible for all! Klinkowström used to say that it was mankind's greatest enemy, that even the Mongol Turks were nothing to it. Millions it has taken to their graves, millions upon millions—and it's an awful death, some say the very worst of deaths. It attacks every part of the body: not only the skin with ten thousand vile malignant pustules that burn like fire and are hard indeed to look upon, but the throat, the heart, the very lights and tripes of a man. The smell is so disgusting that gravediggers have died of that alone, they say. We must flee from here, Hänschen, cravenly flee and hide in the forest till this thing has burned itself out for want of victims. The physicians have no cure for it; they may bleed you by the basinful, wrap you in scarlet broadcloth up to the eyeballs and give you *ptisanes* of sheep's dung and mulberry wine to drink, but it's all in vain. Like as not they themselves perish of it, the poor loggerheads!"

I tried to sound knowledgeable, repeating what I had been taught at Rostock: "But don't Avicenna and Averroes recommend the red treatment to draw out the evil humours?"

"The old wives of Constantinople know better than those two dismal villains did! Don't argue with me: I have seen a hundred pustulated wretches die like dogs. Just pack up quick and let's get the hell out of here."

"And so we did," TF said to Mehemet de Koroni, the Elector's valet at Herrenhausen. They had met in the Morea, it seemed, when Mehemet was taken after the fall of his native town. Klinkowström later made a present of Mehemet to George Ludwig, along with another Turk, Mustapha de Mystra (The Knights Hospitallers passed out *Beutetürken*—"booty Turks"—like candy in those days.) And if I may be a bit subsequent, Mehemet became a Christian, married a Wedekind girl, he being forty-five and she just fifteen [*so they were a bit like us, Sarie*], and the Elector, later still, kindly made him a German and ennobled him—he was in fact the son of the Osmans' Griffin governor of Koroni, so, you see, he was already quite *adel*; he chose to take the name *Ludwig Maximilian Mehmet von Königstreu*, or "True to the King." [*You can*

see Mehemet and Mustapha painted on the wall at Kensington Palace,
Sarie, because George Ludwig took them both to England with him.]
    We went to live in an abandoned forester's hut in the deep
woods. But I caught the *petit vérole* anyway, of course.
    I became delirious, and in my feverish sleep dreamt a dream
in which we were visited by a pair of highwaymen named Henni
and Tönjes, along with the bedraggled whore of one of them, big
with brat, who presently gave birth to it on the cot across from
mine. Tönjes snipped the cord, "baptized" the baby boy with
dishwater, pronounced a formula in thick dialect that I could not
smoke for the life of me, then flipped the little body up in the air,
adroitly caught it in one big dirty mitt . . . and choked it to death
with the other. Whereupon he drew his dag and sliced off its little
right paw and handed it to Henni, who popped it into a small
casket strung on his belt. Seeing me gazing at him in horror, he
grinned and winked and flipped this open to reveal several such
baby hands, half buried in salt. "Fine magic candles the little
fingers of these hands of glory will make of a midnight," he said,
"when a person's filling his *Plündersack* in a pretty parlour!"
    My stomach churning, I fell witless, and when I awoke, there
was no sign of such robber folk. I must have imagined them!
"What? Who?" said TF. "No. There's been no one here."
    But on the floor I thought I saw what looked like a tiny pink
fingernail. When I looked for it again, though, it was gone, must
have slipped between the planks, if it was ever there.
    It was TF who pulled me through my illness, Lord love him!
Liberating a box of lemons and a little sack of sugar from the
Palace pantry at Herrenhausen one night, he lugged them out
to our refuge in the woods, rolled up his sleeves, and made . . .
lemonade, gallons and gallons of it, of which he obliged me to
drink a pint twelve times daily, downing it very freely himself
too, dosed with gin or schnapps as the fancy took him.
    Gradually, I recovered. I was all pocked up. The scabs
dropped off, and I was wearing that mask now until they healed

over a bit better. Actually, it wasn't that bad. I was very lucky. But I've always been lucky. Runs in the family.

"Lucky!" I thought, reflecting on the splitting headaches, raging fever, and puking I had endured in that ghastly hut, and the pruriginious pustules that had covered me from scalp to scrotum, down to my toes.

"Lucky indeed," said TF. "Christoph Bernhard's kids are dead."

Taking a stab in the dark, I said: "And what about Henni and Tönjes?"

"Broke on the wheel, and from the bottom up too, this past Tuesday in Paderborn," he said forgetfully. "Good riddance to bad rubbish, I'd say!"

"There are quite a few who go masked about the court these days, especially among the ladies," said Mehemet. "And Herr L.—that's Godfrey William—had some of those *famous lozenges* fetched from London after he read about 'em in *The Review*. I've also got some Greek salve for the skin that works wonders—my Griffin grandmother's recipe. She was from Sparta, and they used it there against the pox even back in the days of the Great Peloponnesian War, you know, of which Thucydides writes."

"How was your grandmother a Griffin?"

"Well, when they came into Greece in the Fourth Crusade, the Franks called us 'Griffins.' The name stuck, and some still call us that five hundred years later," Mehemet said. "The Hospitallers are nothing if not traditional-minded. But why they called us Greeks 'Griffins,' I don't know. Perhaps they found us rather spikey! Come, let me take you to Herr L. He'll look after you. He's very kind. That's the kind of man he is."

And indeed he was. "Bijou is in heat, I fear, *rollig*, you know, and things are a bit rackety, but I must put you in the Tower room with the cats," Godfrey William said, "while Thomas here goes about his business, which is not mine to find out, much as I love to find things out. Meanwhile, Mehemet has gone to fetch you some of his grandma's ointment, excellent fellow. You mustn't believe the lies the Pretenderists spread about the Elector 'keeping two Turks for abominable uses' and 'backstairs duty' and all that. Though he was a very comely boy indeed in his young days, George Ludwig is no tartan cat; he's straight as a row of marquees—that's army tents, not lordlings—and Mehemet loves his wife, Hans and Sophia Wedekind's daughter Maria. She has just presented him with a son, Johann Ludwig, whose *Patenonkel*—his 'godfather,' as the English say—I have the honor to be."

[*Should I describe GW? No need, I think: Christoph Bernhard Francke has painted his portrait, very true to the life, with the kindly expression and the great black Allongeperücke he wore—it kept out the cold, he said. Being of a delicate disposition, he also donned an extra mantle and weasel-fur stockings at the slightest chill.*]

As he spoke, he conducted me up a winding stair to a massive brass-bound door on its final landing.

One of the happiest weeks of my life was about to begin.

"Now we must get you measured up for some new clothes," said GW. "If you are to be my cipherer and indexer, you must be properly dressed. Perhaps you should wear red. It is said to be good for the small pox. An English alchemist of my sometime acquaintance, Mr Isaac Newton swears by it: his counterpane, curtains, cushions, hangings and upholstery are all crimson, and he drapes himself in a vermilion cloak."

I noticed that Godfrey William himself wore a dark red dressing-gown.

He introduced me rather formally to the two cats and showed me where I might sleep, where the door to the jakes was, which depended over a little moat, and where I might wash at a basin set on a stand. Here, my eye immediately fell on something that I had longed for in our woodsman's hut, though it was doubtless as well that I had not had it there: a silvered looking glass. And much as I enjoyed the speech of my distinguished employer, I longed for him to be gone so that I might see how I appeared—so far, I had only what TF said to go by.

"Well, then, I must be off. I have an appointment to meet with the Elector and tell him of the latest progress on his *historia domus*, which I hope will satisfy him for a while!"

Immediately the door was shut, I snatched off my buckram vizard and snatched up the looking glass.

"Why, it's Orion!" I said, "but luckily without his club and shield—that would have been a bit of a muchness." Counting, I found just seven large pockmarks that looked as though they meant to hang about: I identified big Betelgeuse on my upper right temple, smaller Bellatrix a bit lower down on the left side, Rigel, biggest of all, on my left cheek, with smaller Saiph on the right cheek, just above the jaw line, and askew above my nose, three declivitous relicts about the same size as the Saiph pock, making up Frigg's Girdle, whose star names are Alnitak, Alnilam, and Mintaka (which as you know, Sarie, are called the "three kings" in Dutch). I recognized the pattern because I had been looking at maps of the heavens at Peter Motteux's in London just before we left—he had explained to me that the lovely names of these stars (except Bellatrix, of course) are all in fact Arabic and were bestowed on them by the old Saracen astronomers.

My lesser pockmarks were fading and would doubtless disappear with time, or mostly. So, perhaps not too bad! But when would I be able to shave again? I truly looked a barbarous sight with the scars of my forest battle glinting pinkly amid the bristle. Buckram would have to be my social phizz for some time yet.

One of the cats rubbed itself against my leg, and I felt a spasm of contentment: not because of the animal's affection, but because *I would never more again have to fear getting that sickness.* And the fact that I had survived a satanic scourge before which even *Kurfürsten* and kings trembled was surely a sign of God's grace. The Sun King himself, I reflected, did not have that good fortune, although His Highness the Elector did, having survived the small pox as a little boy, Mehemet said.

And now I was in this sunny tower, serving GW, one of the greatest philosophers in the world, with shelves of books to read and two very pretty animals for company. So all seemed indeed for the best in this best of possible worlds of mine.

But what was this? On a table in one corner was a strange device. Perhaps some new sort of glockenspiel?

"Ah," said Godfrey William later. "That is my *Staffelwalze,* or *machina arithmetica,* with which all manner of calculations can be performed. With such a computer the adding, subtracting, multiplying, and dividing of large numbers becomes simple, even for a peasant." And he went on to expatiate at length on what he called his arithmetical "Calculus," reflected, he said in Creation and Divine Providence Itself, explaining: "Die 0 ist das Nichts, die 1 ist Schöpfung und Fügung." Go figure! I simply report what I remember of the great genius's thoughts. Seeing me quite at sea, however, he changed the subject, saying: "But since you are by profession a cipherer, you will be more interested in my *machina deciphratoria.* It is employed as you play a clavichord, making a letter almost as easy to encipher or decipher, even in the most difficult insoluble codes, as it is simply to copy it. Unfortunately, no prince as yet wishes to pay for such a machine to be built to my specifications. How empty of sense most crowned crania are!"

GW presently presented me, vouchsafing me to be his assistant, to Herr von Görtz, the chief of spies, or Secret Man, of the Elector's *Kabinett,* who questioned me closely about my family, made me speak the Lord's Prayer in Lübsch to him, wormed the story of the fatal duel at Wismar out of me, smiled a little at it, and gave me a ribbon with a silver token on it to wear at all times in the palace; for, he said, it would not do to have masked persons such as myself wandering the corridors without identification. By this sign, his hatchet men would know and respect me; whereas if I did not have it, these *sbires* (as Beaumarchais calls such filth) would remove me to a dungeon beneath the palace until further notice, or perhaps forever, as an agent of the English, "so villainous a people, as the Prince-Elector likes to remark." From which I deduced that Görtz knew perfectly well that I was an English agent and wanted me to know that he knew it.

GW then asked me to draft a memorandum for him from books in his library on various stones that are specific against poisons and disease, such as the bezoar, or *lapis bezoarticus*, which is found in the stomachs of goats and rhinocerots; the stag's tear, or *lacrima cervi*, of which Julius Caesar Scaliger gives an account, which forms in the corner of a stag's eye when it is a hundred years old; and the *aetites*, or perdicle, found in the nests of eagles in Saxony and other places, which inter alia enables the detection of thieves and prevents miscarriages when bound to a woman's left thigh. "I do not ordinarily concern myself with these matters," he said, "but I have received an enquiry about 'em from Mr Erskine, chief apothecary of All the Russias and first physician to the emperor Peter, who is very much interested in such antidotes, since his tsarish majesty lives in perpetual fear of being poisoned. Mr Erskine is a Scotsman and a Pretenderist, but I have high hopes that Peter may one day make me a privy councilor—there is no monarch in Europe who is a greater friend to natural philosophy—and Erskine undoubtedly has his ear."

This task pleased me; I like nothing better than to read old books in a sunny spot, and with Bijou draping herself on the floor alongside me, displaying her pretty belly, and Bressler perched sphinxishly on the table, I was soon happily immersed in Scaliger's *Exotericarum exercitationum* and Cardano's

De subtilitate. These studies engaged me until, famished by my researches, I went in search of something to eat.

As I had discovered at the Château of Saint-Germain-en-Laye, a royal palace is an enormity, and Herrenhausen, believe me, went on and on and on. My nose should have led me to the kitchens, but the mask I wore blocked my sense of smell, I realized. Just when I was about to take it off, however, a slight female person, also masked, and wearing a pleated tabby mantua, appeared in the passage before me. On a ribbon round her neck, I noticed, she wore a token very like mine from the Secret Man.

I was lost, I said, and was looking for a meal. Could she direct me to . . . the Ordinary? *Mensa? Speisesaal? Lieu de dîner? Refectorium? Pincernaculum?* She seemed nonplussed behind her mask, which was faced with red silk, like her mantua. Surely she must know one of these words!

"Oh," she said in English. "You want supper. Well, I'm going to the Buttery too. It's this way. Since we are both vizarded, it seems all very well that we should go in together. I have tickets for two, if you lack one."

This was very forward for a woman, and I wished very much to know who she might be. She seemed quite young. Her voice was well-modulated, and her hands were exquisitely formed, smooth of skin and perfectly tapered fingers, neither too large nor too small.

[*Very like yours, Sarie—I've always been one for lovely hands on women!*]

"I was brought over to be governess to the little Griff—Frederick Louis, that is, the son of George Augustus, the new duke of Cambridge—I suppose he may be king of England one day, after his father! Then I had to go back to Norwich to nurse my aunt, who had fallen very ill. There I contracted the small pox, alas. My aunt died—not of the pox, it was a dropsy of the brain, Dr Browne told me—and I recovered, of course, but so badly marked that I am now obliged to vizor my face."

"I suppose they will pack me off. I've become such a sight to be seen! Lady Caroline is very kind—she had the pox herself, you know, just after Griff was born—so she sympathizes. But Cambridge likes nothing but pretty faces in his household. His wife's pockmarks he must put up with, but he can do without poor mine."

"I have seven big . . . well, the others are just little ones," I said. "They form a pattern rather like the constellation of Orion, if you know it."

"I should like indeed to see that," she said. "For I too have my constellation."

"Well," I said. "I'll show you mine if you'll show me yours."

She had the most charming laugh, and she laughed long, stopping still in the corridor and leaning on a windowsill.

I realized that I had been bolder than I had intended and blushed beneath my mask. But yet I blundered on:

"Saint Augustine tells us," I said, "that God created the stars to console those who must do their work at night."

"My dear fellow," she said. "What an ingenious flirt you are! But I fear you'll be disgusted. For Ophiuchus, the Serpent Bearer, is my cruel array! 'Incensed with indignation Satan stood/Unterrified, and like a comet burned/That fires the length of Opiuchus huge . . . and from his horrid hair/Shakes pestilence,' don't you know?"

"Serpens, which they call the thirteenth sign of the Zodiac," I said. "Milton, *Paradise Lost*, is it not?"

"Book 2," she said. "But 'paradise lost' indeed! Alas, you'll never know how fine I used to be."

"But I can easily tell already how fine you are now," I said.

"We are moving along a bit too fast, I think, sir," she said. "Though a penniless wretch, I am a lady of sorts. My father was a justice of the peace and a poet. But here is the Refectorium, as you put it. Let's go in and hope they have something besides *Sauerbraten* and dumplings today.

Much as I like them, I could do with a change. The food at
Herrenhausen is really too dull."

Sauerbraten! I salivated.

"By the way, I am Johannes Tornarius, secretary to Herr L,"
I said. "In English I'm called Jack Turner."

"And I'm Serpentaria, trampler of Scorpius," she said.
So; we were introduced.

"But how did you know that Scorpius ruled my nativity?" I
said, telling what I hope was a white lie: in fact I was born on
New Year's Day under the sign of the horned goat, Capricornus,
but didn't like to admit it.

"I didn't. But I do now."

We took a side table, to be more private. There was beer and
cold venison pie. I consumed more of both than I should have
and felt more stuffed than I had been since leaving France: *Satt
ist satt!*

"So your father was a magistrate," I said.

"But a poet and a musician too. He played beautifully, even
as a boy, mother said. He was what they call a *Geigenwunder*
here in Germany—a 'violin wonder.'"

"Do your parents know of . . . your illness?"

"My parents are both dead. I am an orphan," she said. "And
you?"

"My father died last year. I believe my mother is still alive,
but I have not seen her for a long time. It's complicated."

"So we are both alone in the world."

"I'm not, really. My great-uncle August Hermann Francke,
who is a professor at Halle and a protégé of the king of Prussia,
helps me. It was he who recommended me as an amanuensis to
Godfrey William—you know, the Elector's *Geheimrat*. And then
there's my cousin Thomas Frederik; well, he's actually a second
cousin, and he's much older, but we are good friends. He's been
all over, fought against the Turks and the Spaniards, speaks at
least ten languages, and is a dead shot with a flintlock pistol."

"Herr L. is the Elector's councilor, but I don't think he is a *Geheimrat*."

Wasn't Godfrey William a privy councilor? I blushed again behind my mask.

"Perhaps I am mistaken. I've just entered his employ. I am still finding my way."

"No matter, sir."

"Whereabouts in England did your father serve as magistrate?"

"Nowhere in England, though we are of an old Norfolk family that came over, they say, in 1066 with the Conqueror. No, it was in the shire of Henrico in Virginia. I was born there."

"Then how on earth do you come to be here in Hannover?"

"I am actually named Zipporah, not Serpentaria—that was a joke, of course."

"What a beautiful name!"

"They call me Zippie for short. It's the American way. You can too! After my parents died, I was sent to my father's sister Maud in England. I was just about ten years old, and we lived quite on the frontier in Virginia, so I could not stay there. My father's few slaves were sold for my portion, but they did not bring much. Aunt Maud brought me up and educated me at her own expense. It happened that she was a particular friend of Mr Toland's and through him obtained me the patronage of the Electress Sophia, who kindly recommended me to Lady Caroline. I thus came young into the hurry of the great world."

"Mr Toland," I said. "I know that name."

"He's an Irish philosopher who wrote a book called *Christianity Not Mysterious* that was ordered burned by the public hangman in Dublin, you know," she said in a very soft voice.

"So, the Spinozist?"

"Not so loud. But yes, and I think the Electress may be one too. *And* Herr L."

"Never on your life! He has expressly written in refutation of the licentious doctrines of that anathematized lens grinder."

"Well, so he would do. He's not a *Geheimrat* yet, but he hopes to be one, don't he? And he can never succeed in that ambition if he is taken for a Spinozist."

Not liking this line of chat much, I switched it. "I should very much like to visit America," I said. "Do you remember it well?"

"Perfectly well. We had a little house all surrounded by woods on the banks of the beautiful Hardware River—the name is, in fact, a corruption of our own family name, which was originally spoken as Ardois, though my people were certainly no haberdashers. The place is very near where the Hardware joins the James, a mighty flood named for the late King James or his grandfather, I forget which, of which you have surely heard tell?"

"And were you not afraid of the wild Redskins?"

"Not a bit, for there were none thereabouts. They had all gone over the mountains, like the buffaloes. Or died perhaps of the small pox. For they cannot live with white men, and white men cannot live with them, it seems. I wonder why."

"And did not Mr Toland write a book called *Letters to Zipporah*?"

"Ah, you know a lot, Mr Tornarius! Yes, he wrote a book of that title, and he may have appropriated my name for it, but I am not the lady of the title, as you can see by the fact that he addresses her as 'Madam,' and when he wrote it, I was a girl just turned fifteen. She is quite another. A great lady, I think."

"A princess, perhaps, whose real name he could not use in a Spinozistical book like that?"

"Perhaps. It also happens that a sort of relation of mine, Mr Robert Paisley, works in the Elector's cipher room—the Black Chamber, as they call it."

Paisley. The name struck a chord. Hadn't Nairn spoken of "Rabbie Paisley, an alchemical sort of bloke with a nasty ginger beard," to whom we were supposed to show the medal TF carried in the heel of his left boot?

"Mr Paisley has an apartment in the north wing of the palace, where he kindly accommodates me at present. You might call on me there if you wish."

"And Mr Paisley would not object?"

"By no means. I feel sure he would be most interested to meet you. But unfortunately he has gone to Potsdam on business."

Rondo alla Turca

THE great *mensa*—as we called such places at my *alma mater studiorum*, the good old Universitas Rostochiensis—was crammed with court officers, visitors, and parasites like myself, supping away at the Prince Elector's expense, stuffing their faces, hubbing and bubbing. But through it all I distantly heard a booming set of accents that made my blood run backward. Though I then knew no word of Turkish, I sensed at once that they were speaking that language—and that they had dropped from the jaw of King Carel's Osmanli *Drabant* Attila, murderer, for no good reason, of my brother Berendt.

I peaked over my shoulder, and it was indeed Attila. With him were Mustapha de Mystra and a man in a nasty magpie's nest of a wig. Ali perhaps? I couldn't be sure. They were combustively debating over something.

But what was Attila doing there? That I thought I could guess. Carel XII was an enemy to the Elector and also (though an Evangelical) to the Hannoverian succession in England; Godfrey William had said, I recalled, that the *heldenhaften* Swedish king actually planned to invade the British Isles to back a Jacobite rising just as soon he returned from Bender on the Dniester, where he had been obliged to accept the hospitality of his ally the Grand Turk ever since the Swedes' catastrophic defeat at Poltava the previous summer.

"Scotland is less than two days sail from Bergen in Norway," GW had mused. "And the Swedes mean to make themselves masters of Bergen's Hanseatic Wharf just as soon as they have seen off the Russians in the east. Meanwhile the Elector himself, I don't mind telling you, is very ambitious to gobble up the duchies of Bremen and Verden and sundry other Swedish dominions in Germany."

These thoughts whizzed through my brain: Godfrey William claimed the Hannoverian succession in England as his own diplomatic masterstroke: it was he, after all, who had got the electress Elizabeth to persuade William III to agree to it when he visited Celle in 1698.

George Ludwig, the one likely now to don the British diadem, didn't seem terribly interested in becoming King George I of England, however; he'd almost rather have had Bremen! But so it was, and in the end, the Saxon stallion would get Bremen and Verden too. In any case, as the self-supposed *éminence gris* behind all these important plans, Godfrey William was most anxious to defend the possibility of their realization. And as GW's appointed amanuensis, so was I, of course, bound to be, and was.

Attila had clearly come to foil the Protestant Hannoverian Succession, and since he was a professional killer, he had no doubt come to kill someone. But who? Why, George Ludwig, of course; his son, George William, no doubt; and probably also *his* son, the boy Frederick Ludwig. Perhaps even the dear old DE too—why not, after all, go for a clean sweep? Then the Blackbird could march down from Scotland on London, in alliance with Carel of Sweden, there to reign happily ever after as James III of England and VII of Scotland, with Lewis

Baboon and the Pope rejoicing and Sultan Ahmed, Tsar Peter, the Emperor, the Danes, and the Catalans all gnashing their teeth in the wings.

Could I be imagining things?

"We could go there now if you like," Zippie was saying. And she was in scant doubt, of course, that I'd like. "I'll go ahead. Follow from as far off as you can without losing sight of me," she said.

None of the Turcophones so much as glanced at us as we passed, being too busy with their debate—and even if he *had* looked up as I passed, I reflected, Attila could scarcely have discerned my identity behind my buckram'd mask. I presented a front fit for Philip of Spain's mechanical monk, and felt a bit like an automaton too—if clockwork could feel.

As instructed, after exiting the Refectorium, I followed Zippie from a discreet distance as she glided down corridors and up flights of stairs. Eventually, she entered at a door, leaving a thin strip of light in the hallway. I entered too and found myself standing very close to her in a narrow antechamber. Our hands met. She trembled, which both moved and excited me. Soon I found myself in a bedroom on a bed with her. We did not touch. We were both fully dressed.

She was as eager as I. "I don't think I'm ready to show you my face yet," she said. "But . . ." And she drew up her skirts, exposing the location where I might insert my virgin yard.

Our swiving passed all too swiftly. We both remained masked, her red silk pressed closely to my black buckram. Gazing on her as she lay there afterwards (as she permitted me to do upon my explaining that I had never seen a woman's quim before), I thought, a bit vaingloriously: "Ma main a bien osé toucher ça! Ô vraie amour!"

Now that bastard TF would no longer be able to make jokes about my maidenhead!

"You must go!" she said, straightening up her mask. "Quickly!"

"Will you see me tomorrow? Perhaps we could meet in the Gallery—as though by chance?"

"Yes, tomorrow, in the afternoon, around three, but in the Orangerie parterre, by the gilded gate through the hedge across from the fountain."

So it was arranged, and I left, noting on my way out a portrait of the Elector scowling at me in the half-dark from the vestibule wall.

Once I became acquainted with Zippie, we saw each other on many occasions in the public rooms of the palace. (She must clearly have been there before too, but being one of many, without my registering her presence.) Observing her in close conversation with a Count Palazzo, who was something or other in a Venetian minister's train, after a performance by the Elector's mummers on the subject of kidnapping an heiress, I fell into a fit of despair. Zippie, when I told her what troubled me, quickly sought to relieve my jealous agony, saying with a smile, "Why, Jack, to prefer a poltroon like Ugolino to you would be like renouncing Apollo to venerate an insect! You need not be concerned."

But he was a man, not an insect, after all, and possessed a man's tool and a man's wiles. And in any case, I thought, no one has ever worshipped an insect! I was mistaken there, of course, for as I would discover at the Cape, the Bosjesmans do indeed adore an insect: a slim green locust that Afrikaanders call the Hodmadod god, which extends its forelegs in such a way as to make you think it is praying.

"Ugolino" was what Zippie had called the Count. The familiarity of it made me want to puke, and I began to think how I might make away with the man. Would it be possible to pay some ruffians to give him a thrashing? I had read of this being done by noblemen in novels. But I was no nobleman, knew no ruffians, and had no money to pay them if I did. Then it occurred to me: I could call him out in a duel on some pretext. After all, I had killed Axel, even if by accident, showing that I was a natural good shot, and I could perfectly well slay this Ugolino that way too.

"And if things go wrong and he kills me, it would at least be the end of my suffering," I told TF, who grinned.

"I think," he said, "that on the Whale at Wismar was probably the only time in your life that you have wielded a pistol in earnest. So I should give you some lessons. But then again, have you thought that if you challenge him, he will have the choice of weapons and, being an Eye-tie, might well opt for swords?"

I had not thought of that.

"Somehow I don't think you're exactly the fellow for *l'arme blanche*," said TF. "What you must do is insult him in such a way as to make him challenge you. Then you get to choose your weapon."

With this plan in mind, we went every afternoon into the forest, where TF taught me to fire at marks on the trees.

I swole with pride on finding that I was a fair shot and could well and truly plug a thin birch at thirty paces.

Then suddenly as it had come, the Venetian mission packed its bags and returned to the Serenissima, taking Ugolino with it. I thus no longer had need to put my newfound marksmanship to use. All my pistol practice had been a waste of powder!

I longed though for the time when Zippie would remove her vizard, for if her beauty were as much impaired as she said, the number of her admirers would be lessened, whereas I should love her, I knew, no matter how badly pocked she was— not even if she had lost her eyebrows. The expressive brown orbs that looked from within her mask, not to speak of the lithe body that she revealed in our private moments, were too precious to me for such minor infringements to matter.

La petite vérole stands ever ready to put its marks on a pretty face, after all, and they are but to be expected.

Not long after I crossed the Great Garden and ran, full tilt, up the stairs to GW's Elaboratory, where he sat in a stream of late afternoon sunlight, flanked by his cats, all gazing intently at an engraved portrait of his English colleague Sir Isaac Newton, pinned on a board, while he thrummed on the table with his fingers, as he was wont to do when disturbed in his ratiocinations about the distinguishing characteristics of hypothetical and absolute necessity.

"A new edition of Newton's *Principia Mathematica* is being prepared," he said. "I must lay hands on a copy. Great man though he is, both Bernouilli and Bressler's [*hearing its name senior cat arched its back*] estimable discoverer have asserted in papers in the *Acta Eruditorum* that he bases his calculus of fluxions on my own differential method. I don't care about the priority myself—I suspect we both came on it independently, as often happens when something is 'in the air,' so to speak—but I do painfully feel the attacks Newton has made on me in the Royal Society. Of course, he is practiced upon by his 'ape,' that wretched little watchmaker Faccio, although who would credit a man of that kidney! I hear say he was condemned in London to the pillory as a common imposter."

"Indeed, I believe he wore the wooden ruff at Charing Cross, and would have been bombarded to death with trash by the mob had not Lord Ormond ordered the beadles to stand by to prevent it," I said. "But he was convicted of putting about millenarian prophecies and pretending to save the world, you know, which seems to me perhaps madness, but no crime."

I did not mention the report circulating in the Moon Calf Club that Faccio was the Master of the Mint's punk; who is to believe such tales? and men's lives are put at stake in circulating them—if *penetratio et emissio seminis* in a detestable manner were believed and proven, Faccio and even Sir Isaac himself (I supposed—but they'd surely find a way to pardon him) might swing for the crime of *peccatumque illud sodomiticum, anglice dictum Buggery* (5 Eliz. c. 17), rather than the unnatural Helvetian merely having to stand a few hours in the nutcrackers and be pelted with bad eggs and horseapples by hoi polloi, unpleasant though that must be to a man's amour propre.

Mint-Master Newton had dispatched many to Tyburn to be turned off for counterfeiting Birmingham groats to escape *la misère*, and he was said to be the very devil for entrapping them. He showed no mercy bringing a coiner before a commissioner of oyer and terminer to be judged worthy of dancing to the hangman's merry tune.

"There is a most wicked man come to the Elector's court," I said. "And I thought you should know it. His name is Attila, and he is an Illyrian Turk in the service of the king of Sweden—a murderer certainly and, I believe, a spy. I have just seen him in the Refectorium jabbering in Turkish with Mustapha de Mystras and another. He would have recognized me but for my mask, for we fought a duel once."

"A duel? I wouldn't have taken you for that sort of young twit!"

"It was on an island at Wismar. There were three on a side, and my brother Berendt was killed by Attila. I didn't wish to fight, I was forced into it."

"I think men usually are forced into it. But they are willing to be forced, and in that sense if no other, they choose it of their own free will. But I am sorry your brother died."

"Shouldn't we speak to Mehemet of this?"

A footman was sent to summon the Elector's major domo. Meanwhile, Godfrey William for some reason seized upon the opportunity to discuss religion with me. He hoped that I was a good Lutheran, he said.

With an uncle like Uncle Augie and a father who had been *primarius* pastor of his town, I certainly should be, I said. What's more, I was descended from the *Doktor Augustinianus* of Herford and so in a way was a spiritual sprout, albeit at many removes, of the saintly bishop of Hippo himself.

"Ah, yes, Augustine," said GW. "Nothing worse than a reformed rake! Julian of Eclanum says Augustine invented the idea of Original Sin. Not quite true, of course, but he did invent the notion that Original Sin, translated to us over the ages from Adam by carnal generation, is a *moral evil for which we are liable to answer* and inexpungable without God's grace. He thus held that even little babies who die unbaptized, even unborn children in their mothers' wombs, are damned. Wicked notion—and even if it were true, he should never have proclaimed it! It's more than people can stand!"

"But if Original Sin is not a moral sin, what is it?"

"Dear boy, you must understand that there are three kinds of evil, *videlicet*, physical evil, or *malum poenae*, which is earthquakes, plagues, and things of that nature about which nothing can be done; moral evil, or *malum culpae*, which is human sin; and metaphysical evil, or *malum in se* or *defectus*, which is the evil of imperfection from which we all suffer as creatures created *ex nihilo*. The sin that led to the Fall was undeniably a *moral* evil on the part of Adam and Eve, but merely a *metaphysical* evil for the rest of us."

My confusion must have shown on my face.

"Oh, for goodness sake!" he said. "Think of it mathematically. Let us say that God is the great, perfect, primitive unity, 1, and nothing is 0, which by definition is privative, lacking any character or perfection. God brought us, and indeed the world, out of nothing, as Augustine himself confirms. So our natures result from the action of the perfection that is God on the limitations of nothing, which may be expressed as combinations of 1 and zero. From this arise our souls, rather in the way that an imaginary number such as the square root of a minus can give rise to real value. However, we suffer from our original lack of perfection, which is metaphysical evil."

At least I *think* he said something like that. He went to a shelf and brought back a book, published in Amsterdam in the year MDCCX, which he slapped into my hand. Its title I saw was *Essais de Theodicée sur la Bonté de Dieu, la Liberté de l'Homme et l'Origine du Mal* (which in English means "Theodician Essays on the Goodness of God, the Freedom of Man, and the Origin of Evil").

"Read my new book," he said.

I have it still, but I must confess that I have never yet actually *read* it (although I have *skimmed* it). Perhaps I shall one day soon, now that I am old and need more than ever to know about these things. However, I have always suspected that Godfrey William proposed his philosophy tongue in cheek. After all, he could not come out and say that he *agreed* with Spinoza and Bayle. He would have been instantly discharged from all his offices—and worse. Besides, he was such a jocular sort of man. "It is not for philosophers always to take things too seriously," he once said to me.

I had not yet fully understood at that time that people, even philosophers, lie, incessantly and without pity.

Mostly to themselves, of course. Then they believe themselves and tell those lies to others.

When I was in London, I gave GW's *Theodicée* to Peter Motteux to read. He did, and said: "It seems to me the man plays with words, and perhaps he does not really believe what he says. All his argument depends on the existence of an all-good, all-powerful God. But what if there is no such God, or a God very different? The gods of the Greeks, for example, were a thoroughly bad lot. I have lately been reading Mr Dryden's *Iliad*, and it seems to me that Homer is nothing but a satire on religion and war! The Olympians fornicate, murder mortals, and cheat one another like a set of Mohocks. Jupiter is all-powerful but he hangs up his wife from his chair with anvils chained to her ankles to punish her. Minerva, whom the Greeks call Athena, is among the worst—even her brother Mars condemns her as a wild, pernicious female—yet Pericles had the Parthenon erected in her honor! But no doubt the old Greeks, too, like your friend, saw that piety is a necessity, even if untrue."

"But if it be so, we Christians have been bubbled ever since Golgotha!"

"Perhaps so. But perhaps mankind is still in its infancy and only beginning to learn the laws of bubbling. What saith our English Theophrastus? Men talk as if they believ'd in God, but they live as if they thought there were none. And boys are commonly bubbled when they first begin to play at cards! Tell me, though, does your Godfrey William go to church and receive the sacraments?"

"Very little, I think," I said. For indeed I had never known him to do so.

He smiled. "Come," he said. "Let's to the Ram and have a bottle."

It was our familiar haunt in those days, a jolly tavern by the river, whose painted sign was a great white-fleeced ram caught by his horns in a thicket of thorns and so saving Isaac from the paternal carving knife.

"Bishop Julian believed that the Roman Catholics were actually Manicheans in disguise, you know—and he was right in my opinion," Godfrey William said. "Augustine certainly had been a devotee of Mani when he wasn't out chasing sluts! (He was a Scorpio you know!) No, it was Julian who ought to have been canonized. That's where it all went wrong, if you ask me. But for that we'd never have had this terrible schism in the Church today! It's all Augustine's fault."

He was becoming very heated, so to change the subject, I mentioned that there were some things in Scripture that troubled me.

"Like what, for instance?"

"Well you know how in Genesis God orders Abraham to sacrifice his only son, Isaac? And Abraham takes Isaac into the mountains with enough wood for a burnt offering, without telling him what's going to happen and even makes him carry the wood, while he carries the knife, and when they get there he builds an altar and stacks the wood on it and ties poor Isaac up and puts him on top of the pile and gets ready to cut his throat and at the very last moment, just as he's about to, an angel of the Lord shows up and tells him, 'Abraham! Abraham! Stop! Don't do it!' And Abraham just happens to find a ram stuck in a bush out there in the mountains—a likely story!—and sacrifices that instead. Well how do you think Isaac felt about all that? Don't you think he would never have trusted his father again about *anything*? Or ever again trusted *anyone*, for that matter? After his own Dad tried to make a burnt offering out of him!"

"Ah," said GW. "God in commanding Abraham to sacrifice his son demanded obedience. 'The firstborn of thy sons shalt thou give unto me,' he commands in Exodus 22. But He did not in fact will the action, which we see He halts in the nick of time. We might say that God, by virtue of His sovereign goodness, always a priori intends every bad action ultimately to fail. But the best possible design of things may require that the good must sometimes be enhanced by evil, so to speak, in the same way that shadows serve to set off the sunlight in a painting. By reason of his own supreme goodness, God can neither exclude this evil nor introduce good that doesn't belong in this plan without wronging His supreme perfection. And because the analysis of the continuum extends to infinity, it follows *infallibly* that we live in the best of all possible worlds (even if not *necessarily*, as we philosophers say). In any case, you'll be a happier fellow if you believe it. The alternatives are Pyrrhonism or dogmatism, neither of which is a comfortable position!"

"I think it's all an allegory," I said. "We can't be meant to take it literally. Perhaps Abraham in this parable *is* God. After all, he does God's will without questioning for a moment, even when He wills this unbelievably terrible order to kill his only begotten son. And he can't be just a little bit of God, either, as Spinoza supposes. We know from the doctrine of the Holy Trinity that God has three parts, but they form an indivisible unity. Abraham, and the angel in the story too, must simply *be* God. And then Isaac, the son, is *us*, humankind. God sacrifices us but also saves us. We find the same thing in the Crucifixion. Christ, the Son of Man, is sacrificed but resurrected after the three days."

I thought that pretty smart of me, but I never did hear GW's rejoinder, or to mention to him as I intended to do, that my mother laughed when I was born—because I emerged with a tuft of wild red gold hair, which the midwife declared eased my way into the world—just as Sarah laughed in the Book of Genesis (21:6) when Isaac was born—in her case, it seems, out of sheer astonishment and relief at his bestowal on such extremely elderly parents—to which Godfrey William would doubtless have responded, as was his wont, invariably leaving me crestfallen, "What's that got to do with the price of eggs, dear boy?"

This was because at that very point, Mehemet came in and heard my report about Attila. He frowned and had a private word with GW. When I mentioned TF's part at Wismar, they wanted to know where he was now. I couldn't help them out there. After handing me over to GW, he had vanished. Earlier this had bothered me. But now I thought only of my appointment with Zippie.

"He goes off like this and doesn't tell me where. He thinks it safer that I don't know."

"But now we must consider the safety of the Elector and his family," Mehemet said. "My fellows will find him."

"Perhaps we could give out that the Elector is going to visit Duke Anton Ulrich in Wolfenbüttel," Godfrey William said, "while they in fact go to Schloss Celle? They'll be safe at Celle, and if this Attila heads for either place, we can pick him up and put him to the question. He'll have a hard time explaining himself."

"Do we tell the Elector?"

"If Attila really represents King Carel XII, whose *passeport* he indeed carries, it might be diplomatically very difficult just to hang him as he deserves. So the Elector must know."

"And what part does Mustapha play in all this?"

"Attila claims to know his family in the Peloponnese. He is clearly briefed with all the names and details needed to make it seem so. And since Mustapha hasn't been back home for many years, he is very out of touch with things there, as am I. We have both in fact for all practical purposes become aboriginal Krauts."

GW possessed in his tower apartments a cache of alchemical materials, among which were some pigments, and to pass the time while they debated, I carefully designed with *blanc d'argent* the seven great stars of Orion on my mask, where they might confabulate with the seven primary pocks beneath them.

"As within, so without," thought I. "As above, so below. *Pallidus in Side silvis errabat Orion.* Which to say, he wandered palely in the forest out of love for his beautiful wife, whom jealous Hera pitched into Hades, so says Ovid."

"If you don't need me," I said to Mehemet and GW, "might I take a walk?"

"Go, go, by all means, boy," said GW, waving me away and turning back to the fuming Mehemet, who continued inconsequentially to bewail and rejoice in his Teutonic metamorphosis and to exalt by contrast his natal Mani—its sea, its skies, its fish, its men; the wild greens of its mountain slopes (ἄγρια χόρτα του βουνού) that put Hannoverian sauerkraut to shame; indeed, nothing even on the German emperor's table— and he had sampled such stuff in Vienna—could rival his mother's simple *prosphagion*, washed down under the mulberry trees with a jug of retsina wine: bread hot from the oven and the sheep's milk cheese made by the monks of the Pantokrator. He smacked his lips magniloquently and called on God—or perhaps it was Allah?—as witness.

There is much to be said for being a nonentity and insignificant in the scheme of things: I gladly embraced that role. If ninnyship excused me of responsibility for dealing with Attila and his bully-backs, then a ninny I would be. My only proviso was that Zippie not perceive me as one.

"Oh," said Zippie, when we met yet another afternoon in the Orangerie parterre. "Mr Paisley has returned. He desires me to go to Hamelin to help look after a sick child there, the daughter of one of his acquaintances. For, he says, the infant's mother is also very unwell, and I have such experience now of nursing my aunt! But I should be back in a week. It's not far. Then we shall see each other again."

We parted very tenderly, and I returned to my business. For I now had the wherewithal for an important letter to Mr Harley, which then also needed to be ciphered and then carefully copied in lemon juice between the lines of a letter to Jenny Cutlett, who would give it to Dan'l.

The next morning, Herr von Görtz summoned me.

He motioned me to sit on a stool facing his desk, where I felt a bit of a dunce. He said, "The Elector and his family have gone to Schloss Celle. Thanks to you."

I was filled with pride. No longer was I a mere pawn in the affairs of the world.

"I know! They will be safe there from the Turk Attila."

"They were in no danger from Colonel Attila, who is the personal representative of King Carel," said Görtz, "but rather from that little trull Zippie Sowieso with whom you have had congress, don't tell me you haven't, and from her scheming 'Uncle' Robert Paisley, whom we have long known to be a Pretenderist of a singularly unsavory nature, who insinuated himself into our service long since for that very purpose."

"But Zipporah is just an orphaned girl," I exclaimed, surprised in the first place at his so cruelly mangling my darling's name and enraged, in the second, that he should dub her "What's-her-face" (which is what *Sowieso* comes down to). But I dared not show my anger to the Secret Man, and I added somewhat sotto voce: "And her uncle has sent her to Hamelin to nurse the child of his friend there."

"And that child has measles, a disease that kills more than one in three of its unhappy victims, which La Sowieso will surely herself contract in Hamelin and bring back here to Herrenhausen. Before the signs of the disease appear on her, she would, had he not been evacuated to Celle, have introduced it into the Elector's household, and indeed into George Ludwig's bed itself! The outcome might have been the death of the whole Electoral family. Such was Paisley's scheme, hatched no doubt at Saint-Germain. The girl did not know of it herself, of course."

"The Elector's bed . . . !"

"Georg Ludwig has been swiving her almost nightly ever since Paisley brought her here to inveigle His Grace's affections. La Schulenburg was getting very suspicious of her, however, so they came up with the scheme of sending the girl back to England, from where she returned masked, supposedly hideously disfigured. But her pretty face is in fact completely unmarked, I believe, behind that vizard."

"But . . ."

"She may well die, of course, of the measles. At least then I would no longer have that beanpole La Schulenburg breathing fire at me over her."

I departed, and back in the tower room sat down again before my half-written letter to Mr Harley, which must now take a very different tone.

It took me all the rest of that day and half the night to write, and after I had dispatched it by "the usual channel," I lay on my bed and wept a little.

However, I do believe that letter of mine had a far-reaching effect, for in 1712, someone played the very same trick on the dauphin of France and his family. The sweet, clever *dauphine*, Princess Marie Adelaïde, was infected with a *rougeole pourpre* by a measled *dame de palais* who had been newly introduced into her service (some said she was a secret *orangiste*), and Marie Adelaïde presently died, ravaged by the emetics and exsanguinations of the royal quacks. Her husband, the duke of Burgundy, caught the sickness from her and followed her into the grave only a week later, as did their elder son, the five-year-old duke of Brittany. Lewis XIV was thus left with only a feeble baby as *dauphin* and heir to the throne, who was also measled but was saved and lived to be king in his turn because his governess foiled the Faculty in their intention to bleed the child, as they had done his parents and brother with such fatal results, by locking herself in a room with the baby and refusing them entry. Few people doubted then that there was a plot to destroy the royal family. Indeed, the *dauphin* had been warned of it in a letter from his brother Philippe, the king of Spain.

Some said the Dutch were responsible. Grand Pensionary Heinsius was surely too honorable a man for such work, but there were men in the service of the United Provinces who would not have scrupled at it. However, Matt Prior, in his cups, once muttered to me, "Bolingbroke read your report. He exclaimed over it to me. And that man stopped at nothing, you know. He is perhaps the only person I have ever known who is truly, truly amoral. *Torcy thought he was behind the measling of Louis's family.*"

[*By an enormous joke of history, no one will ever know, Sarie, that I, your own good Isacq, thus saved the entire royal family of England from extermination—and that the royal family of France was decimated and very nearly wiped out also through my agency, albeit quite unwitting. Up on Mount Parnassos, Cleo must bepiss herself laughing when she thinks about it! Always assuming, of course, that the Muse of History actually thinks, something of which there is scant evidence!*

Who's this pissing Cleo? You haven't mentioned her before, said Sarie.]

Well, I should see Zippie very soon now, and she would explain everything, I thought the following bright Westphalian morn amid the fountains and geometrical topiary of the Great Garden as my feet steered me, almost of their own accord, it would appear, for I had no sense of directing them, toward the Orangerie, where perhaps she would even let me gaze on her face.

It was not to be.

Wheels crunched furiously on the raked gravel behind me.

"Hop in!" TF cried. "Hop in and be quick about it."

"Where did you get the *Kalesche*?" I said, admiring his phaeton.

"There's a *calèchier* in town," he said in French. "But do hop in! I've found us a splendid pair of sluts. You'll lose that maidenhead this day, my lad, or I'm an ape's uncle!"

I should have said, "It's lost already, you bastard! Call me a virgin no more!" But what I said was: "I fear I have a prior appointment with my Zippie."

"You young spark, you! But no matter. Pose the drab a *cuniculus*! A court lady will not lightly be cullied, and these babes of mine are both willing and ready."

"Tommi," I said. "I think I'm in love."

"Alas for you, then! But no matter. I met an old mate of ours at that Tingeltangel—you know, the Hedgehog, over Braunschweig way, where we had a few beers that time? Do you recall Attila the Stockholmish Turk? You could have knocked me over with a feather when I spotted him there. He'll be game, I'm sure. See you, kid!"

And before I could say another word, he whipped up the horse and blasted off in his dainty chariot.

I thought sadly a few moments of my late brother Berendt Jacob, with whose murderer TF now proposed to go wenching. But I knew the sorts of things TF would say if I challenged him: Attila had done nothing wrong; he had simply acted as any soldier would, as *un homme de cœur et d'honneur*. Why, he had even helped us afterwards! If anything, too, it was he himself, TF, who had precipitated the duel. And in any case, we had all been in drink and combusting when the challenge was so intemperately issued. Berendt Jacob's death had indeed been a cruel blow—but life was short, and these things were in the lap of Fortuna, *imperatrix mundi*, ruler of our world here down below. Fate had struck down my good old brother—but God must have willed it in his mysterious way—Uncle Augie had said so. There was nothing left to do but weep for him.

No, I didn't buy it! Even now the wheels I had set in motion were a-rolling. The Elector's lifeguards would dog the Turk Attila and catch him; and then perhaps he would yet swing from the Electoral gallows.

Thinking thus, I proceeded to the Orangerie.

There, alas, I found not my mistress in her vermilion mask but a barefaced serving maid with very ugly hands indeed, who made an obeisance, Saxon-clowness style, and put a folded paper in my way.

"I deeply regret, sir, that my aunt requests my immediate return to England," the note read. "But perhaps you may be kind enough to write to me in care of the Grecian Coffeehouse, Devereux Court, off Fleet Street.—Z. Ardis."

The drab's hands under my eyes called to mind a song I had heard among my brother Moon Calves: "Tho' her Hands they are red, and her Bubbies are coarse,/Her Quim, for all that, may be never the worse."

But I thought to myself: "No, no, damnation take it!" So I gave the girl a pfennig and off she scurried about her business. I was pleased to find myself less corrupted by idiot lust than I might have supposed.

What became of all this in the end? Mehemet's men did not catch Attila, assuming they even tried to do so, because he did not follow the Elector and his family to Schloss Celle, where I believe they spent a pleasant few weeks until the danger was supposed over.

The Turk must have smoked from TF while they were debauching themselves in the Tingeltangel, or whatever the place was called, that I was on to him. Nevertheless, I credit myself by these proceedings to have saved the lives of two kings of England, to wit, George I and George II, as well as of course of the electress Sophia and of the Prince of Wales, who will one day be king in London in his turn.

[*Not a bad day's work, don't you think, Sarie? But it will never be known that it was I who accomplished this. And, don't you know, it don't bother my head a bit! For I have no desire for fame. In fact, believe it or not, I should thoroughly dislike it if it ever befell me.*

I'm glad you didn't fall into the clutches of that Zippie, Sarie said. Something tells me she was what they call a trollop! And Sir Isaac must have been perfectly horrible to commit such an unnatural crime. It's hard to believe that people actually do such things. I hear Ouma Koekemoer's knecht out Riebeeck's Kasteel way was arrested the other day for—she let her voice drop to near a whisper—abusing it to a sheep like that. I suppose they'll hang him too.

And the sheep as well, I said. Unless it was under the age of consent. In which case, they'll just cut it up for lamb chops.]

But Herr von Görtz was right, alas, I discovered: my Zippie was nought but a common jilt. For scarce a fortnight or so after our first masked congress, I was smitten with a dysury, accompanied by a whitish secretion from my *meatus urinarius* (I learned these terms from the learned Hannoverian quack to whom Mehemet referred me): in short, I was afflicted with a *chaudepisse*: it burned like the blazes.

The repugnance I felt at this disease—whose emissions seemed a nice parody of love's divine utterances—was as nothing, though, to my despair at the betrayal the girl—*my* girl, as indeed I thought of her—had inflicted on me. I was mightily afflicted: all unbidden, thoughts of self-murder sprang into my brain. But luckily, restrained by its native horror at the idea of doing itself a hurt, my body played the coward.

The Electoral physician kindly offered to pump a stiff dose of mercury up my poor old tool with a syringe, but TF had warned me against this Paracelsian treatment, for, said he: "In the army, I've known mercury to cause men to lose their hair and teeth and even their sight and hearing. As physic, it's much worse than the clap, which I myself have had more than once. Here's what you do. A *sage femme* in Toulouse turned me on to this. Anoint your manly organ with plenty of good garlicky chicken fat. Human lard is even better, of course. Perhaps the local executioner sells it? *Weiß der Henker!* Meanwhile, knock back a draft of pounded cardamom and *cubèbe*, or cubebs, which is a kind of pepper, in half a pint or so of ginger wine three times daily. I can tell you, it clears the clap up real quick—and the stuff tastes not bad either."

GW seconded this advice. "For God's sake, no quicksilver, boy! It's deadly poison. But that fat and garlic are helpful in many diseases is well known, and the cubeb wine can surely do no harm. The pepper might well expel the *moleculæ gonorrhoeae* from your tarse by stimulating the *glandula pinealis*, or *conarium*, which, as you perhaps know, some physicians call the yard of the brain, since it resembles in shape a man's prick (though some say more like to a pineapple in form) and evidently governs the virile member. It's a well-founded phenomenon! Descartes actually believed the pineal to be 'the habitation of the soul' but he always went too far. Try, too, wearing red underclothes—Newton swears by scarlet as a panacea and he's a cunning bloke, even if besotted with his vials and trumpets."

"When England's Gloriana came down with the small pox, the court quack brought in a bolt of scarlet English broadcloth and wrapped her in it from head to foot—and as you know, she lived, did the Virgin Queen," said TF.

I observed what they said; I got tipsy at breakfast, and my nethers reeked of schmalz—the Elector's trusty old *Henker* (who, astoundingly, turned out indeed to be a Herr Weiß) unluckily having no human grease for sale at that time—and garlic. The symptoms of my *chaudepisse* duly abated. I remained in a despair about Zippie, but the weeks slipped by gently enough at Herrenhausen. Life as an Electoral parasite was not unpleasant. My duties as GW's amanuensis were light; often enough they consisted in reading and summarizing interesting books; and the food in the Refectorium was usually excellent, if a bit monotonous.

Then one day Herr von Görtz summoned me again. He sat back in his chair and looked me up and down. I was elegantly dressed and thought I should pass muster: my coat was a pretty light camlet faced with red velvet and had silver buttons. By this time I had ceased to wear my mask too.

"The small pox touched you but lightly, and word has it that you have also just overcome a clap," he said. "You are a very fortunate young man indeed. A very fortunate young man."

"Thank you, *Exzellenz!*"

"No need to thank me," he said. "It has been decided that you are to go on a mission. Grand Admiral Wassenaer will sail soon from the Texel for the Mediterranean with the Dutch squadron of the Allies' spring fleet, which will touch on the island of Sardinia. His Highness wishes to have a confidential agent go there to who knows English and Latin: English to be able to converse with Her Britannic Majesty's officers; Latin so as to communicate with the islanders, who evidently speak some sort of ancient Carthaginian called 'Sardish.'"

This was the first time I had heard of Baron Jan Gerrit van Wassenaer, Heer van Rosenburg and Prefect of the Rhineland, who was to play such a part in my future, and from whose coat of arms I later borrowed the crescent moon I put on my own *wapen*, signifying that I too had had a run in with the Saracens.

[*He ate himself to death, did old Wassenaer, you know, Sarie. His gullet burst from his stuffing of it, it seems, and when they opened up his corpus delicti, the whole dissecting room reeked of beer and duck, Jean Blignaut told me who came out as a cadet in the year of the eruption, 1723, to teach Daniël Hugot's children, and then married Hugot's widow, founding a dynasty of postmasters. Blignaut said he had it on good authority.*]

I was to go as soon as possible, Görtz said, on board Admiral Wassenaer's flagship, called *The Province of Utrecht*, which I would find at the Texel in Holland with a few weeks.

"And, sir, may I enquire, will my cousin Thomas also go?"

"That ruffian! Yes, he may as well go too. You may need someone like him if you fall in with brigands, with which the island is said to be infested. In any case, he's more trouble than he's worth here. Men like him were made for war, and if there's no war, they turn naturally to crime, for which their military experience equips and encourages 'em."

GW was clearly in the know, for he was unfazed by the news of my impending departure. I begged him for his blessing; but he averred that this fell beyond his remit, he being neither my father nor a clergyman, albeit a jurisconsult, a philosopher, a mathematician, a privy councilor, a mining engineer, the official historian of the Guelphs, and so on and so forth.

"However," he said, "in my jurisprudent capacity I shall recommend to you as my parting advice that you make your guide the charity of wisdom—in the language of the ancients, *caritas sapientis seu benevolentia universalis*—and benevolently esteem all those with whom you chance to meet."

[*Whatever you might think of his theodicy or his priority in the matter of the calculus, Sarie, there is no doubt in my mind that Godfrey William was the very best if men. I do believe that he wished everybody well—even Turks and Sir Isaac Newton!*]

TF and I packed up our few things and set out the very next day, Baron Görtz having made it clear that there was to be no shillyshallying: *Winkelzüge*—"dodges"—was the term he used.

Amsterdam, where we soon enough found ourselves, is, of course, the largest, richest, most populous, and most beautiful of cities. The endless streets, with their intersecting canals, their biscuit paving bricks, and their beautiful linden trees, are bordered by the most splendid houses. The dwellings, the shops, the warehouses were replete, it seemed, with all the riches of the world.

"It's a poxy good thing we are gentlemen, you and I," said TF, as we sat drinking our beer at the Gaaper, a tavern proclaimed by a sign that showed a fool in cap and bells gaping immoderately. "The last time I was here, I was a penniless bird of passage, a young *Zugvogel*, on my beam-ends and in imminent danger of going under. I dared not beg, since I might be arrested and sent to the workhouse if I did; and if you steal, the penalty is, of course, hanging—and they are quite firm about it too. But luckily then, I met a lady . . ."

We made our way to the Prinsenhof, where the Dutch Admiralty had its seat, and presented our papers.

Soon enough then we were on a launch being rowed to the
Provintie van Uytregt, a seventy-two gun monster with a huge
oranje-blanje-bleu tricolor flag flapping at its stern. The ship
towered overhead as we got near it. I'd never seen one of the
line before, except from a distance, and I was stunned by
the ingenuity embedded in every lineament of this immense
naval machine.

We were given hammocks among the *adelborsten*,
or midshipmen, youths of good family beginning their
naval-military careers. No sooner were we nicely settled in
at the midshipmen's mess, however, than we were brought
on deck and told that we would be going to another ship, for
Admiral Wassenaer, to whom our arrival had been reported
evidently said that he would have no such Hannoverian tittle-
tattlers aboard and ordered us transferred to a brig that was to
accompany the fleet, loaded with pitch, spare sails and tackle,
and suchlike. She was called the *Troost* and was commanded
by a young Dutchman named Captain François Zegers, who
turned out to be a very amiable fellow and became a good
friend of mine.

Al-Djezaïr al-Gharb

THE fleet set out the very next day and we had smooth
sailing until we came to Cape Finisterre, where the
weather turned very savage and black clouds covered
the sky, lowering right down to our mastheads. When the next
morning broke, we found ourselves between a gargantuan green
sea and a mountainous rocky shore on our lee beam, which
threatened to founder us in short order. There was no sign of
the rest of the fleet, and an icy wind blew. Captain Zegers then

attempted a tactic called "club-hauling"—"that is, bringing the ship's head around by letting the lee anchor down as soon as the wind shifts and then slipping the cable and trimming the sails," said TF, who came forward to assist in this procedure, which I am told is always a last resort.

It succeeded, but "I'm glad we can both swim," said TF. "It always amazes me that most of these poor sailors can't."

The poor old *Troost* was badly injured in this encounter with the elements; several men were washed overboard to drown, the taffrail was busted to splinters, and the sprit-sail was demolished. We were obliged it seems to "bagpipe the mizen" and take other nigromantic nautical measures of that kind, incomprehensible to me, as we limped on toward Gibraltar.

Once past the immense Rock, the *Troost* made for the great fortress of Port Mahon, on Menorca, in possession of the Allies since its taking by Lord Stanhope in 1708. A few leagues south of the small island of Formentera, however, we became aware of a trio of lateen-rigged xebecs closing in on us. They were Algerines. Zegers ran out his gun and sought to bombard them, but the scant carnage that resulted was mainly among the unfortunate rowers, Christian slaves chained to their oars. Once the awful bashibazouks were alongside, there was simply no resisting the horde of ferocious, saber-wielding mustachoes who soon swarmed over us.

"This has a depressing air of déjà vu," said TF. We raised our hands in the air and yelled, as we had been advised to do by one of our shipmates, "Merhamet etmek!" which is "Have mercy!" in Turkish if you don't know.

A jihadist with a red pique-devant beard, speaking Zeeland Dutch, advised us to remove our clothing, and we were quickly examined all over by Turks, *soi-disant* Turks, and their Moorish comrades and made to prance about on the deck, prodded with the point of the sword, to reveal any defects. It must have made a comical site, for the Mahometans all laughed heartily. Our tarses were examined for signs of the pox. Our ears were carefully checked for piercings, which might indicate wealth and the possibility of ransom. Some who had such were set aside. Thirteen of us, TF and I included, were selected to replace the dead and injured rowers. Captain Zegers and the remaining crew would remain on board under guard to convey the *Troost* to Algiers.

First we were set to work swabbing down the blood-stained decking of the xebec. Then, after donning the ragged pantaloons and shirts that had belonged to our predecessors (whose poor corpses our captors indicated by hand signals and shouts we should shove overboard), we were chained, each one by the left foot to the bench and the right hand to an oar. The surviving member of the bench, an Italian named Fabrizio, bade us a melancholy *benvenuto*.

Seemingly content with his prize, the *raïs*, or captain, of the jihadists set course south for Al-Djezaïr al-Gharb, the Islands of the West, as the Saracens call Algiers, which was formerly flanked by four small islands, now incorporated into the fortifications.

Arrived in Al-Djezaïr, we were disconnected from our oar, which we had luckily not had to employ much, the wind being very favorable, and marched through the streets, jeered at by spectators and bombarded with trash by boys. For we still had to be sold. From the cash profits realized from the sale of the cargo and slaves, after the Beylik and the ship-owners had had their shares, the *raïs* got forty parts, the seamen, the gunner and the troop commander three each, the helmsmen and foremen two, each soldier one and a half, and the cabin boy one part, while the Christian slave oarsmen, however many there might be, divided three parts among them all.

The conclusion of our march was a dungeon, a den of stone reached through dismal passageways, where we had to dispute the food flung to us with an army of rats. Being more experienced and quicker, the rats mostly won. I did not sleep, but passed the worst night of my life thus far. Then after not waking, I passed the worst day of it. Only the terrible nightmares with which the pox had smote me in the forest hut in Braunschweig could compare.

The manners of the *adjak* who had charge of us were as brutal as his face. The Dey had lately been assassinated by the janissaries, who were now permitted by the Porte to elect his successor from among themselves; all check on their wantonness having been removed, they did what they pleased. I was a prisoner in a place where murder ruled, where even the Dey himself stood little chance of dying in his bed, where men were routinely impaled . . . in short, I was fucking doomed.

"No, no," said the Spaniard shackled next to me. "There are cushy jobs here. You won't perforce have to dig salt, shift boulders on the mole, or be a rower frying on the bench of a *xabeque*. You could become a cook, for example, in one of the barracks. How are you with barbecue? If you can cook, you should let 'em know. The *yoldaşlar* are quite kind to their slaves—although they tend to bugger one senseless from time to time, as womenless men in a strange land might be expected to do."

"Who are the *yoldaşlar*?"

"Why, they are the Levantine Turk soldiers, of course. It means 'comrades.' They're not bad fellows on the whole. Their pay is miserable, forty sols every two months. But to supplement these starvation wages, the Dey allows 'em much freedom to pillage the Arabs and Kabyles of the countryside pretty much at will. And, of course, they have their shares of prizes taken at sea and slave raids along the coasts of Europe."

Diego—that was his name—spat and said, "The ones you want to watch out for here are the *kouloghlu*—half-breed spawn of janissaries and Moorish females. The name means 'sons of slaves.' Most folk around here are half-breeds. You may have noticed that the citizens of Algiers are very pale-skinned for inhabitants of the Æthiopian continent. Vicious they are too! The Levantine Turks won't admit 'em to be members of the garrison, or to any high office, because they're what the French call *mauvais sujets*—always plotting to expel the Turks and rule in their stead. Why, a runnagado European can do better than a native mongrel in Algiers! A runnagado, for example, may become a two-moon agha or a vice admiral; many do, even some that don't speak Turkish or Arabic, but one of these *kouloghlu* has little hope of it." He sighed. "You should definitely convert if your conscience will allow it. Mine won't, alas! We Spaniards are very proud."

"It does seem rather shameful to do a thing like that."

"Indeed, contemptible, unworthy of a man of honor. Yet better to blush than to be bastinadoed, as they say. It's a dilemma. So, then, become a cook! Or a choker. That's what I'm hoping for myself."

"A choker?"

"Well, yes. You see the Turks think 'emselves too nice to strangle or hang a man. But the Dey is always condemning people to be executed, and someone has to do the job! So who do you think? Jews, of course, or Christian slaves! A Jew called Mohel does it at present, but he's getting old and losing his grip. So I'm hoping the Agha will soon appoint me in his place."

He flexed his muscular arms to show off the strength that qualified him for this task, crossing his wrists and making a sharp tugging motion, accompanied by a gurgling sound in his throat, something like the keel of a boat scraping on marshy shingle.

"The thing that I fear most though is that the Agha may introduce here the Moorish custom of 'tossing.' In that case, he would have no need of my own services, for all that is required are a few muscular blackies. I have heard in fact that he has sent an emissary to Salé in Morocco, where they are trained for the purpose, to purchase a set of just such men."

["... *the person* ... *to be thus punished is seized upon by three or four strong negroes, who, taking hold of his hams, throw him up with all their strength, and at the same time turning him round, pitch him down head foremost; at which they are so dexterous by long use, that they can either break his neck the first toss, dislocate his shoulder, or let him fall less hurt. They continue doing this as often* ... *as ordered," Thomas Pellow, a Cornishman who was long a slave at Salé, explains. There is no end, I reflected, to the ways our species has devised to torment itself! One cannot but admire human ingenuity in such matters, although regretting, of course, our mutual unkindness.*]

We were driven the next day, TF and I, to the auction ground by *kouloghlu* wielding cudgels and bull's pizzles, arrogant spurleathers who spared not our hapless Christian bums in the least. There we were made to perform again our nude prancing for the benefit of shoppers. The depths of misery engulfed me as I performed for potential customers and let them examine my teeth and my tarse. But as Godfrey William insists, this is the best of all possible worlds. And indeed the *deus* in the *machina* was not long in putting in an appearance. ("This is pure vulgar Newtonianism," Godfrey William exclaimed long afterwards when I narrated these events to him, or would have if I had done so; "I do not subscribe myself to the notion that God makes periodic adjustments of that kind to the functioning of His world!")

TF and I were "waiting in the wings" (so to speak) while some Iberian maidens were being bargained for: a bearded face, surmounted by a crimson turban, clasped with an enormous lapis-lazuli broach, suddenly appeared before us and burst into hoots of laughter.

"Attila Effendi!" TF said.

"Thomas! Hänschen! What are you doing here? When were you taken?"

TF explained our bad luck.

"I shall buy you," Attila said. "A hundred and fifty Venetian sequins for the pair of you should do it! Damned if he don't take it! I'll knacker him if he don't!"

TF said: "Fifty louis d'or! Why, we'd surely be a bargain at that price!"

Attila counted out the cash and our chains were struck off by our jailer, suddenly grown obsequious. Soon the banter flew gaily as we were headed up a steep street to a door in a high wall draped with wisteria. Soon we were reclining on pillows on a charming verandah overlooking the bay, drinking coffee and pomegranate sherbet with Attila and an Albanian friend of his called Adnan. Soon too we saw which way the wind was blowing for us.

"You must both turn Turk," Attila said. "It's the easiest thing in the world, my dears. A lesson or two in the Holy Quran, a little snip down below, Mohel the Yid can do it for you, he's had lots of practice, so it won't hurt much, and the *grand Seigneur's* your uncle."

Seeing my puzzled look, TF whispered in my ear: "On appelle communement l'Empereur des Turcs, 'Le grand Seigneur.'" The emperor of the Turks is commonly called the Grand Seigneur.

And seeing my puzzled look, Attila exclaimed, "The circumciser doesn't have to be a Muslim."

"Islam is the religion of the future, you know," Adnan said. "All the Christian nations pay tribute to us, though we enslave their subjects at every opportunity and flog 'em all over." He snickered: "Literally!"

"I bet there are a million Christian slaves in North Africa," Attila said. "Europe's high and mighties are always too busy fighting one another, it seems, to be bothered to do much about it. Lucky for us! Nip across to a northern shore, load up the old xebec—take your pick—with a bunch of Spaniards, Sards, or Sicilians, and its raining sequins when you return! Of course, the market is badly oversold right now. The wretched *kouloghlu* have become so lazy, what with white slaves doing everything for 'em, that they scarcely lift a finger anymore. But the demand remains enormous. Every little *shaikh* in the Maghreb wants palefaces to tend to his nasty whims and gratify his guests."

"We'll think on it," I said.

TF gave me a wink and said: "What was the Sea Beggars motto in the old days, eh? *Liever Turcx dan Paus!* Better Turkish than Papist!"

"That was over a hundred years ago," I said. "And King Philip's bones have long been removed from the *pudridero* in El Escorial."

"Don't take too long about it," Attila said. "If I may be permitted to quote the Prophet, peace be upon him: 'Revolted by the piddle of the uncircumcised, the very earth cries out to God for forty days.' And remember, too, that you still legally belong to me, and I desire this."

A sudden chill descended, though the African sun shone as hot as ever, and I sneezed.

"Yarhamuka Allah!" Adnan said. And he translated: "God bless you!"

"Gesundheit!" TF said.

"Çok yaşa!" Attila said, scowling a grin. "À vos souhaits! Meanwhile, Adnan and I have business with the Agha. We'll be back in an hour or two. I strongly advise you to stay indoors here for now. Take it easy. Smoke if you like." He indicated the gold-topped hookahs with a nod. "I'll send a slave with some food."

"We are most grateful to you, Attila Effendi," said TF.

When they had gone, I said: "Perhaps we should make a run for it."

"Don't think you he expects just that? He's playing with us. Didn't you notice the *yoldaşlar* or whatever they are, with scimitars and pistols all stuck in their belts lurking in the back of the courtyard as we came in? I fear we wouldn't get very far if we ran! Better to be patient. And why not convert, after all, if it comes to that? What harm would it do?"

"As the poet says: 'Some have turned Turks for gain, yet live despised/After they've but been circumcised.' Don't you want to go back to Europe some day?"

"Why couldn't we though?"

"Why, the first whore in Christendom who saw your cropped tarse would tell, and since no one, I think, would take you for a Jew, the law would judge you a turncoat renegado. Which would be true if we go coursing with Attila. We might also have the bad luck to be taken by a ship of one of the European navies and hanged from the yard's arm."

"We could say we were forcibly trimmed out of spite by the Algerines."

"Also, it probably hurts like hell, no matter what he says. He doesn't remember—he was cut as a kid, and they say babies don't feel a thing. Anyway you can't do anything about it then; you just have to accept it because your mom and dad command it."

I simply *couldn't* turn Turk. After all, I was the descendant of the *Doktor Augustinianus* and a long line of pastors, *all of whom had moreover borne the identical name: my own, and honorably retained their prepuces.* How could I betray the memory of all those pious namesakes? I cited to my yawning cousin a family legend, inscribed by Vati on a flyleaf of the big Bible in the Grube parsonage's parlour:

In 1532, Bishop Erich of Paderborn, who also owned the adjacent bishopric of Osnabrück, negotiated with the bishop of Münster, Friedrich von Wied, to buy the latter's bishopric, for which he bid 20,000 gulden. The archbishop of Cologne, Hermann von Wied, backed this bit of simony, in part on the grounds that his brother Friedrich—whose hobby of working a lathe (*Drechseln*) had earned him the nickname of "the Spindleturner" (*der Spillendreher*)—had no interest in spiritual matters in any case.

Erich borrowed the money to buy the Münster bishopric from the Protestant Landgrave Philip ("the Magnanimous") of Hesse, who greatly relished helping the Roman Church shoot itself in the foot. Pope Clement VII (alias Giulio de' Medici) approved the deal and Erich was duly invested. The feasting and libations upon Erich's entry into his new see of Münster were so lavish, however, that the chief celebrant himself—Erich— dropped dead in the middle of them, thus leaving all three Westphalian bishoprics (Münster, Osnabrück, Paderborn) simultaneously vacant.

This ecclesiastical vacuum was just the opening Westphalia's Protestants needed. At the nearby Hanse city of Herford, founded in 789 by Charlemagne at a ford on the river Werre, the citizens and city council invited a fierce young preacher, like Luther a former Augustinian friar, to draw up a new constitution (*Kirchenordnung*) for their church, because they reckoned that no one in town could best him in argument. D—— himself may have nudged them toward this step more quickly than they otherwise would have by letting it be known that he was planning to leave town soon if they didn't give him the job.

Born around 1500, Johann D—— was the son of Bernhard D——, a councilor in the Hanseatic and Imperial free city of Lemgo, located in the Bega River valley in the Lippe Uplands, a region bordering to the south on the Teutoburger Wald, where the ancient Teutons massacred Augustus Caesar's legions in the famous battle Luther later dubbed the *Hermannsschlacht*. My father suggested that some early D——s had been in Hermann's army.

Lemgo had become a Hanse city in 1324. The Lemgo D——s traded in cloth via Lübeck with Scandinavia, and Johann's uncle was Dr. Hermann D——, the provincial superior of the Order of Saint Augustine in Saxony and Thuringia, and before that a professor at Rostock University. Like Luther, Hermann and Johann D—— were Eremites—members of the Order of the Hermits of Saint Augustine—and not, like their great contemporary Desiderius Erasmus, of the rather less strict canons regular. In either case, they were sworn to poverty, chastity, and obedience.

After Luther's theses were read from the pulpit there around 1518, a Reform movement rapidly developed in Lemgo. In 1528, still only in his twenties, Johann became known as the author of a radical exposition of Scripture. Then, in 1530, he shed his friar's habit and went to Wittenberg, where he met not only Martin Luther, but the famous theologian Philipp Melanchthon, called the *praeceptor Germaniae* (teacher of Germany), and the latter's confessor and wingman Johannes Bugenhagen *Pomeranus*.

Bugenhagen had warned him that Herford was a dangerous place, where Protestants might meet with violence, and on his return there, Johann found himself unable to preach the new doctrine in the Münsterkirche. Undaunted, he went out and preached it in the town cemetery, where growing crowds came to hear him. He probably felt like one of the Holy Apostles.

On April 7, 1532, *am Sonntag Quasimodogeniti*, which is to say, the Sunday following Easter Sunday, a new church constitution, *Ordinantie kerken ampte der erliken Stadt Hervorde dorch D. Johan D——*, received a full public reading. Bugenhagen, who had written several such constitutions, including that of Lübeck, supplied a preface to it praising Johann D——. As chief author of this *Kirchenordnung*, D—— became the first Lutheran minister at Herford, acclaimed as the *Doktor Augustinianus*.

However, D—— soon found himself in conflict with Luther himself. In Herford there had long been a community of the Brethren of the Common Life (Fratres Vitae Communis), committed to the so-called *devotio moderna* (modern devotion) movement and linked to the Augustinian canons regular. The related Sisters of the Common Life also had a house in Herford. The Fratres espoused Lutheranism, but the radical Herford city council nevertheless moved to secularize their houses and their persons as early as 1525. They were ordered to move into private accommodation, dress like everyone else and receive the sacraments in the city's churches. Needless to say, they objected to this leveling.

Now as it happened, Luther had himself attended a school of the Brethren of the Common Life in Magdeburg when he was in his early teens, and he remembered them fondly. Moreover, the Herford Fratres had adopted his doctrine of salvation by grace alone. On January 31, 1532, in his usual irascible way, Luther therefore responded to the Fratres' appeal to him against the dissolution of their order by denouncing his own adherents Johann D—— and his comrades as "raging, licentious, and undisciplined spirits," even going so far as to identify Satan by name as their inspiration. Condemned by the "Pope of Württemberg," D—— was obliged to step down as Herford's priest. He took his pregnant young wife—following Luther's example, he had married a former nun—to Minden, a backwater not far away. There, alas, the Ur-Johann died young, of anguish, or perhaps of accidie, around 1544, leaving five children, three of which presently died too in an epidemic of measles, leaving one, Hinrich, who followed his father's example by becoming an Augustinian, and a second, Johann, who followed his father's example by becoming a Lutheran pastor.

"Be bloody reasonable, for fuck's sake! How can you decide based on that old family bullshit? In any case, that was all back in the Dark Ages," said TF.

"It wasn't 'the Dark Ages.' It was what we call 'the Early New Time.'"

"Well, be a fanatic if you want, kid. Me, I'm getting myself cut just as soon as Attila can fix a date with Mohel the Yid!"

And so it was. TF surrendered his foreskin, turned Turk, adopted the name Touma Raïs (he was not, in fact, a captain, which is what *raïs* means, but he had always asserted that rank in Europe and was now, he claimed, admitted to the debates of the *taiat-al-raasa*, or guild of captains), wore silk, and had roast lamb and sherbet for breakfast, while the Dey presently ordered me put back in chains on a diet of black bread and water with the other pious pricks.

"I'm sorry, but there's nothing I can do about it," said Attila. "He could have me impaled, you know, if I don't obey orders. I suspect he'd be glad of the opportunity, too. He gets off on impalings, and the grander the one impaled the better as far as he's concerned. Pray for both our sakes that the strangler's bowstring may encircle his repulsive gullet sooner rather than later!"

And with that he tightened the silken points of his yellow tie-front Cassimeer breeches—a fashion favored by modish runnagadoes in Algiers—and exited my cell.

My comrades in incarceration included Irish fishermen, made captive in their native waters, and even two Icelanders, Sturla and Snorri, identical blond twins. Snorri told me that he and his brother were the only survivors at this time of forty or fifty of their countrymen who had been kidnapped from their village in the Westfjords of Iceland by Algerian raiders two years before. All the others had died, mostly of plague, but some murdered by their *kouloghlu* jailers.

Also among us—we were an international set—was a Frenchman named Benoît Venture de Paradis, who contended that if liberty were a matter of doing what one wanted, we should merely be slaves to ourselves. "'*Amor fati*' is my maxim," said Benoît. "Love your fate. Only he who learns to be content with the small part of the Great All that is his lot and go gladly wherever Fortuna may lead can be said to be truly free." Benoît confessed that he derived this doctrine from Marcus Aurelius.

"Insha'Allah," said I. "He was the emperor of Rome, wasn't he? Easy for him to talk! If he had been a galley slave, he might have sung a different song." Although it seemed to me that this *Amor fati* business fit well enough with GW's belief that this is the best of all possible worlds, which I was prepared to accept, if only because it pleased me to do so, it was hard to be *glad* to be in this dismal hole. Benoît, however, did not dispute his case, being of a whorish unresisting good nature—just the sort of companion you would want in adversity.

We were put to work in the dockyards. And hauling rocks and timber, over the months I gradually built up a powerful torso, which would later stand me in good stead as an oarsman.

TF visited from time to time, bringing meat and dates and dried figs in his pockets for me. "I am trying to get you out of here," he said. "So, I think, is Attila. This is the strangest place I've ever known—and some of the strangest people! The sheer queerity of things in these parts takes my breath away!"

"How's your tarse doing?"

"Terrific! Just itches a bit now."

He frowned narrowly at the pigeons strutting on the next-door roof.

"I think we shall be going a-coursing soon. All is very near in readiness."

"Oh, Tommi!"

"Touma Raïs, if you please. I am to captain one of the xebecs. There'll be three. A big one and two smaller craft. Attila is to be our leader—he's in line now to be *wakil al-kharj*—secretary of the navy, you might say. A sort of mutual fund has been formed by the Pasha and some wealthy Yids to finance us."

"And where shall you go?"

"Northeast coast of Sardinia, I think. Easy pickings there, they say. Hasn't been raided lately. You may be coming too."

He slipped this last in so softly that for a moment I hardly noticed.

"Why me?" I said at last.

"Because you wouldn't renege, that's why! You're a slave and the Pasha wants you for his galleys. They're rounding up all the oarsmen they can find. There's a shortage. The plague cut quite a swath through the slave quarters and everywhere else last winter. I'll look out for you though. I should be able to get you assigned to my xebec."

"I'm not strong enough to be an oarsman. Surely they see that?"

"Crap! You're as strong as an ox!"

"Well, I don't *feel* strong enough. That's what counts."

"Tell it to the *çorbacı!*"

"*Tazir!*" I said. "Shut up!"

We had switched to Levant jargon, what they call "la Franque," or Lingua Franca—the lingo of the Frankish crusaders long ago in the Holy Land, well salted with Turkish, Greek, and Arabic, with which runnagadoes and *yoldaşlar*, slaves and *kouloghlu* communicate in Barbary, and that I too had been obliged to learn over the course of the past few months in the *bagnio.*

There was no getting around it: I was indeed a slave. And when the corsair fleet assembled in a week—a huge war galley with twenty-four oars to a side, and two smaller ones each banked with twelve—I was there on one of the latter with Sturla and Snorri, slave caps of red cotton on our shaven heads. We were lucky, we were told, not to have been branded with crosses to mark us for the Christian dogs we were.

"À brebis tonduë Dieu mesure le vent," said my French friend Benoît, who sat on the bench behind us: "God gentles the wind to the shorn lamb."

Could this be true?

If so, it seemed to me a matter of great importance. And to tell the truth, I didn't feel nearly as bad about my predicament as my rational intelligence informed me that I *ought* to feel.

I had heard, too, that men in the last extremity are often very calm about it. And in fact I had myself been witness to an Englishman standing with other condemned persons on the gallows at Tyburn, the ropes already fixed around their necks, addressing his last words to the parson urging him to repent: "I came here to be hanged, Sir, not to pray!" and then leaping off the platform of his own accord, so that he preceded his fellow sufferers into eternity by several minutes. Of course, the English are famed for their careless approach to dying: English criminals often laugh, sing, cut jokes, and insult the spectators at the place of execution, and it is said that an English lord at Paris who offed himself gave as the reason simply that he could no longer endure the tedium of having to get dressed each day (notwithstanding that he did not perform that task himself, but had it done for him by his valet). Finally, of the English, I would note that there were a quite disproportionate number of them among the runnagadoes.

"Less babble, more brawn, Monsieur," said Touma Raïs, who was indeed, it turned out, to command our xebec, which was named *Ghazi* (the other small one being called *Bône*, and the great galley *Mezzomorto* after the recently deceased Turk grand admiral Hüseyin Pasha, who was given this odd nickname—"half-dead"—by the Venetians after a battle where he was wounded but to their annoyance survived).

The Epirot boatswain Enver stepped forward to give the philosophical *crapaud* a wack or three with the stretched bull's tarse that was his wand of office. Prodding Benoît gently with his toe, Thomas showed the bosun the palm of his hand to hold him off. The Griffin turned pale with rage at this *mountza*, a gesture supremely opprobrious among citizens of the whilom empire of Byzantium, but there was nothing he could do but droop his stretch of taurine prick and bear it best he could. No one challenged the *raïs* on an Algerine xebec (unless it be the captain of the janissaries).

"How are you doing, slave?" TF said.

"You talking to me?" I said.

We rowed on across the great bay, past Cape Matifou and northeast through the waters of the Mediterranean. My hands soon hurt like hell, even though I had taken care to smear them thickly with mutton fat, and the pain in my shoulders was such as I could scarcely endure. Luckily, Sturla and Snorri were excellent rowers—descended perhaps from a long line of Vikings? They sang softly to themselves, but I did not know the words of their chant.

We raided mostly in Italy and Sicily, descending before dawn on sleeping coastal villages, slaughtering their strong men and carrying off as many of the rest as we could load into the xebecs. Then when we got back to Algiers, it rained Christians, as they say. You could buy yourself a slave for a song.

So it went for many a month until I wished that as the Greek seamen tell, the sprite Arethusa would rise from the waves and demand of us in a voice like the wind itself:

"Where is the Megalexandros?"

If no one can answer her riddle, the enraged naiad immediately stirs up a storm and the ship is sunk. The correct answer, though, is known to all Greek skippers, so this seldom happens. It is, of course:

"The Megalexandros lives and reigns and conquers."

That said, Arethusa is content and returns to her lover Alpheus in Arcadia, leaving the vessel unharmed.

But if the waters stormed around us, and we feared for our lives, we were entertained by no watery enquirer about the Great Alexander.

"What nonsense those Greeks do talk," said Benoît. "They've got their ancestors' legends all mixed up!"

"The oar handles are rough as sharkskin; our hands are cut to the bone; our hair is plastered to our heads with salt; and the gums in our gobs are raw as butcher's meat," muttered a toothless old character called Kipple, or something like that, who claimed to come from a place called Kakamuchee, or something like that. "They whip us if we don't row. Who has time for stories? It don't look too good, so don't talk too wise." So ran the conversation among us rowers.

Then one day, somewhere in the midst of the vast, heat-hazed ocean sea, in the late afternoon, we sailed into a dense bank of fog; then the wind shifted swiftly, a weird grayish orangish sky lowered above, and we were abruptly lashed by gale upon gale of fine dust. Sahara sand covered everything and penetrated every fold of my clothing. My eyes stung like fire and I held my cap over them with my free hand. There was no rowing. You could not see twelve poles' distance in any direction. But our sails bore us on to the northeast.

The sirocco wind blew for about three hours. Just when you thought it would never cease, it ceased, and the fog gradually dispersed to reveal the great *oranje-blanje-bleu* of the Dutch Republic reared on the stern of a great ship scarcely a quarter of a mile away.

Blinking, I presently recognized the 64-gun ship of the line *Wassenaer*, commanded by Captain Cornelis van der Graaf, who had once said a kind word to me at the Prinsenhof, and then the *Uytregt* herself, the 72-gun flagship of Admiral Baron Jan Gerrit van Wassenaer, from which, above her stern, depended also an orange-white-blue tricolor and a very nearly equally large personal banner bearing his coat of arms, with its salient crescent moon, adopted by some distant ancestor of the Wassenaer race to memorialize his exploits in the Crusades.

This Wassenaer *wapen* was doubtless puzzling to some of our Turks, since its crescent moon was also, of course, their own Ottoman ensign. In any case, the *Mezzomorto* did not at once take to its heels (if I may put it so), as it should have done had Attila not been in a hashish stupor. Enver, thick-headed as a caulker's beetle, took the warning *coup de semonce* for a comradely salute and failed to understand for some time that we were heading straight into a Dutch armada. Thomas to no avail at all waved his arms and shouted across at the *Mezzomorto*. Then he gave the order to put the *Ghazi*'s head about and run for the horizon as fast as possible. The sails were struck, and we were painfully encouraged at our oars by Enver, who had no desire to be hanged for a pirate at anyone's yardarm. But we were rowing against the wind.

I'll say this for him, Jan Gerrit wasted no time. A single cannon shot rang out from the *Uytregt*, with a delicate little puff of white smoke standing out against the tattered fog. "Voila, le coup de semonce," said Benoît behind me. "What point in a shot across the bows, when they'll sink us certain as shit if they catch up with us," said his benchmate Smeaton. "And they have the wind now behind 'em in their sails."

Then, only minutes later, the *Uytregt* and the *Wassenaer* commenced all at once to thunder their broadsides; splinters could be seen to fly up from the *Mezzomorto*, which was closest, and a pair of frigates flying the *oranje-blanje-bleu* tacked quickly to cut off the *Bône* and *Ghazi*.

As we watched one of the trim Dutch warships plowed into the *Bône* amidships, slicing her frail form in two and sending 72 manacled slaves to the bottom with despairing cries. The heads of the few Turks aboard her who could swim bobbed amid the waves. The *Mezzomorto* would have suffered the same fate had she not already been sinking, with her freight of 144 doomed Christian rowers. The second Dutch frigate bore down on the *Ghazi*. In moments it would be our turn.

"Unshackle the oarsmen," TF cried, himself leaping to do so.

The bosun roared some obscenity and moved to stop him. Plunging his dag into the Epirot's gut, TF shoved him pop-eyed into the splashing brine. The other janissaries all followed Thomas's lead, and soon all the oarsmen were free and leaping into the sea, not waiting for the fatal impact that would sunder the *Ghazi*.

Neither did I wait. The sea foamed about me and washed off the mud that coated me. I realized that even a man on the brink of death could take pleasure in something. I did not see the *Ghazi* smashed and sunk. I was too busy keeping my head above water.

But I was one of those who could swim, and we were soon being hauled into Dutch longboats and taken aboard the *Uytregt*, where the corpulent Jan Gerrit stood on the high quarter deck surrounded by his officers and contemplated his triumph.

"Christian slaves to be brought to the nearest Christian port, and to a port held by the Sea Powers if they are Protestant; Turks, Moors, and Coologles to be conveyed to Leghorn, there to be sold to the highest bidder and the proceeds paid out as prize money to the fleet; runnagado dogs to be keelhauled without delay—after so many months at sea, we should have a fine crop of barnacles down there to greet 'em en route to hell." So said Jan Gerrit.

The bedraggled rescued were inspected one by one and divided first into Christians and Muslims. The Christians— about forty or so—were all from the *Ghazi*. The surviving Muslims were also about forty or fifty in number. Attila and Thomas were brought forward for Jan Gerrit to interrogate; the *raïs* of the *Bône* had drowned. In their sodden Cassimeer breeches and other dandyish finery, it was easy to see that Attila and Thomas were not mere tars or grunts.

"Pull down those fancy pantaloons and inspect their tarses," said Jan Gerrit.

Sailors seized and debagged the two, and the ship's chyrurgeon stepped forward.

First he looked at Attila. "Cut in childhood. Chronically clapped," he said.

Then he looked at Thomas. "Looks like a fresh job," he said. "Still a bit inflamed. No sign of clap."

He stepped back to where a sailor waited with a basin and towel for his hands.

"A runnagado, eh," said Jan Gerrit. "Score one for the mollusks!"

I stepped forward. "Sir," I said. "I was assigned to your service at the Prinsenhof but the ship I was in was captured. It was the *Troost*, under Captain François Zegers, sir. He was sent back to Algiers with a prize crew and I became a slave rower."

Jan Gerrit looked at me closely.

"Ah, yes, the little Hannoverian latinist foisted on me by the Elector."

I shall not attempt to translate his vulgar Hollands speech.

"I can testify, sir, to the fact that the condition of Touma Raïs's virile member is due to an unfortunate encounter he had with a witch. It has been the talk of the slave barracks in Algiers for several weeks, sir."

"A witch? Explain. What happened?"

"Well sir, have you heard of what is called *vagina dentata*, sir?"

"Pish, man! I'm no latinist. What is it?"

The chyrurgeon stepped forward and whispered at length in his ear.

"But is that not a mere fable?"

"No, sir. Pliny the Elder speaks of it. Paracelsus wrote a monograph on it, I believe, which has unfortunately been lost."

[*"The Byzantine Greeks I knew on Kerkyra record something similar," Benoît told me later. "They call it* farmakomoeni—*poison cunt. A man who copulates with such a woman dies in agony."*

"But I made that stuff about Pliny and Paracelsus up myself!" I said. "It was Thomas himself who told me about vagina dentata. *Said he knew a Sorb in the army who was bitten. I thought at the time that he was just shitting me—as usual. In fact, I still think so."*]

"Well, what happened to the *raïs*?" said Admiral Jan Gerrit.

"Touma Raïs was on a journey to a desert oasis in the far south when he crossed paths with this Touareg bitch. They dye their skin blue, you know, to amaze their victims. He couldn't resist . . . and to cut a long story short, she bit his tarse most painfully with the teeth of her quim."

"Good Lord!" said Jan Gerrit. "Well, since you vouch for it! We'll send him to Livorno then with the other Turks to be sold. He's a strapping fellow. Should fetch a pretty penny!"

"He saved all these men," I said, gesturing at my sodden companions. "But for him we'd all have gone to the bottom like the chained slaves on the other xebecs! Surely, sir, he deserves better." But Jan Gerrit had already turned away; lunch awaited him in the admiral's great day cabin, all finished out in mirror glass and red mahogany.

The heads of Algerine slave rowers are kept closely shaved, and the next thing I noted aboard the mighty *Uytregt* was that a fine layer of stubble was already making itself evident on my scalp. I ran my hand over it and almost laughed; so quickly the body adapts to liberty! The next thing I noted after that was Snorri staring fixedly over the rail at the waves; Sturla was among those not saved, and his brother still hoped that he might yet be found clinging to some bit of wreckage.

The janissaries were crowded together under guard by Dutch marines in the aft orlop deck; going down there, I was able to speak to Thomas.

"Sorry about your being sold off," I said. "Where's Livorno anyhow? I thought all the Turk captives were being sent to Leghorn!"

"It's Legorno. Leghorn is what the English call it in their vainglorious way. Like the Dutch they are always changing the names of everything to suit 'emselves. But the Roman name was Liburnus, so Eye-ties who study what they call *rinascita* prefer 'Livorno,' and hoitys like the admiral have adopted the fashion. It's kind of like Algiers actually. Very cosmopolitan and everyone and his uncle trades in slaves. Why not? Swapping a braid of garlic for a Muslim in the Piazza Grande in Legorno is just like swapping a bunch of onions for a Catholic in the Casbah at Algiers. I know some Jewish dealers there, and one of 'em is bound to cough up for me. It'll be like when Attila bought us—déjà vu all over again! Don't worry—I won't end up a galley slave, not me."

I could tell he was putting a brave face on it.

When I left, I saw that he and Attila had fallen to dicing, although how they had concealed their beloved ivories, I can't imagine, since they had been stripped even of their Cassimeer pants by the Dutchmen and knelt there now gaming in their small clothes.

Feeling suddenly very lonely, I sought the company of Snorri and Benoît, who stood gazing still at the sea as *Uytregt* set her course toward "the nearest Christian port held by the Sea Powers"—presumably Mahon or Cagliari in Sardinia—followed in close rank by the *Wassenaer* and the rest of the Dutch flotilla.

"He's drowned," Snorri said. "My dear brother with whom I have kept company from before my birth is drowned in the ocean."

"He's with God," said Benoît.

"I know how you must feel," I said. "For I saw my own beloved brother Berendt murdered by Attila Raïs."

"That lustful fiend brought Sturla here to his death," Snorri said. "He must be killed—it's my *faida* now to do it. What you Germans call *Blutrache*—blood vengeance."

"But how?" said Benoît. "The Dutchmen won't let you harm a hair of his head. A great man like him is worth a fortune in ransom money to 'em! The Pasha will surely pay many, many Venetian sequins to get his *mazoul agha* back, and every man aboard this ship may hope to get at least a little of that gold as his portion."

"You won't have long to extract vengeance," said I. "We'll soon be put ashore and then they'll take him to Leghorn."

"But why would they if they're going to sell him back to the Pasha 'emselves?" said Benoît. "The *yoldaşlar* will be sent there, of course, but not the *raïs*."

"You're right," I said. "And perhaps Touma Raïs will also be held back despite what Jan Gerrit said about disposing of him to the highest bidder." And I thought immediately that perhaps I could bring this about. All I'd need to do was persuade the admiral that TF was ransomable too.

But this was of course easier said than done. I was a rescued slave—at best, if anyone remembered, a luckless *secrétaire-interprète* foisted on Baron van Wassenaer by the Hannoverian Elector, he believed, to spy on him. I scarcely had the Grand Admiral's ear—in fact, as soon as I came to his attention at the Texel, he'd transferred me to the *Troost* as a nuisance. I'd be lucky even to set eyes on him again.

"Perhaps I might address him as a member emeritus of the faculty of the Collège de Genève, founded by the great Calvin himself," said Benoît, who read my thought. "I was too, you know. Perhaps I even am still, providing my brother pedants have not yet had me declared dead. In any case, I've heard it said that our admiral is a Gomaerist—that is, he reveres Calvin and must believe that our fate is absolutely predestined. And if you'll swallow that, you'll swallow anything!"

I'd never heard of François Gomaer before but from the disquisitions of Professor Quistorpius, my docent at Rostock, I knew a bit about supralapsarianism, the old Netherlandish counter-remonstrants, and the horrid judicial murder of Oldenbarnevelt. And Godfrey William had elucidated the doctrine of predestination for me: "The point is that we cannot know what the case may be. Since no man is truly prepared to believe himself to be damned, Calvinists necessarily act as though they were saved, which means they generally act better than they might otherwise have done. However, since they believe their fate to be absolutely predestined, they also feel freer to do as they wish—since whatever it is, it must be God's will—which makes 'em more energetic than they might otherwise have been, and in particular more *commercially* energetic. That is perhaps the chief reason why the Dutch Republic is the greatest trading nation on earth. You might almost say that Calvinism willy-nilly makes possible the more flexible functioning of free will. It provides those who in England and Holland are called capitalists (because, that is to say, they are *taxables par capitation*) with a moral fulcrum for their business operations. Thus we may detect the functioning of this best of all possible worlds even in the odd notions of the Puritans and the Calvinists—and your Uncle Augie and his Pietist friends hold rather similar views, of course, though moderated in their case by honest North German practicality. A sense of balance is always what is needed in matters of religion."

"There was one thief saved and no more, therefore presume not, and there was one saved, and therefore despair not," said I. "So, someone says, said Saint Augustine."

"Exactly," said Benoît. "I'm a bit of an Arminian myself, but there's no need to tell *Mynheer* the Baron Admiral that."

I felt the delicious tingling of the skin that comes over you at the prospect of action.

Later it was revealed to me that Benoît was not from Geneva at all, but from Marseille, and that his surname was not Benoît Venture de Paradis but Philibert Rusé. Neither was he an Arminian—or even a Protestant: he was a defrocked Catholic priest who had been condemned to serve in the royal French galleys for committing what they call "spiritual incest"— which is to say, copulating with a girl under his ecclesiastical direction—and had subsequently been captured and enslaved by the Algerines. He was a compulsive liar—as the French say, a *menteur comme un arracheur de dents*, which is to say, he lied like a tooth-puller, which I suspect he may at some points in his career have been—and loved nothing better than to make up stories about himself. But I thought him an excellent chap, and he certainly fibbed to good purpose to Jan Gerrit's benighted sky-pilot.

The aforesaid *predikant* then reported to his master that a philological paragon from the Collège Calvin in Geneva was among the rescued Christian slaves. In no time at all "Philibert," as I might perhaps now call him (not that I shall), was seated at the admiral's table sipping Tokay, nibbling Jordan almonds, quoting Scripture in Latin, Greek, and Syriac, and setting forth that Touma Raïs was the darling of the current Algerine two-moon agha, who would likely pay as much ransom to get him back as the Pasha would for Attila Raïs himself.

"Most interesting!" said Jan Gerrit, and took the bait. For although a dashing sailor of great courage, and at this time in his heyday a fine figure (he spoke very passable English too), *Meneer* the Baron Admiral was a marvel of greed and could never get enough of desideratums, be they bankable, fuckable, potable, or edible; which finally did him in: as I have wrote elsewhere, in retirement he gorged himself to death: his surfeited *œsophagus*, being discovered at the *autopsia cadaverica* to have exploded, spewing roast duck and Flanders brown ale into his chest cavity.

But that was many years later, and I digress again.

In short, Thomas was ordered not to be sent to Livorno but confined with Attila in Fort San Felipe at Mahon on the island of Menorca, conquered a year or two earlier by the English under General Stanhope, until such time as a deal could be worked out with Agha and Pasha. For it was to Port Mahon, reputed third of the Mediterranean's safe havens (the other two being the months of June and July) that we were now bound.

Did we get there?

We did not. The month was neither June nor July, and a day and a half's sail later, one of the treacherous storms typical of those waters blew up out of nowhere: the Netherlandish armada was fortunate to limp battered but undiminished into the port of Callaris or Càller (in Catalan), now called Cagliari, the capital of Sardinia. I thus never saw Mahon and can give no account of that commodious and excellent harbor, allowed by all to be the finest in the Mediterranean.

O, du lieber Augustin

C AGLIARI: the name comes I surmise, since the ancient Romans ruled it for six centuries, from the Latin word *coagulare*, which means "curdle"; and for witness there was much cheese for sale there: to name a few kinds I can remember, *brocciu*, *cagliu*, and that horrible Sard cheese called *casu marzu*, said to be an aphrodisiac, but which even the most impotent of rakes might resist consuming, since live maggots are of its essence.

In August 1708, Sir John Leake, Vice-Admiral of the Blue, representing the Sea Powers, issued an ultimatum to the Spanish viceroy of Sardinia, the marquis of Jamaica, inviting him to surrender. Then, without waiting for a response, Leake impetuously permitted a bombardment the same night. Six score or more shells were lobbed into the unfortunate town. Come daylight, notwithstanding his eighty-seven brass cannon, Señor Jamaica capitulated, and the city's gates were opened to the invaders. Thus was Sardinia with its 300,000 inhabitants conquered by a mere flotilla, an island so fertile that it been the granary of the ancient Romans (as the Whig Junto in London well knew, all of them having had fine classical educations) and abounding in remounts for the Allied cavalry in Catalonia. Fourteen hundred tons of wheat were immediately requisitioned and transported to Barcelona for the nourishment of the Imperial forces and their Anglo-Dutch allies.

The English soon came into conflict with the Sards, whose vegetables they made free to plunder and whose womenfolk they tormented in their nautical way. One of the crew of an English 70-gun third-rate ship of the line, HMS *Northumberland*, that stood in the harbor, unwisely ventured into the upper city with too few of his shipmates and got drunk there. Unknown persons thereupon took the opportunity to get their revenge on the resented interlopers, murdering him "very barbarously," said Leake.

So when we arrived, we found ourselves in a place buzzing with rebellion and patrolled by squads of English marines, to whom Jan Gerrit now added their Dutch counterparts while he refitted his armada. The Sardinians gazed sardonically (say it I must, think the worse of me if you wish) upon these sweaty, red-faced, musket-toting foreigners. But they weren't dying laughing, as eaters of the *herba Sardonia*—a sort of *Ranunculus*, or buttercup, that blisters the mouth when eaten, Benoît said— are reputed to do. They were sick and tired of the Wars of the Spanish and English Successions, one explained to us, and just wished their "liberators," of whatever nation, would go away and leave them in peace.

"They celebrate the feast of Saint Lucifer here," an officer of the English marines, one Captain Herbert, told me. "Damme! A bit odd, what!"

A spikey, opinioned little man, the captain had got himself a mistress from Metz, Kunigunde von Welcherlei, or something of the sort (whom he rudely persisted in referring to, even in her presence, as "the queen bee"). He had some kind of hold on her, knew something that it would be to her disadvantage if revealed. We met—and it was to be a most fortunate acquaintance, as you'll see—when she heard me singing in the street, you know, the charming Viennese song that goes:

> O, du lieber Augustin, Augustin, Augustin,
> O, du lieber Augustin, alles ist hin.

Our common Germanity established, Kunigunde and I strolled in the marketplace admiring the profusion of strange produce, unfamiliar to Teutonic eyes, but some of which I had already seen in Algiers and could name for her: Those are *alcachofas*, or cardoons ("We call them artichokes," she said); these are *melongenas*, or *berenjenas* ("We call them aubergines," she said).

We gazed into one another's eyes standing very close together in front of a mountain of aromatic minions and nectarines—or do I embroider? I thought myself with the lovely *Baronin* in some peach orchard sheltered by an ancient, moss-grown wall. From somewhere, very far off, the melancholy Carthaginian ululations of the fruit women impinged.

"Let's get some of these lovely big ones, then," said Kunigunde.

The look on my face must have conveyed something. She said: "How old are you, Johann?"

I was twenty-one, wasn't I? Or was it twenty-two?

"I had supposed about eighteen," she said. "But you'll make some lucky woman a wonderful husband one of these days."

Aside from us, the liberated captives of the Algerine corsairs, and the troops of the sea powers in their red (for the English) or iron gray coats (for the Dutch), there were in Cagliari three classes of humans: the once and future Spanish masters, sweating in their wigs, who were as ruled by fashion as much as any London or Paris gutter jumper; the ragged, shackled Muslim slaves, of course, for all the world indistinguishable from the Christian slaves we'd been ourselves in Africa; and, finally, the Old Sards in their country garb: striped dresses, scarves, and mantles for the women, and the men in short black capes, white linen shirts, and black *sobrapantalones* of homespun frieze, with white trousers tucked into gaiters and big fezzy stocking caps of black or red, flattened on top and usually folded forward to shade the eyes.

Why I know not, but I felt myself very comfortable there with these Sardinians. They seemed proud and pleased with themselves and struck me as very fine in comparison with the ill-humored continentals. I liked their Carthaginian bonnets. This might be a good place to live. And after all, a man must live somewhere in the world.

"The *mousquittes* are awful here though," said Kunigunde, when I suggested this to her. "Satan must have created the horrid things to torment us! What other purpose could they have? And then the mal'aria that rises from the marshes every summer kills one. The only cure is Jesuits' powder—you must get some if you value your life."

"Come along, QB," Captain Herbert said grumpily. "I want my tea." And he took her firmly by the arm and hauled her off, which having enlisted as his hussy, she could not, alas, refuse, nor I reasonably object to.

"I am so-o-o sick of your teas, Mr Herbert!" she said for all to hear as they departed.

Once we were disembarked from Jan Gerrit's fleet, he and his officers paid us no more attention. Attila and TF were confined under guard in what was, by reason of a small statue of that animal adorning it, called the Elephant Tower, which served as the city's jail. As far as the Hogen Mogens were concerned, the rest of us were simply free to go wherever we pleased.

We liberated "chaps" (I've found this handy word in Mr Steele's magazine *The Spectator*, so make free to use it) were destitute, however, our only possessions being the clothes and boots Captain van der Graaf had kindly procured for us in place of our Algerine slave garb. In theory, we might expect to be paid a few farthings of the money to be got from the sale of the captured *yoldaşlar* in Leghorn, and from the anticipated ransoming of Attila and my cousin by the Pasha and Agha, if it ever happened (in practice, it would be a very long time coming).

I requested in vain to be taken back into Jan Gerrit's service, but the Baron Admiral allowed that he had no further need of me—I being no sailor and he having no instructions to conduct operations on land—and he recommended that I apply to my countrymen, as he called them. I would find the Austrians at a place called Sassari in the northern part of the island. The Imperial forces were settling in there as the new rulers and would take control of Cagliari too just as soon as they could. For their part, the Sea Powers would be glad enough to hand over Cagliari to Archduke Karl, who in his capacity as His Most Catholic Majesty King Carlos III of Spain was, they postulated, its rightful inheritor.

"Let's go to Sassari then," said Benoît. But Snorri wished to remain in Cagliari to have his family *faida* out with Attila, and I couldn't leave without TF. "We must find some way of getting 'em out of that prison," I said, and surrendered to febrilous day-dreams of getting into the Elephant Tower under pretense of being munitioners and then carrying out TF and Attila past the guards in hampers or lowering them down on slings. It has always been my way to think foolishly, if not always to act so.

Captain Herbert had permitted the three of us, Benoît, Snorri, and myself, to inhabit a sort of booth, or hovel, at the foot of the castle that crowned the hill, in which his men sheltered from the heat of the day and we at night too after they had returned to their hammocks aboard the *Northumberland* (for they did not venture to patrol after twilight); but for this kindness, we should have had nowhere to rest our heads. Where the other liberated Christians went I know not. They had scattered through the city to try their luck with the inhabitants and probably got as good as we did, for the Sards were on the whole a generous people.

We had no lamps nor any candles and so on moonless nights crept to bed on our heaps of straw and rubbish in the inky blackness. The smell of dust was in our nostrils—not a bad smell really when it settles down with you—and the cats and rats, or whatever they might be that scurried about in the night did us no harm. We were in a kind of limbus, neither damned nor entirely saved, and could only wait for something to happen, or so it seemed to me. After a while, too, we saw no more of Captain Herbert and his mistress—they had gone somewhere. I endeavored to put Kunigunde out of my mind, assigning her to that dim Platonic catacomb of dreams in which my surviving notions of Jenny and Zippie also resided. I wonder what they would have made of keeping company together in this way had they known it, the three ladies; but thus we all of us are jumbled up and stored in the memories of others, willy-nilly, without so much as a by-your-leave. Even our own parents likely catalogue us on the same shelf as other children they have known in their lives: not only themselves, but their sisters and brothers; cousins; neighbor children; and children in books and stories, even in pious cases the baby Jesus, paragon of infants. They mean no harm by it, and neither did I.

Jenny, Zippie, and Kuni would none of them, I think, have *entirely* resented being memorialized in this way: any woman not a whore or a harridan admits the spice of romantic worship in the composition of a pretty gallant, such as I hoped they found me. The fact is, I thought of them all three very fondly indeed, and would have found it better reason to turn Turk, and that my tarse be trimmed, than Attila's threats and blandishments ever were, if I could have married them all three (and under the law of the Prophet, I could, of course, even have added a *fourth*, further compounding my imagined happiness).

As a good Lutheran son of my saintly father and nephew to my dear Uncle Augie, to whom I owed so much, I adhered with all my heart to the *Confessio Augustana*, however, and not to such Mahometan conceits and circumlocutions, and so I strove manfully to think of Jenny, Zippie, and Kuni as three sisters of mine in Christ.

I was reflecting on all this while lying wakeful in the dark of early morning, looking for dawn to break over the Gulf of the Angels, or Bay of Cagliari, while gently favoring my wanton tarse so as to bring it to a more civil frame of mind, when I heard a whistle, so low as to be scarcely audible, that could have come from no other lips than those of my cousin TF. Many a time had I heard it when we were hunting in the woods and fields of Pomerania.

"Come," he said. "Attila is waiting with mules and tackle."

The guards at the Elephant Tower had, it seemed, been set a-doze by Kunigunde with a tincture of Greek valerian, the drink they call Jacob's Ladder, since it is a staircase to dreams, mixed into some strong Jerez brandy, and she had then released the prisoners, not only our two, but fifteen others, common scape-gallows of the city, who had swiftly fled far and wide once their cell doors were unlocked.

Two of the latter had, however, been suborned by Attila to steal a fishing boat in the port and sail it to the island of Santu Antiogu to the west so as to throw the searchers who must surely pursue him off the scent. "They'd naturally suppose us to escape by sea, you see," said TF. "They'd never expect us to head north inland. And once we are in the Barbàgia, they'll never get us back. Spain's writ never extended there, and Cagliari's certainly doesn't."

I gathered that this Barbàgia was a savage region of the interior, and that Attila had found one of the ruffians held in the Elephant Tower who came from there and would be our guide through the mountains.

"What shall we do after that?"

"I shall go to join His Swedish Majesty, Demirbaş Şarl, at Bender on the Dniester river," said Attila, "where he has lived as the guest of my other sovereign, the Sultan, having lost at Poltava to Tsar Peter."

"And I shall go to Vienna with Kunigunde," said TF. "I hear Stranitzky is packing 'em in at the new Kärntnertor Theater with his Hanswursts, and I have a mortal urge to see some clowning. Why don't you come with us?"

"I shall go to Sassari first," I said.

Benoît said he would like to go there with me. Snorri feigned to snore. And as everyone knows, it is very difficult to wake a man who is not asleep without doing him injury. So I let him be. He had his reasons, which involved a well-honed eight-inch blade he kept under his bed-board.

Where had they gotten the mules? The animals had, it seemed, been impounded by Captain Herbert's naval detachment for patrolling purposes, and Kunigunde knew where they were stabled by the careless British tars, who had other things on their minds.

After riding all night, we came at first light to a plateau called the Giara de Gestori, where we sheltered in one of those ruins called a *nurake*, of which there are many thousands in this island, built by giants of old, they say, longtime before the Romans and Carthaginians fought here. It seemed a hill much like any other, and you would not have thought there was anything special there, but our guide, a villain called Zuannantò, brought us by a hidden path into the center of it, where we found a shaft lined with massive rocks that led deep down into rock, by which you could enter through a narrow, stone-linteled casement into a succession of large, dry chambers, each perhaps twenty feet in height by fifty wide and long. In one of these there was a spring from which a thin stream of clear water ran down through a crack in the rock into a small pool, which must have drained somehow at an even rate, for it never got deeper or shallower either. Here folk of thousands of years past had once found refuge from their enemies, who must have been terrible, since the makers of the *nurake* had gone to so much trouble to create such shelters, and so many of them—the whole island must have been consumed by fighting. "Probably it was from their own close kin that they fled to these fortresses," said TF. "For there is no struggle as cruel as that among brothers, as our foreparents found in our own country during the Thirty Years' War, when one German in three died at the hands of his ilk."

In our *nurake*, upon an ancient hearth built before the time of the Caesars by unknown hands, we made ourselves a fire, on which we carbonadoed for breakfast an enormous large hare Zuannantò had brought down with his *frundza*, or slingshot (see, I was learning Sardish). This we ate with apples and pears he had in his *bisaccia*, a sort of knapsack with large pockets at each end, such as you might drape over a donkey, but that Sards wear over their own shoulders, so that one pouch handily hangs down in front of you and the other at the back.

Then we slept. Kunigunde lay near TF in a room thither from the one where we had eaten, and where I and the others lay ourselves down.

Later—it was after I had failed to hold Ziza too—I asked Doctor Efix, an old Sassari physicianer who knew all the answers, why it was that I always struck out with women. He stood back, squinted at me for a few moments, and said: "It is because in making you, Providence departed from the Golden Rule. Your left leg is longer than the right; one eye rides higher than the other; one ear sits lower on your head than the other. Women don't know that they see this, but the female demon in their bellies takes note and cuts off the flow of desire."

What he said was true, I realized. Like anyone else, I had observed myself in a looking glass many times, and I knew that my ears were mismatched: and my spectacles had often slipped awry in the days before they were miraculously made redundant by that fatal duel in Wismar.

"You are right, I am a bit lopsided. But what can I do about this? Is there any cure?"

"The only cure is not to beat about the bush with women. Say simply, 'I am a crooked man, I know. But I will love you better and more faithfully than a straight man would. For straight men are rigged up by their pride and vainglory, but I am modest and kind and aware of my faults, so you will not need to tell 'em me.'"

I awoke before the others—sleep does not rest easily upon me—and climbed out onto the slope, where I sat in the strong afternoon sunlight watching the rock lizards in hues ranging from dark green to cinnamon brown to lustrous black. Zuannantò came out to sit with me and indicated with the help of dumb signs that the people hereabouts called these reptiles *aligestra*. Supposing, it seemed, that I wanted to eat them, he pointed out as an alternative a lumbering tortoise, what is known to Germans as a shield toad, which he thought, if I correctly understood him, we might roast for our supper. Faced with this unappealing prospect, I quite without willing it shook my head and, somewhat to my own surprise, said: "Baa, baa!"

Zuannantò grinned and replied: "Baa, baa!" He motioned me to follow him, and I did, up the gulch and out into the flattened top of the *nurake*-hill. Taking me by the arm, he pointed at a slope opposite, across which a stream of grayish whitish flecks could be seen flowing. "Baa, baa!" he said, pantomimed cutting a sheep's throat, and quickly tapped first my chest and then his own.

We had found a common language it seemed, and I had unwittingly hit upon Zuannantò's profession. He had, I later discovered, been instructed to refrain from pursuing it until further notice, but he now wishfully took that as given, and without further ado led me down the gully and into the scrub land below, seeing no sense in eating rabbits and tortoises in a land of mutton.

I stumbled after him along a hedge of prickly pears, as the Algerines call them, but whose Latin name is *Opuntia*. It was only natural that they should be found in Sardinia, I mused, since according to the elder Pliny—who says unequivocally that they flourish *circa Opuntem*—they take their name from Opuntian Locris, a region of Greece near to the pass of Thermopylae. Professor Quistorpius had set me to read Estienne's edition of Herodotus (the beautiful 1592 one, that is), so I was very well informed about all this.

Presumably, Sardis was also overgrown with these same, misnamed "Indian figs," which botanizing whifflers now assert to be Mexican. How curious the mania for assigning an American origin to strange plants and creatures! The exact same thing occurs with the *indianischer Hahn*, that ugly black fowl of indifferent, dry meat, which the Greeks and Italians call a "French bird," and the English, rather more sensibly, a "Turkey." The Turks, who know very well that it came to them from India, call the creature a *hindi*, from which their allies the French clearly derive their own name for it: *le dindon*. Nonetheless wiseacres are abundant in the London coffee-houses who will tell you with the greatest confidence that the bird makes its original home in the forests of North America!

Thus I scornfully dogmatized to myself, but now know the opinions I then held to have been fatuous. We crouched behind a screen of acacia and Zuannantò silently pointed out to me a flock whose shepherd drowsed beneath a shrub.

"Let the baa-lambs be, my dear!" said TF, who had come silently up behind us. "That's all we need now, to have the locals breathing down our necks. Zuannantò was raised a robber. He's a fool, and they'll hang him or have him row in a galley one day, but he's good at what he does. You on the other hand were raised to be a Lutheran pastor and a metaphysician, and I don't think you'd be much cop as a rustler of livestock!"

Roast tortoise it was, then, for supper. Not much meat on those things. But we had prickly pears aplenty.

Our plan was to ride by night and rest during the heat of the day in some lonely place, and this we did. Zuannantò each morning ventured forth to seek what provisions might be found, acting the part in the villages along our way of a disbanded recruit returning to his home in Gallura in the north of the island. But one day in the middle of our journey, he did not come back. It was near a place called Orgòsolo, inhabited by descendants of the most ancient original inhabitants, who for three thousand years have been at war with the successive invaders of their island—Phoenicians, Carthaginians, Romans, Byzantines, Pisans, Genoese, Catalans, and Spaniards—and are thus famed for their tenacious ferocity. They post up the names of those they plan to murder on the church door and exterminate whole families in their feuds. Or so the story goes. "I believe they must have killed him," said TF. "Poor fellow! He wasn't a bad lad in his way, though a villain."

That night we continued on our way, using an old ship's compass to check on the route through the mountains.

Next afternoon when I woke groggily from a heavy, stupefying slumber—we had stopped at a desolate, empty shepherd's hut on the slope of a table-topped mountain of gray granite—I found that Attila was gone too, taking with him Kunigunde. TF said nothing, but I could see even he was downcast and felt closer to him for it. If even he, with his bully demeanor and eighteen-inch calves, could lose a woman like that, I didn't feel so badly about having done so myself (not, of course, that I'd ever had her in the first place).

"She was just a bloody trull," he said.

"We would have parted soon anyway," I said, "since he was heading for Olbia, where he expected to find a fishing boat to take him over to the free port of Civitavecchia on the Continent—from where he might make his way to the lands of the Great Turk." At Olbia, Snurri would be waiting for him with his blade. But I did not say this, because TF wasn't supposed to know. But perhaps he would have liked to know it now.

Who knows what happened to them? People come into your life, and whether you love them or hate them, or are indifferent, eventually they disappear and there is no more news of them. Did Attila escape Snurri's dagger? Did the witty Kunigunde end her days in a seraglio in Bender, or on the Bosphorus, nibbling *loukoum*? She would shortly have been glutton'd with that, I think, even with the constant round of stranglings and drownings the Turks are famed for (though it may be a libel).

Attila had kindly left us our mules—and I was pleased not to have lost my own particular mount, an intelligent gray animal of which I had grown fond, and dubbed Adel, or Noble. We also had the *bât*-mule that bore our scant wherewithal and remaining provender, such as it was—mostly fodder for the animals themselves and a bag of what the Spaniards call *garbanzos*. I guessed that Attila planned to ride hard now for Olbia and thought he would have no further use for a *bât*-mule.

But he took the compass. It was his to take, after all—I believe he had dipped it, in the first place, from the pocket a Spanish captain confined in the Elephant Tower for peculation. The Spaniard received it from King Carel's Turkish *drabant* in exchange for his freedom, but unfortunately died, not long after getting it, in a dockside mêlée, while attempting to acquire the wherewithal to sail for Santu Antiogu. It was a curious thing about Attila that he seemed so often to bring bad luck down on those who had to do with him.

"The Greeks have a word for such bad-luck-bringers," said Benoît. "But I forget what it is—*palaeo*-something-or-other. They invite the evil eye."

I for one was delighted now to be free of his insidiously menacing presence, which at times seemed to me almost satanic. Even though I had fought his second in a duel and killed my man too (although entirely without wishing to), I was always a little afraid of him: he was like some terrible force of nature, a volcano maybe, that might erupt at moment.

I mounted on Adel, and TF and Benoît on their unnamed beasts, we struck northward again as soon as dusk had fallen: TF claimed he could steer us from here on by the stars, having learned to do so in the army. We were now in a region called the Logudoro, which it had been since the time when the island was ruled by Byzantine magistrates called the Judges, as I was told by a Benedictine whom I encountered at his church in the town of Ardara. On a tombstone in the floor there, of which all else was pretty much effaced, I deciphered an epitaph: *Quod potui feci; faciant meliora potentes*; which means something like: "I did what I was able to do; let those who can do better." I thought this very fine indeed and resolved to adopt it for my own sepulcher.

[*Please arrange that for me, Sarie. I've written the words down on a paper with my will and testament.*]

We gave up traveling by night and resting up by day once we had said good-bye to the Barbàgia. The land through which we now passed was fertile and rich in corn. So it must also have been in ancient times, which must have aroused much envy, for we saw many a *nurake*. I had supposed that the name Logudoro must mean something like "Place of Gold," alluding to the profusion of wheat that sprang from it, but my learned Benedictine said, no, it was a corruption of Giuigadu de Torres, or Magistracy of Torres, the old name of the country, dating from the era of the emperor Justinian, the greatest earthly *iudex*, he of the *Codex Justinianus* that gave all Europe its laws.

Sitting by a little stream while Benoît went into the bushes for a moment, I watched a brownish sort of bird, perhaps about seven or eight inches tall, with a pretty black ruff under its throat, a lark, I think, from its song, take a leisurely bath in a puddle between some rocks, then gracefully sip its bathwater with an air of greatest contentment. Ah! If only human life could be so simple, without need of laws and judges, wars and whores!

It was beautiful here indeed: a forest of reeds nodded around us under a perfect blue sky. Only the innumerable *mousquittes* made the place less than perfect. I slapped one furiously. Kunigunde had been right—they were surely Satan's creatures.

"Tommi," I said to TF boldly, "do you not miss her? I do."

"Hänschen," he said. "Let me tell you like a brother something that probably no one else would tell you. Inside every pretty girl, there is a tube full of shit. Of course, there is also an immortal soul in there someplace. And the same is true of you and me too, needless to say, and of all men. I believe that is what Uncle Augie means when he says that we humans are nobler than the angels, but lower than worms. Do angels void? If so, is our dung somehow less foul than theirs? Is worm shit? It's a mystery, and you can spend your whole life thinking about it, as I have, but in the end, you just find yourself back where you started. So in answer to your question, yes, I do miss darling Kunigunde. I miss the bitch's naughty heart and the shape of her arse, and her tits and lovely smile that can cut into a man quick as a poleaxe splits a Turk's topknot. But believe me, I truly do not miss her shit!"

At which remarks I held my tongue, if not my nose. Still, I was flattered that he said this "like a brother." I meditated on the question of whether any angels I had seen depicted, whether in oil or marble, had arseholes. If not exactly shown, I decided, they were at least *implied* in some *putti* of Donatello's. Whether these are properly angels, I must leave it to the reader to determine.

Benoît then returning from the *locus in quo* in which he had eased himself, we remounted and rode on, scratching the bumps inflicted on us by the satanic *mousquittes*. Godfrey William would no doubt be able to shed light on why they existed in this best of all possible worlds, but I was much out of humor with them!

We rested up the next night in a sort of cave we came across, one of those places I later learned was called a *domus de janas*, or fairy house. Inside, it had been crudely hewed, as though by children, into the rough simulacrum of a dwelling; the lintel and frame of a door that led into solid rock were carved into one wall—only a spirit could have passed through it, and that was no doubt the idea. It was a door into the realm of the dead. I realized this when I awoke, and grasped that we were almost certainly relaxing in someone's tomb. But it was cool in there, and no spirit came to object to our presence.

Going out into the light, I found standing there, peering in, a portly man in a black (or was it gray?) friar's habit. He smiled at me and extended a hand in blessing, saying in a firm voice: "Dominus vobiscum." To which I, of course, replied in words I had spoken many times in my father's church in Grube: "Et cum spiritu tuo."

Here was yet another of those eremitical Benedictines who seemed to be found everywhere on the island—and just as well that he was, for we should not have been able to exchange an intelligible word had he been a common Sardishman. As it was, Brother Barisone expressed surprise to me in Latin that we should have chosen to stop here, when the magnificent city of Sassaro lay but a mile distant. There, he promised, we should have beef and manchet bread and all that civilization allowed. The arrival of an Austrian regiment under Count von Wieheißter and a horde of Imperial bureaucrats, bringing with them all manner of matériel and sparking a great demand for labor, had created a boom. There were now even coffeehouses in which *Strudel* and *Kipferl*—croissants, the French call them, but they were actually a Viennese invention—could be had. The *Streusel-Nuss-Hörnchen* at the Goldenes Dachl especially was "to die for!" (so he expressed himself).

I explained to the estimable friar that even though ourselves Germans, we were but humble recruits to the Allied forces and could not afford such delights. We should be perfectly content with some bread and cheese, perhaps washed down with a glass of beer. I wondered if he could recommend some modest inn where we might be accommodated and set us on our road there.

As to beer, Brother Barisone could not speak too highly of the famous Pilsner of Bohemia; as to inns, well, there was one run by a man named "Uldank Artissunk" (perhaps an "Ulrich Sunk"?) and his Sardinian lady, but he could not speak to its merits, never having resided there. We could enquire for it when we reached the city gate.

I had hoped he might propose we accept the hospitality of some monastery or other ecclesiastical *Stiftung* of that ilk, such as TF and I had enjoyed in France traveling as Franciscan friars *de couvent en couvent*, but no such luck.

"I could use some of that famous Pilsner right now," said Benoît, who had joined the conversation. Since I did not know that he was himself a former priest, I was a little taken aback at the fluent Latin in which our friend formulated himself. Brother Barisone took it in his stride, however, perhaps assuming that we all spoke Latin—since aside from a few who spoke Spanish, Count von Wieheißter's officers doubtless also perforce communicated with the locals in that tongue—and soon the two of them were embarked on a discussion of the merits of various beers from Bohemia to the Lower Vorarlberg. This was as might be imagined a comical performance in the language of Cicero, but I shall not venture to reproduce their conversation here.

TF said nothing, but he started to load up the *bât*-mule. Adel wandered over and gently sniffed the back of my neck.

"Well, I must get going," said Brother Barisone. "I am expected in Castheddu. They have a donkey for me, you know. God be with you, dear gentlemen!" And he picked up his staff and headed off down a path.

I was both glad and sad that this journey was coming to an end. Glad because I was saddlesore and my clothes were filthy with the grease of the road. Sad because I felt very fond of my two companions and loved the curious clarity of traveling nowhere in particular, and this was now coming to an end. We were about to be precipitated into an outcome. Simple ponderability would dictate our friends and our enemies: duty would ally us to them and make us love them if they were Protestants or Imperialists; difference would compel us to betray and even murder them if they were Pretenderists or the Sun King's servants. And all to what end?

I tried to recall the broad thrust of Dan'l's directions: I was to state rumors such as they might be reported by Grub Street and report rumors so that they might be asserted in Parliament. Public opinion was all; it was all in the *minding* of things now: what people *minded* or could be led to *mind* by pamphlets, gazettes, news-letters, and rumors in London, Paris, and the Hague would determine the course of history. Meanwhile, the war ground on. Everyone was determined to settle, everyone was determined to fight. No one wanted to settle, no one wanted to fight. "No peace without Spain," said the Whigs—who by "Spain" meant only keeping tight hold of Gibraltar and Mahon and getting into the bargain the *Asiento*, which is to say a monopoly for England of selling Negroes to the Spanish in America. "Moderation" was Lord Treasurer Harley's principle, who would be moderate always provided he could break Marlborough and Bolingbroke, see the Dutch ruined, the emperor sunk, the French bankrupted, and himself continue in office forever, or as near as possible. Of Bolingbroke and Marlborough, it was hard to say that they *had* any principles: each simply wanted to exclude the other from all preferment, build the most magnificent palace set in a park of the latest design, and never be short of gold or anything gold could buy. To that end all of these men would deal shamelessly in secret with England's poor old counter-king, the phantom of Saint-Germain-en-Laye, and through him with the cosmic puppeteer Lewis Baboon at Versailles. As for the Queen, she was dying. Eighteen of her children had preceded her to Heaven; there were none left now. As for the Elector of Hannover, much as Anne hated it, he stood waiting in the wings to take his turn just as soon as she turned up her toes. (Indeed, rumor had it that he would not wait much longer either, but would very soon replay the Glorious Revolution, to which end, it was claimed, an invasion fleet was even now being assembled in the Netherlands to convey a German army to England, which would swiftly take charge there, as William III's had done before it.) As for Carel XII, he was at Bender—or was he perhaps already heading home across Poland to launch a counterinvasion of Scotland and set the Blackbird on the British throne as Sweden's tool? As for the Tsar, who knew? Was he a philosopher king and the savior of the world, or a drunken madman who had more luck, good and bad, than was had by any prince since Nero?

And as for Mr Swift, who caused so much trouble with his pamphlets and satires, "He'll never be a bishop," said Dan'l, who hated Swift (and the Dean in turn made fun by pretending to be unable to recall Dan'l's name, calling him instead "that fellow who stood in the nutcrackers, don't you know").

It was enough to make one's head spin. And of course Dan'l had never intended I should be in Sassaro, or in Sardinia at all. I was only here by accident. I should have been back in London by now, or at least in Barcelona or Naples or someplace where useful rumors could be mustered.

Meanwhile, Cousin Tommi continued sad and silent. He rode ahead of us lost in thought.

"I think he really does miss Kunigunde's shit," said Benoît.

I rubbed my chin. Our beards had grown. "Soon we shall have to submit to the torture of being shaved three times a week," I said.

"But we shall console ourselves afterwards by taking coffee and a *Streusel-Nuss-Hörnchen* at the Goldenes Dachl," he said. We both laughed with joy at this thought. "We are not in Sassaro yet," I said, "and we have only the honest father's word for it that such a place even exists. It may be a mere *fatamorgana*."

"To think that not so long ago we were a pair of galley slaves straining at the oar on a corsair xebec!"

"Fate's wheel has turned, and Providence has favored us. We must have been doing something right," I said.

"Touchons du bois!" he said gaily.

And suiting the action to the word, he grabbed at a branch of the huge carob tree under which we were passing. At that very moment, his mule happened to catch its foot and lurched forward to free itself. Benoît must have gripped his branch too hard; but though the wood of this tree is reputed very hard, in this case it was rotten, and it snapped, and he took a tumble, striking his head against a rocky outcrop that sprang up there.

"Benoît!" I said.

He lay silent, and I dismounted. A thick thread of blood ran from his left ear into his whiskers. He still clutched a bit of carob wood in his hand.

TF, who had heard my call, was soon at my side. We crouched together over Benoît, trying in vain to arouse him. "He's dead," said TF at last. "But what on earth happened?"

"We were just talking about our good luck, and he said, 'Touch wood!'"

I shivered in the strong sunlight. TF stood up and made the sign of the cross. Slowly I rose too and did likewise.

"When your time comes, it comes," said TF. "He was lucky indeed. That's the easiest death I ever saw or could even imagine. And as you know, I've seen plenty."

Thus suddenly concluded the earthly career of my dear benchmate and fellow slave Benoît, alias Père Philibert of

Marseille, forgiven now for his sin of spiritual incest I had
no doubt. We buried him there in the shade of the ancient
kerátion that had been chosen by God to end his life: no ignoble
instrument, indeed, for the seeds of this kind of tree, which are
called carats, have time out of mind been the measure of riches:
a Greek obol tipped the balance against three of them, and a pure
gold solidus of Constantine weighed exactly twenty-four. Pearls
and precious stones such as diamonds are assayed by them too.

The carob tree does not bear fruit until it is seventy years
old. He who plants one thus does so, not for himself nor even
for his children, but for his children's children, if not his great-
grandchildren. It must have been there a long time that tree, I
thought, to grow so wide and so tall. Who knew, perhaps it had
even in its day looked on the elvish rough-hewers of the *domus
de janas* in which we had passed our night? And during all those
long centuries, this eventual purpose had been in store for it, to
deliver his death to Benoît!

"They call these pods Saint John's bread," I explained to TF,
"because these and honey were what the Baptist had to eat in
the wilderness. Some say he ate locusts and honey, but who
save a fool would eat a grasshopper!"

"Hänschen," he said, "what a poxy lot of things you know!"

"Try one," I said, handing him a pod.

He chewed into it tentatively. "Not bad," he said. "Have we
got any honey?"

When Benoît was tucked into his sleeping-place, we prayed
over him, meditated on the Resurrection and the life, and
sprinkled a few drops of crimson Cannonau wine from the *bota*
on the mound as an oblation of sorts. Then we rode on.

What else, after all, could we have done? That's the way of
this world. One moment you're there, the next you're not.

Danse Macabre

WE were soon enough in Sassaro, or Sassari, as they call it now, and a fine city it certainly was. But we did not stay there very long. Indeed, I could scarcely conceive of taking coffee and *Kipferl* at the Goldenes Dachl now. My very throat shut up in melancholy at the thought. However, a merciful glass or two of beer (Zur güldenen Sackpfeife) eased it. There, too, one of Count von Wieheißter's aides suggested we proceed straight to Alguer (the *r* is silent in Catalan, mind) on the coast, not far away, where we would find need of our services, since shipments of horses, wheat, and matériel from Sardinia to Barcelona and Valencia passed through there. He gave us the name of the chief of the Anglo-Dutch office there, Lord Burgo Cinquebars. The address was simply "Palazzo Doria."

When we got to Alguer, I felt immediately that this was a place that would have special import for me. We circumnavigated the town wall till we came to a gate among the usual aloes and prickly pears, where we were mobbed by swarthy, half-naked children. They scattered, however, at a word from a charming lady of a certain age, as they say, bearing a parasol and leading a large seagull with a crippled wing on a leash of ribbon. Going up to her, we introduced ourselves in our bad Spanish. She could speak French, however, and told us that she was Madame Zoccheddú; the bird's name was Mouette. Madame Zoccheddú kindly described the layout of the town and told us which way to go to find Lord Burgo. Indeed, she said, she would walk that way with us. Ciceronied so agreeably, we smiled at our luck.

The harbor was swarming with people of many nationalities—this was a world war, after all. Some were buying fish from the fishermen; others were engaged in loading barges with sacks and boxes that would be conveyed to a large three-master that could be seen at some distance. English and Dutch marines, in their red and iron gray uniforms respectively, patrolled up and down in squads, just as at Cagliari.

"That's the cathedral," said our adorable guide. "But doesn't the spire look just like a carrot?"

The Palazzo Doria was the grandest house in town, with marble tiles on the floor and a marble staircase, under ceilings frescoed with what we were told were scenes from the life of Brancaleone, husband of the last of the Judges, Eleanor of Arborea, who defeated the invading Aragonese and promulgated the *Carta de Logu*, the Sardinian Magna Carta, which remained in force on the island until it was replaced by something less advanced four and a quarter centuries after Eleanor died of the plague. Branca was variously depicted in a toga and as a Roman general in armor.

Our interview with Lord Burgo was brief. He told us to come back the next day, because he was engaged with a Chinese gentleman, the first I ever in my life saw, dressed in a scarlet coat with silver buttons and a fine tie wig.

"I must speak to that man," said TF as we departed. "I shall ask him if it is true!"

"If what is true?"

"Why whether the sacred cleft is indeed horizontal there, as Attila told me. Or vertical as with us."

"What cleft, Tommi?" I said, mystified.

"Why, the most important cleft of all, my dear—the cleft of Venus!"

Alas, we never again saw this Celestial. He was an interpreter of oriental tongues aboard HMS *Euryalus*, Lord Burgo told us later. But that vessel sailing soon after for Persia, and he with it, we got no answer to TF's question.

I had been feeling poorly ever since we arrived in Alguer, and now my head began to ache and spin. Unruly notions raged muzzily through my brain, my brow seemed afire, I shivered and shook, and in the summer heat, sweat poured from my body, soaking my shirt. There could be no doubt: I had been stricken by the quartan ague, or "mal'aria," as the Italians call it. I had seen it happen to others in Cagliari.

"Tommi, I'm as sick as a dog," I said. "Get me to a bed and some Jesuit powder, for God's sake!"

Every bed in every hostelry in the town, such as they were, had been occupied by the warriors of the Sea Powers, however, and we dragged around in vain looking for one. I should no doubt have died in the street had not Madame Zoccheddú suddenly reappeared (now without Mouette) and come to our aid. Having heard of our plight, she insisted that I be taken to a house belonging to her family outside the town wall. I was aware of being half-carried, half-dragged through a tumbledown archway into an overgrown garden where quinces hung golden on the trees.

I have no memory beyond that of my descent into an agonizing slumber. Dreams I have always had, like other men, but these were of a quite different order: I dreamed myself a wolf perambulating a world of indescribable evil, peopled by an army of fiends in human form. Neither Bernd Notke's *danse macabre* in the Mariankirche at Lübeck (which it is a pity all the world cannot see) nor even Pieter Breugel de Oude's Last Judgment, *De triomf van de dood* (which I viewed once when I had the honor in the Netherlands of being in the entourage of that peerless *cognoscente* Prince Eugène) begin to convey the horrors of the nightmares inflicted on me by the mal'aria of Sardinia.

What is seen in dreams is impossible to be accurately painted or sketched, of course, even by an artist like the elder Breugel. It can only be conjured in the mind. We had in our vicarage at Grube a number of little figures of souls in torment, which were said to have been made by the famous woodcarver Benedikt D—— as models for an altarpiece that he never completed, and

I think the memory of these, which I had even played with as a child, was the fodder of my nightmares.

I remember them well, tiny figures whose bodily and facial expressions spelled out the registers of damnation and horror. Nothing was being done *to* them; no one was breaking them on the wheel, crucifying them, flaying them alive, impaling them, pitchforking them into hellfire. Yet such was Benedikt's genius that they conveyed all this with their faces and in the contortions of their bodies.

After Benedikt died around midcentury, those little damned wooden souls must have lain about Pferdemarkt No. 5 in Lübeck gathering dust for decades. Somehow, though, a hundred years later, they found their way into my father's possession; seeming mere toys, probably no one else wanted them. Or perhaps they were handed down and played with by generation after generation of infants. And so I eventually got them as my childs-part, treasures kept in a little brass-bound chest under my cot. What boy has them now I wonder?

When I awoke I found a woman's face looking down on me. I liked it well enough but could not recall its owner. A most delightful scent emanated from her, however, which held me entranced. In the ensuing days, I would discover that one effect on me of the mal'aria was a heightened power of olfaction, which long remained and has declined only recently with my advancing years. Indeed, it seems as though my olfactory nerves had become as sensitive as those of a dog, to which animal *all* smells are clearly interesting, if not indeed delightful. I was able to distinguish between people by this superior sensibility alone. Moreover, my sense of saporousness was similarly enhanced, and for a while I enjoyed a most exquisitely sensitive palate— but this left me more quickly, alas, within a few weeks.

For now, I did not know that I had been thus benefited, however, and I simply assumed that I was in the presence of an angel, naturally dispersing a heavenly odorosity.

"Who are you, O noble lady?" I said. "Where am I?"

"You are very polite to call me so," she said. "I'm Ziza. And you are in Can Jaume, our house in Alguer. The first crisis of your illness has passed now, I think, so you should drink this. It's a tincture of Peruvian bark, wormwood, jalap, and rhubarb, which I have mixed in a glass of wine. You will find it bitter and purgative, but it is the best medicine we know of for an *intemperie* caused by the mal'aria such as you have."

"Oh yes, I remember you now," I said, for it was Madame Zoccheddú. "Where is Mouette?"

"She's in the garden eating snails, which she loves above all things. Drink up!"

Bitter and purgative the tincture was, but it worked. If my recovery was but very gradual, it was mostly because I wished it so. I delighted in Ziza's company, and she, it seemed, in mine. TF, who was busy with his own affairs, did not seek to detach me from my willfully protracted convalescence, simply dropping in from time to time to dine or take a glass with us.

Ziza was a widow, about twenty-nine years of age at that time. Aside from the bird Mouette—which recovered faster than I did, not realizing that in so doing it risked losing its sinecure and being returned to the ocean to seek its living among the fish—she led a solitary life among her domestics, who consisted chiefly of a maidservant named Grixenda and an old man whose name I forget, he worked in the orchard. I gathered that she had inherited sufficient property from her husband, Giuannú, eighteen months dead of a quinsy or angina, to have no need to remarry—even had it been possible in a world that considered a woman of her years to be no better than a crone. She would have liked to remove to France or Savoy but was restrained by the need to watch over her senile father, who had not quit his house in Sassari for the past five years, believing that he had enemies—quite fictitious, Ziza told me—who planned to murder him. If she went to Milan, say, as she would like to do, he might die, and she could never forgive herself. Conversely, he seemed likely to live forever, for he was as hale in body as he was sick in brain. Her other great regret was that she had no children. She had married Giuannú Zoccheddú as a young woman because her father, who was the bridegroom's friend and close contemporary, had wished it, and old Giuannú had been unable to engender any new ones, much as he had wished it, and his sons and daughters from a prior marriage all being dead, alas, of various illnesses and calamities, he had none.

Ziza suffered under a great handicap: she was a woman of superior natural taste and intelligence who found no peers in the provincial society into which she had been born. Luckily, she possessed a library—her father's, which he no longer used, having inexplicably after a lifetime of bookishness lapsed into illiteracy.

But though I love them dearly, books are a poor substitute for friends!

It was now late summer of the year 1711. TF brought news. Mr Handel's opera *Rinaldo* had opened at the Haymarket. Harley had become earl of Oxford and Lord High Treasurer. Archduke Karl had become Holy Roman Emperor of the German Nation, his brother having died and left him that post. Mr Hume the philosopher had been born. And the very latest was that, at a cost only of some ten thousand lives, all told, Marlborough had broken through the French Ne Plus Ultra line and captured the city of Bouchain, opening the way to Paris. Final victory for the Allies was thus surely at hand. Lewis the Sun King was well and truly screwed. He was said to be raving about dying in a final charge at the head of his household cavalry and thus winning in his end the sublime glory that had always eluded him in life. "Poor old fucker," said TF. "They say he has scarce a tooth left in his head!"

Once TF brought with him Piers Prettyman, one of Lord Burgo's aides, who had become his good friend, and we made up a merry supper party. The discussion was all, of course, of the winding down of the war and the dramatic events to be expected. In particular, it was anticipated that the duc d'Orleans must become regent of France, since King Lewis could not be expected to live long—he was now above seventy-three and in very bad health.

"The physicians," said Prettyman, "only keep him alive by regular bleedings and administration of an elixir made from powder of crab's eyes and the lichen that grows on the skulls of men who have died violently. Such crottle is worth its weight in gold—the imported headpieces of Hibernians left hanging on the gibbet go for half a guinea or more in London, depending on how much moss they bear. But who can say whether it is effective? In his final apoplexy the late King Charles was also dosed with *liquor cranii humanii*— and he died, of course. In any event, d'Orleans is a very sound, sensible man—we shall have none of this *merde à la roi soleil* with him in charge in Paris."

"Merde à la roi soleil!" said I, who was growing saucier by the day. "You turn a fine phrase, Sir Piers."

Merde or not, the reason for the occupation of Alguer by the Sea Powers was clearly rapidly dissipating, I reflected later, walking in the orchard. Sardinia would henceforth be governed by the likes of Gundaker von Wieheißter, and the Sards would sensibly learn to speak German. So why should I not marry Ziza and remain there?

Marry Ziza? Where had that idea come from? I had paid no court to her. Indeed, I always treated her with the greatest respect and deference, as befitted a penniless guest in her house. And she had treated me with the greatest generosity, not only caring for me in my sickness, medicining me, feeding me, and sheltering me, but bestowing on me from an antique wardrobe articles of the late Giuannú Zoccheddú's highly unfashionable clothing, a little too tight in places, and a little too capacious in others, so she had Grixenda resew them—or even, I suspect, did so herself. At least the shoes fit well enough!

Remain there? Did I wish to spend my life on a remote island, among folk who spoke a language heard nowhere else in the world? True, I was picking it up with my usual facility; at root, it was much closer to the Latin of the ancients than French or Spanish . . .

"Quisquis, quaequae," said the birds in the orchard trees, some of them so big and ancient that they might well have been there, one thought, when Rome ruled here. "Cuiuscuius, quarumquarum. Cuicui, quibuscibus. Quamquam, quasquas. Quaqua, quibuscibus. Quisquis, quaequae."

Whatever, whoever: a man must live somewhere, and if a man marries it must be to some woman, mustn't it? The choosing was all. A cascade of imaginings I had never had before overcame me. Might I not have children? Ziza was not past child-bearing age, after all. How old did a woman have to be for that. Probably forty or so at least. And it was normal to be a father. All men wanted sons, did they not? And a daughter or two would be nice too!

If I lived on the island, I reflected, I would become a subject of the emperor, whose territory it now was—or would be, since he had not yet been crowned. Had I not been the subject of his brother Joseph (who had died of the smallpox in April)? Holstein was part of the empire. So I hung in a void between two emperors, the dead one and the one to be, like all the other Germans, or most of them, not to speak of the Bohemians, Moravians, Styrians, and what have you.

However, I supposed Charles would rule Sardinia as king of Spain, so I'd be a Spaniard!

Extraordinary though it may seem, I had never reflected on this issue of nationality and what I "was." I had never thought myself anyone's subject. My father, who regarded himself as a citizen of the Imperial free city of Lübeck, had never spoken to me of such a status, which struck me as rather contemptible. True, my mother was Danish. But I had matriculated at Rostock with the designation *Holsatus*, so on that basis I was clearly Holsteiner.

The passport with which I had been supplied in London was, however, English. Was it too much to fancy that I had really acquired that happiest of nationalities? Unfortunately, the passport was made out in a false name. Well, sort of a false name—after all Tornator and D—— mean the same thing. What a nonsense it all was! Charles Frederick of Holstein-Gottorp, who had succeeded to his dukedom at the age of two, was still a small child. By what right could he consider himself my liege lord? At least the future emperor Charles was a soldier, if only a few years older than I was. He had nobly defended Barcelona. Everyone said so, except the former generalissimo in Spain, Lord Peterborough, whose vanity was at issue, since if his orders had not been ignored, the city must certainly have fallen to the French. The peripatetic Peterborough—"Mordanto" was Dr Swift's teasing nickname for him—was by report now traveling through Germany representing himself as an English diplomat. He would not get far with the Hannoverian Elector, who did not like him.

Such was the disconnected jumble of thoughts that rushed through my brain. Unfortunately, having thought them, I found myself no wiser or decided than before. Of whom could I enquire about this? Why, TF, of course!

"For myself, I believe I am no one's subject but my own," he said. "As for old Mordanto, I suspect he is about the same business as we are, although on a more elevated level. Devious devil! He used to be a Whig; now he's a Tory. What is one to think?"

"I don't care about him. What I want to know is how to project my own course."

"Well, what do you want it to be?"

"That's the trouble! I don't really know. I think I'd like to be English and marry Ziza."

He looked at me quizzically.

"Not possible in either case," he said. "No one can *become* a John Bull. *Personne ne devient pas un anglais, on le naît.* You have to be born to the manner. Well may he have overcome the islanders and disposed of their property and titles to his Netherlandish favorites, not even King Billy himself was ever an Englishman. To his British subjects, he was always 'Dutch William,' just as the Elector of Hannover after he accedes to that dignity will always be 'German George' to them—unless they choose to call him something less polite. And you can't marry Ziza either."

"Why not?"

"Why because she has already agreed to become my wife."

A clear sky fears no lightning, they say, but for a moment it seemed as though the heavens overhead had been bolted into pieces and were tumbling down on me. *That* possibility I had never entertained. How could it even have come about? I had not thought TF properly even *knew* Zita. Had he seen her other than when he came to visit me? She wasn't his (slack-mannered, full-uddered) type.

And he couldn't be Ziza's type!

Could he?

"It was as the French say, *le coup de foudre*: love at first sight," said TF. "Do you remember when we first saw her with her tame sea-bird? That was when it happened, the very moment we set eyes on each other. So it was for me, and she has confirmed that so it was for her too. Ever since then, we have met in secret. Piers has been of the greatest assistance in making it possible for us to see each other without exciting the many old wives' tongues in this city."

"Yes," I said bitterly. "I know him for a very accommodating, whorey sort of fellow."

"Ah, Hänschen, that's unfair to him. I know the other young
scarlets on Lord Burgo's staff call him 'Whorey Tory,' but Piers
is a very honest decent bloke. What's more, your remark is
unkind to Ziza and to me."

That was true, of course, and I blushed. It *was* unkind to
them. And for that matter I liked Prettyman myself. He had
taken me to some mirthful gatherings in the town where with a
band of elegant young Imperials and Sea Powers we had drunk,
sung, danced, and ruffled with a gaggle of the jolly goslings who
had flocked by the score to Alguer after its occupation by the
Allies. Piers and I had moreover lain with two of these young
women at the nannyhouse where they resided, as TF knew,
since I had been unable to resist boasting to him of it.

"And what, pray, were *you* doing, when you overheard him
through the brothel cloison pronounce to his Barcelona bawd,
as you told me, 'Come, come, my sweet Conchita, I know very
well that you've had a tarse in your mouth before and like the
taste'?"

There was nothing I could say to that. I had so told him,
thinking the tale a *piquant* one that would make him smile.

"I must admit that both you and Piers have picked up Catalan
something marvelous," said TF. "But then you have learned it
in the best *horizontal* academy, haven't you?"

There was nothing at all I could say to that. But, pox take it,
why had Ziza chosen to fall in love with him and not with me!

Meanwhile, it was reported, the Queen had gone to the
House of Lords in Westminster, sat herself down, and with
Prince Eugène standing beside the throne, approved the Act
giving precedence among the peers of her realm to the duke
of Cambridge, which title now belonged to my old master the
Elector of Hannover.

Godfrey William was no doubt delighted, and wondering
what he should take with him to London. In the event, he took
nothing, because he never went. The Elector himself vetoed his

passage there with some relish, still mad at Herr L's failure to complete the wretched history of the Guelphs whose writing had been assigned to him years ago, but which GW in private dismissed as "Sisyphusarbeit"—a labor akin to old Sisyphus' rolling his boulder up the hill forever in Hades, only to have it forever roll down again.

The Queen had assented to repeal of the Foreign Protestants Naturalization Act of 1708, I was informed by *The British Apollo*, a dilapidated copy of which newspaper came into my hands. If this applied retroactively, my poor descendants (if I had any) might one day lament not having British passports. Damn pernicious doxy! Why had the English not like all sensible folk adopted the law of the good old Salian Franks, which denied females the right to inherit thrones! Even godamn Hannover subscribed, godamnit, to the Lex Salica! I raised my glass to Anne's perdition more than once, and Whorey Tory roared out the toast with me, one of Mr Swift's it was—"To the stupidest woman in Europe!"

I had a perfectly vile hangover in the morning.

We having agreed from the outset not to break each other's hearts, I bounced into a dalliance with a charming slut named, or so she said, Eulàlia Crèvecœur—Laia for short. She was the child of a Catalan mother by a Norman father, born in La Rambla of Barcelona like most of the easy girls in Alguer, parents defuncted, mother by the plague, father pierced by a British bayonet, known relatives none, cheerful disposition, smashing smile, no prospects of any description. I wonder what has become of her.

With Piers and his girl (who was by no means always the same one), Laia and I sailed the Bay of Alguer, visited the great grotto called the Cova de Neptú, with its stalactites and stalagmites, lay laughing on wet sand, and fished up strange fishes and mollusca from those waters, from which our *donselas* prepared a delicious dish they called a *zarzuela de mariscos*—and we for our part "the food of the gods."

In these delicious months, I saw less and less of TF and Ziza. My muscular cousin was smitten with his new bride—they had been married twice, once by a Catholic priest and the other time by the Anglican chaplain of HMS *Bicester*, the Reverend Frederick Gedge, who was as good, TF said, as a Lutheran—and they determined to settle down in Sassari and open an hotel for the accommodation of travelers. When I expressed surprise at this ho-hum ambition, he observed that no man lives forever, and that he had already had many reprieves from death. He wanted to take no more chances and beget him some sons while there was still time.

Piers was now my constant companion. Indeed, we were like brothers. From time to time he and I traveled on one of the transports that were constantly crossing to Barcelona, two days' sail at most, loaded to the gunnels with flour, nervous remounts for the Imperial cavalry houyhnhnming away in the sea air and decorating the afterdeck with their dung. In Catalonia, we talked with as many men as we could, whether Catalans, Germans, British, or whatever, treating 'em, hail-fellow-well-met, to whistle-jackets, a knockdown compounded of gin or brandy and black treacle that was in fashion just then among the forces.

I was getting good at this, and kept notes on their opinions, which were read by Lord Burgo and forwarded to Mr Harley himself—or as I should properly call him now, by the office and title he had borne since May, the Lord Treasurer, Lord Oxford—in London. I had even vaingloriously begun to think my role in the war not unimportant, man's capacity for self-delusion being one of the three things that know no limits, or is it seven?

Presently, we extended the radius of our travels to Valencia and even to Zaragoza. Since these cities were now in the possession of the enemy, I journeyed there with some trepidation, but Piers was able to obtain passports from the office of the Spanish viceroy of Valencia and Murcia, Cardinal Luis de Belluga. Besotted as I was, I did not enquire too deeply into how he was able to get these papers.

"What would you say," Piers said, when we were in Zaragoza in Aragon, "to traveling a bit further afield?"

"Why, where would you go?"

"You know that since he was compelled to beat the chamade and capitulate to the duke of Vendôme last year at Brihuega, General Stanhope has been held prisoner at Valladolid?"

"I've heard that, but I do not even know where Valladolid is!"

"It is about two hundred miles or a bit more west of here as the crow flies. We could be there in a week, and if we could communicate with General Stanhope, we should be able to do great service. He is in very miserable circumstances and deprived even of books, except what the Jesuits have, who are no very great bookmen in that country. Do you know, Mr Stanhope wrote in a letter to our common friend Sir John Cropley that when the Fathers sent him a book with *Demosthenes* inscribed on the spine in gilt, it turned out to be Tully when he opened it; and for that matter, 'it might have been the Alcoran for aught they knew,' he said."

I expressed myself suitably shocked at this confusion of Cicero with the Athenian orator.

"Stanhope's men are said to be in a much worse condition, chained up like galley slaves in villages round about, and made to pay even for the water they drink," said Piers. "If some account of these sufferings could be got to England, it would cause a great stir."

So we rode to Valladolid, a very dusty road indeed, but when we got there we found that General Stanhope had been moved, I think to Bordeaux, since he was to be exchanged for the duke of Escalona, the Spanish viceroy of Naples, who had been imprisoned by the Austrians since the capture of Gaeta by Count von Daun in 1707.

In Valladolid, however, I met a gentleman named Don Felix Pacheco who remarked that in his opinion, the novel *Don Quixote* of the renown'd Don Miguel de Cervantes Saavedra, formerly a resident of that city, although the best that ever was wrote was also the worst. "For," said he, "it had a fatal effect upon the spirits of my countrymen, which every man of wit must resent; before its appearance in the world, there were so many Spaniards to be seen prancing before the windows of their mistresses that a stranger might have supposed the whole nation to consist of gallant knights errant. But after the world became acquainted with *Don Quixote*, a cavaliero seen behaving in that fashion was mocked as a madman and slunk off covered with ignominy. And I verily believe that to this, and this only, we owe the poverty of spirit that for a century past has been so little in accord with that of our famous ancestors."

I found this a remarkable instance of the baneful effect of literature in the world, for the Spaniards are undoubtedly much decayed in spirit from what they were a hundred years ago. Subsequently, I told the story to Mr Swift in London as a caution, who made a note if it, and I believe he afterwards put it in a book, changing only the place.

Like me, Cervantes had been enslaved in Algiers, and I thus felt a certain communion between us. "Me tocaron, como a todos los hombres, malos tiempos en que vivir," he is quoted as saying: "I was doomed, as all men are, to live in hard times." (It's actually an old Spanish commonplace, I have discovered, but no matter.) Taking Don Felix's argument to heart, I resolved never to commit the impropriety of writing a romance, and I never have done so neither, though Dan'l recommended that profession to me, which he himself had practiced to good profit.

Sooner an honest spy, I thought, than a scribbler, for telling stories is telling lies, the effect of which on the world can never be calculated.

We then rode back to Zaragoza, and thence to Barcelona, from where we returned by the first available transport home to Alguer, where I dropped gratefully into the arms of my delicious sublunary sweetheart. "I've missed you," Laia said, dear liar that she was, and set her hand to wandering.

Gradually, these our halcyon days slid into what they call "Saint Martin's summer," or the "little summer of the quince."

And it was November.

". . . and the Bey ordered him to be buggered by half a dozen negroes and then impaled." Midshipman Frogley doffed his fringed tricorne bonnet and mopped his brow, as though to emphasize his horror at this.

"Rubbish," said Piers. "There's a lot of talk about impaling but they seldom actually *do* it these days. And the 'six negroes' part is just ridiculous. That tale has been bandied around for years, but it would be quite contrary to the precepts of their religion."

"No," I said. "They do practice impalement. In Algiers there are great iron hooks set in the fortifications and it is said that in the past at least slaves seeking to escape or who murdered their masters have been flung down upon 'em from the top of the wall and so impaled, where they were left suspended until they died. But I am glad to say I never saw it done myself!"

"The mere fact of there being such hooks must have done much for law and order," said Piers. "It would surely make any slave wish to be on good terms with his master."

"It was done even in Hungary during the reign of the late emperor Leopold," TF said. "The Austrians impaled some Hungarians and the Hungarians in revenge not only impaled Germans they caught but also flayed 'em alive. They learned to do such things from the Turks, of course, but there's no excuse for Christians doing it."

"What say *you* to the negroes, sir?"

"Well, it is true that the Mahometans regard blacks as suited by their very nature to slavery," TF said. "And so they would doubtless regard being outraged by a black as being more ignominious than being so handled by a white man. They distinguish between black slaves, who are called *abd*, which means 'slave,' and white slaves, who are called *mamluk*, which simply means 'property.' In Egypt, as you know, the Mamluks are indomitable warriors and have actually ruled the whole country for many centuries now. They were the only men to defeat the Mongols in battle and force 'em into retreat, and they are crueler than most, they say—even for Egypt. Something like that which you recount may well have occurred there."

"They were lucky to have beat the Mongols, who would otherwise have made a pyramid with their skulls, as was ever their practice to do with their defeated enemies," said Frogley. Already past thirty, the tedious windfucker would never be a lieutenant, and after two decades before the mast, he had begun to acquire that sun-baked, oversalted look that one encounters in aging seamen. The convergence of his professional horizons seemed to have calcified his brain, and like some stripling blockhead, he spoke of little else but bloodshed, massacres, and sodomy. Punning on *sard* and Sard, he made a nasty pickle.

"No doubt after first having their blacks bugger 'em," I joked.

Even though I took part in it, I was sick of such conversation. If people are slaves, it is God's will, after all, and they must bear it. It was God's will that I myself had been a slave. Beyond all peradventure, it was also His will that I had been freed in the sea battle and come here to Alguer to drink wine and eat tarts and tid-bits. Filthy things such as those Frogley liked talking about so much occurred in the world, but for all that, it was the *best* of all *possible* worlds, and we should praise God for his care of us and pity those who were obliged to suffer. "Do not expect too much of the world," Godfrey William had advised me in his grandfatherly fashion. "But then again do not expect too little of the world either."

The question was, of course, just how much is too much, and how much is too little? "That every man has to discover for himself," said Godfrey William with a wink.

I had not seen TF for several weeks and believed him to have gone to Genoa, when suddenly he reappeared on our doorstep. After closeting himself with Ziza for some time, he came out and called me into the garden, where we walked among the fruit trees, now hung with only a few shriveled leaves.

"You must get you hence," he said. "I've been in Vienna and have learned that after your latest travels in Spain, the emperor's Black Chamber now quite reasonably believes you to be an agent of the Tories seeking to negotiate a separate peace with France. And there is no doubt, of course, that that is precisely what your friend Piers is about—how else would he be able to come by viceregal passports? In any case, they plan to dispose of you by the simplest means possible, which is to say, knock the pair of you on your heads and drop you in the bay. In fact an old acquaintance of ours has been tasked with the job. Do you remember Rippchen, the Dorset Garden falsettist?"

"You mean Mr Cutlett?"

"Exactly."

"But didn't he . . . wasn't he . . . on our side?"

"Rippchen's on his own side and no one else's. After he was recalled from Hannover for raping a child, he somehow became involved with the Mohocks—you know, that gang of noble young scarlets who were terrorizing London. They merely wanted to raise hell, but there were plenty of pickings on the side for the likes of Cutlett. In any case, Dan'l was obliged to discharge him. Then von Zinzendorf's men got to him and he went to work for the Austrians. He's very good at what he does actually—a valuable asset to any black service. It's just that he's a total shit! I believe he'd sell his own wife and children to the Turks if the price was right."

"How do you know all this?"

"I saw Mr Leibniz in Vienna—he's been made an Imperial counsellor, what the hell! He told me and asked me to steer you right. He's very fond of you, you know."

"What about Piers?"

"Piers must look out for himself. But his uncle Sir Reginald will look after him, I think."

"His uncle!"

"On his mother's side, once removed, something like that. The Cinquebars' family seat is near Rainham in Essex, where Piers comes from, doesn't he?"

"I wonder extremely that the Austrians should think me a Pretenderist, knowing that I serve Grand Pensionary Heinsius and the Amsterdam Prinsenhof!"

"And also Mr Harley, who certainly wants a separate peace, though no Pretenderist. And for that matter, the Elector of Hannover, who has every interest in one too, as long as King Lewis is obliged by it to sell the Blackbird down the river. I fear you have too many masters Hänschen!"

"Well, you serve 'em just as much as I do!"

"No longer. I have made a clean breast of it to His Gräfliche Gnaden Gundaker von Wieheißter and renounced all other loyalties. He's a very sensible bloke, quite unlike most Austrian ministers, whose minds, as the Spaniards say, most resemble goats' horns, being narrow, hard, and crooked. We are like this these days, Gundaker and I."

And he held up two intertwined fingers.

"Where is Cutlett now?"

"On his way to Genoa, then here by the next ship. He has an Imperial appointment that will give him a pretty free hand, though Gundaker doesn't know yet. Prince Eugène himself arranged it. No hard feelings, of course! However, not to worry, there's a berth with your name on it aboard the *Bicester*, which sails in the morning. England is far and away the safest place for you, my boy."

How in the best of all possibles had I gotten myself into such a mess!

"An infinite number of great and small motions, internal and external, determine us, which generally we are not sensible of," Godfrey William explained later. "There are reasons that cause one to set one foot forward rather than the other, though we are insensible of 'em and think we do it of our own choice. What folly! It's as if a needle touched with a loadstone were sensible of and congratulated itself on turning toward the north. The chain of interconnected causes reaches very far—all the way to the Great Monad Himself, in fact."

"By the way," said TF. "Attila reached Bender after all, and King Carel sent him to the Topkapi in Constantinople to beg a favor of the Sultan. Seems our dear Kuni was quickly detached from him there by Ahmed's main French squeeze Ermine (née Jeannette), who got the hots for her and bagged her for the harem in a flash. Nothing Attila could do about it. Seems the poor old Grand Turk is like totally pussy-whipped."

"Might she not yet escape?"

"No way! The Imperial harem is rather like the Neapolitan Camorra—one of those charming societies you don't get out of alive. She'll most like end her days rinsing chamber pots or get dropped into the Bosphorus sewed up in a sack with a few stray cats for company."

"Poor old Kuni!"

"Oh, she'll have a good time for a while. And who knows, perhaps she'll even become a top consort. Ermine herself, they say, is pretty from far nowadays, but far from pretty. So Ahmed might prefer Kuni, who after all is a very talented little bitch." He was still bitter. One could tell.

"Oh, by the way, better not say anything to Piers or to the fair Eulàlia about your sailing tomorrow on the *Bicester*. Just leave 'em each a note."

I put together my few things and boarded the *Bicester* at dawn, where I found the Reverend Mr Gedge kneeling at prayer on the quarterdeck, a sight simultaneously absurd and touching. He rose to his feet at my appearance, crossed himself in the fresh sunlight, and said, with scant pertinence, "I'm a Norfolk man—my Dad was rector of St Saviour's Swaffingham—and such mornings as this always make me think of the Broads."

"My father was the pastor of our church too, at Grube in Holstein," I said. "It's Saint Jürgen's—Saint George's in English."

"And is he no more?"

"Alas, no more. He died four years ago."

"My father died in 1705. They shut up the church after that. Too few people left in the village, you see. The young 'uns all want to go to Norwich, or better, London."

"But you were ordained in your turn?"

"What else was I to do? It was his wish."

"It was my own father's wish also. But I had no calling, and he died with it unfulfilled."

"Better so, if you have no calling. I often feel my own call to be wanting. I married a pair the other day—big German bloke with an amazing scar on his cheek like a fish hook and an island woman with a lovely heart-shaped face—and I wondered even as I pronounced it whether the sacrament of wedlock could be valid if uttered by such a sad dog as me."

TF was famous for that scar even among his fellow *Landsknechten*, who were themselves not without such decorations; in Pomerania, they called him Schmisso, which means "Scarface." He claimed it as memento of a janissary's spear.

"Put your mind at rest," I said. "The power of Holy Orders overmasters any lack in the priest, which is between him and God. I know the couple you mean—indeed, I might have been bridesman to 'em, for the groom is my cousin, but I was in Spain at the time."

"You speak as one with knowledge of theology."

"As it chances, Mr Francke who founded the Pædagogium at Halle is my great-uncle, and Mr Spener, he whom they call the 'Father of Piety,' was a frequent visitor in our house, so I heard much theology talked at home. Then I was put to study it, of course, under Quistorpius at Rostock."

"Indeed, since I was once a serious student of religion before I fell into sin, I have read Francke's *Pietas Hallensis* in Mr Böhme's translation, and have even looked into Quistorpius's *De mysterio magno*."

"Quistorp the Elder wrote that actually. My docent was his grandson—the son of Quistorp the Younger. We students called him the Pisspot. As the story goes, the Quistorps drink ink, piss disputations, and shit *theses theologicae*. Quistorp *der Ältere* and Quistorp *der Jüngere* between 'em scribbled so many that Quistorp the grandson doubtless felt obligated to keep churning them out. It's the family business."

But I wondered what sin so very serious my wan Anglican interlocutor could have fallen into. It must, I imagined be the usual one with clergymen—what they call "self-pollution." But I did not like to say anything to that effect, since he might not have taken it kindly. I see no real harm in boxing the old Jesuit myself. If Providence has supplied us with so obvious a means to pleasure, why not accept it?

I'll not trouble you with accounts of "the blue-green gulf," "the spanking breeze," "the distant shore," "the unanticipated storm," and suchlike. I warrant you've read all that a hundred times. What was a source of interest and much delight to me, though, was that I had found my sea legs: I no longer ran for the railings when the ship yawed and pitched.

It took us about the usual length of time to reach England, and when we got there, that other Eden was still in an uproar over the late duel between Lord Mohun and Lord Hamilton: both were killed, but Hamilton's second said that Mohun's second, one George Macartney, had finished off Hamilton. Macartney had fled to the Continent and was to be tried in absentia. Lord Stanhope was now back in England, having during his Spanish captivity run for Parliament but lost to a Tory brewer who insinuated his lordship to have sodomitical affections. "And he does too, or so the word is," said Dan'l in a collegial *tour d'horizon* sluiced down with mugs of ale.

Unfortunately, he had no further employ for me, what with the war coming to an end. The Austrians had lost, and our Karl would never be His Most Catholic Majesty Carlos III. This was not all that bad for him, of course. He was still archduke of Austria, and since his brother Joseph had died, he had now also become Holy Roman Emperor, as well as being king of Hungary, Bohemia, Dalmatia, Croatia, Slavonia, and Serbia, duke of Burgundy, Limburg, Luxemburg, Gelderland, Württemberg, and Silesia, prince of Swabia, margrave of Moravia, count of Tyrol, landgrave of Alsace, lord of the Windic March (which is someplace east of Venice inhabited by Wends), and so on—I've forgotten a bunch of his other titles. Still, defeat was a bitter pill for us his followers in the Great War that had gone on all those years. "Finis Germaniae!" I said and drained my glass.

"Oh, that's the sort of thing people always say," said Dan'l. "But it never is." He recommended that I try for a job at the Prinsenhof in Amsterdam. The Sooterkins were always in want of recruits, he said, to man their ships and serve in their empire, far-flung as ever, never mind the damned Peace.

A Horrid Sight

P ETER Motteux offered an introduction to a Huguenot compatriot who was lieutenant colonel of the French Protestant régiment de Mauregnault in the army of the Dutch Republic. "The Whig Junto are very exultant these days, and the climate here is growing frosty for Tories," he said. "When the Queen dies—and it is a wonder she has lived so long, poor lady—George Louis will be king, and he hates them all as traitors for making peace with the French and attempting to let in the Pretender, so he thinks, in his place. No Tory will be safe then, not even the Dragon."

"Well, I can scarce believe that! Lord High Treasurer Oxford has done so much good service to his country. And he's such a moderate man, really."

"That's just what they hate about Harley. In a world ruled by parties, there's no love of moderate men who are willing to compromise. In politics, you know, as the song has it, 'Tis fatal to be good.' The Dragon is being forced out and must soon resign his office. I should not be surprised to see him one day being interrogated in the Tower. The Junto are a vengeful lot. They will seek to have some heads taken off when their turn comes."

"But who will assume Lord Oxford's place as the premier?"

"For the moment, Secretary St John, most like. He has wooed Baroness Masham and won her, fond woman, and as long as the Queen lives, Lady Abigail rules."

"Why then?"

"My dear Jack! Because the Queen loves Lady Masham, of course. I shall not say in the Sapphic way, but who ever knows, of course? Before Masham, Her Majesty loved the duchess of Somerset, and before her it was Sarah Marlborough, and both those great dames as good as ruled England in their time. It is not that the Queen is a weak woman. On the contrary, she has been a tower of strength. But she is terribly ill now, and she takes support where she can find it."

"What is your thought concerning Secretary St John, Lord Bolingbroke, that is?"

"Harley's chaplain Willie Stratford once said to me of Mr Secretary: 'He is a sad warning to gentlemen of how little use the greatest parts are to one void of all sense of honor and religion.' And I think that sums it up. Bolingbroke is an unexampled orator. Few men can stand against him in Parliament. He has a world of charm—witness his seduction of Abigail Masham away from her allegiance to Lord Oxford—who is, after all, her cousin. He speaks French exquisitely, even Matt Prior admits, and is a man of great intellectual culture. But he is entirely without morality as far as one can tell. He would betray his own mama without turning a hair."

We stood in Motteux's garden looking at a bed of primroses, the sun slanting down through the trees and illuminating a mossy bust of Flora that stood there on its pedestal.

"So you had better go out of England for a good while, Jack," he said. "For you may be sure that Harry Bolingbroke has been apprised of your meeting with David Nairne at Saint-Germain-en-Laye. Nairne's *huissier*, Arouet, has long been on Bolingbroke's spy-roll—the Blackbird's court can't afford to pay staff much and they must make up where they can. Bolingbroke, you should know, will seek to use you against Harley if he possibly can. Men in your position are helpless against such great ones. Remember the fate of Mr Gregg."

William Gregg, a Scottish undersecretary in Lord Oxford's office had been butchered at Tyburn after having been found guilty of communicating some papers of scant consequence to the French secretary of war. Gregg's pay was little and his family was in great need. The tyrannizing Whig Lords of the Junto examined him and did their best to get him to implicate

Lord Oxford in his treason, but he bravely refused—it would have been a lie—and was hanged and quartered for it.

I'd seen poor Gregg's head spiked at Westminster Hall, much decayed and horrid-looking. Little as I liked to take to my heels yet again, memory of that sight could not but facilitate my departure: I'd best be gone without delay.

But one of my back teeth hurt like the devil and first I needed to see an *arracheur de chicots*—what they nowadays call a "dentist." I had been putting it off, having a great fear of doing so, believing such men to be no better than mountebank torturers, but faced with the prospect of participating in a military campaign, or even a lengthy ocean voyage, I could no longer avoid doing so. I took recommendations from all and sundry, braced myself, and set out to find one.

Toothworms

"I WARRANT you eat a great deal of sugar," said *Signore* Silvio Renzo, the dapper Snow Hill "Operator for the Teeth" (as he styled himself on the signboard affixed to his house) to whom Motteux referred me. "So?" I said. "Who doesn't love sweets, and especially chocolate, anyone eats as much as he can get, but what's that to do with my tooth?"

"Why, it nourishes the worms that are consuming it," he said.

"Worms?"

"Minute microscopical *animalcula*," he said. "Observed by the great Marcello Malpighi, the teacher of my teacher. You can scarce see them unaided they are so small, and they thrive on sugar. Once I've destroyed them with my proprietary fumigant, we'll see if the tooth can be saved. But I most strongly advise you to refrain in future from consuming σάκχαρον in any form, including honey. Or if you do eat some, always to swill your mouth out well afterwards with a cupful of οὖρον."

I could not but recall a proverb they have in France: "He lies like a tooth-puller." If the creatures were feeding on sugar, why should they concern themselves with my choppers? However, one has little option but to bow to the judgment of a professional. Moreover, he clearly saw me for an educated man who knew his Greek, and I appreciated the delicacy of his employing it in this context.

"That of young boys, emitted first thing in the morning, is best in my experience and can be obtained at little cost—indeed *gratis* if you have such lads in your household. One of your people's chiots perchance? I gave the same recommendation to His Grace the Duke of Shrewsbury, and I believe Her Grace Lady Adelaide told it to the Queen herself, who much appreciated it."

Appalled, needless to say, at the notion of Her Majesty adopting so repellent a gargle, I could but stare.

"So I shall first fumigate your dentition, as we call it," Renzo said, very cheerfully. "You know, you really have the most beautiful hair," he added, as he busied himself with pestle and mortar pounding a preparation. "What a pity that this lovely auburn should be hidden under a peruke! But many a fair one must have told you this."

I'd placed my periwig on a form that stood to that end in his examination room, and my head had not been shaved in a fortnight. He reached out and patted my brush ever so lightly.

"Here. Drink this," he said, placing in my hand a cup.

"What is it?"

"Laudanum brandy, with half a drachm of mandragora stirred into it, to relieve you of any discomfort from my operation."

He had laid out on a strip of velvet the tools of his trade— forceps, chisels, scrapers, and another, more frightful-looking device.

"What's that?"

"*That* is what is called a German key, or pelican, for extracting teeth."

"Pelican?"

"So called because its beak"—he tapped it—"is thought to resemble that of such birds. You fix the claw on the tooth, rest the fulcrum—the crescent here—against the gum, and then slowly ease out the diseased fang by turning the screw, here."

He ignited a pinch of stuff from his mortar on a coal of tobacco in the bowl of his pipe (which he had smoked all the while we conversed) and put the stem between my lips, saying, "Draw the smoke into your mouth and hold it there as long as you can; it's henbane and hemlock compounded with onion seed and some other things, my own proprietary mix—fatal to toothworms."

I followed his instruction and presently grew drowsy and fell into what is called a light dog-sleep or cat's-nap. Dozing thus in the chair, I felt no pain, but thought I heard things, although I could not tell what they were, and, it seemed to me, entertained some not unpleasant allusions.

"See," Renzo said, when I awoke, showing a congeries of miniscule wormlike shapes on a piece of black cloth. "Having killed the creatures that were infecting it, I cleansed the cavity they had excavated in your tooth with arsenic and then filled it with an impervious cement. The hurt will cease in a few hours."

I felt a little dizzy, rather as one sometimes feels after being let blood.

"It doesn't pain much. And I am glad that you didn't see fit to venesect me, for I detest a phlebotomy."

"I dislike myself to breathe a vein! When it is necessary, I prefer to use leeches, which can be placed directly on the gum—although one must take care, of course, that the little devils don't make an escape down the patient's gullet."

"Well, thank you, *Signore* Renzo," I said, handing him his fee.

"*Prego, Signore* Turner! And do remember the *gargarisme* I recommend after eating sugar. It's really not unpleasant once you grow accustomed to it."

Unfortunately, no doubt, I ignored this advice, and when we were several months at sea, the same wretched tooth grew painful again, the toothworms having been revived, I suppose, by the treacle water that was our common tonic. Scurvy had loosened it, however, and the bosun of the *Nesserak* yanked it out for me with one quick twist of his powerful finger and thumb. No pelican-wielding alumnus of the University of Bologna, I am sure, could have accomplished it so adroitly.

This was the first tooth I lost, but not the last; and by now, alas, as with all old men, there is many a gap in my poor jaws.

Troppo baddo!

Ysack Dalgú

I T being April and tulip time in the Netherlands, it consoled me to see the glorious show of those charming vegetables. Colonel Chavonnes was mine host's name and he had received me very genteelly in his Amsterdam mansion, which looked out on the Kromboomssloot. I found him there chatting with a group of men, all of them very forceful and outspoken. Among these I was interested to notice Frans Zegers, who had captained the *Troost* on its voyage into the greedy arms of the Algerine corsairs; but being as shy of these smart Dutch Huguenot officers as a crow of gunpowder, I did not at first address him.

Colonel Chavonnes I took to be about sixty. He had the common touch, as they say, and he kindly introduced me to his wife—recognizing me for a gentleman, which I owed to Peter Motteux, whose note I had sent up with a footman. The remarkable name of Madame Pasques de Chavonnes was Balthasarina; apart from that all I recall of her was that her eyes were the color called in Dutch *paars*, and in French *pers*, which to say hyacinth, or violet blue, like those of the goddess Minerva, whose owl so unhelpfully spreads its wings only at dusk. Other than that she was an unremarkable little woman with a pinched face. I suppose she must have been very lovely when young.

"I have a new command," said Frans Zegers when we came to speak. "She's called the *Nesserak*."

"Say what?"

"The name is Syriac and means 'He—God, no doubt—will saw you asunder.' Thus, I believe, the prophet Daniel warns the lascivious Elders in the Book of Susanna."

"'It is a fearful thing to fall into the hands of the living God! They were stoned, they were sawn asunder,' Saint Paul says in his letter to the Hebrews."

"An odd name for a ship, of course. Might as well be called the *Menetekel*, what! Her name was bestowed by one of the Gents XVII, a bloody-minded old Gomarist lord, who apparently has an estate of that wot as well. But she's a beauty, my *Nesserak*, new built just last year at the Amsterdam wharf. They're fitting her out now."

"And where is she to take you to, this *Menetekel* of yours?"

"We sail for Batavia in May. Why don't you come? It's a magic world out there: thousands of islands, each a paradise of its own, each with its spices, never a cold day, blue seas, angel-faced sluts the color of honey, your pockets filled with rijksdaalders . . ."

"And a cruel voyage, cooped up with some hundreds of others in a prison made of wood, which may also serve to drown one, with nothing to eat but rotten meat and nothing to drink but bad water teeming with worms that you must strain through your teeth. Don't they say that a man who has murdered his father and his mother is still too good to be condemned to sail to the Indies! You are indeed inviting me to a Belshazzar's Feast!"

"There are hardships, true. But there are hardships here too." And he added: "If you sail with me, I can offer you your own small cabin and an easy voyage. I shall appoint you my druggerman— you can interpret with the Lusitanians for me, and also with the Moors, should we encounter any—which I pray we do not! For you speak their Arabic tongue, I think you said?"

"I do," I said. "But mostly the language of servitude, since I was a slave to them. And even then they commonly addressed us in the Lingua Franca, which is not the same thing at all as Arabic."

"Be assured in any case that you won't need to play the ape in the rigging. I promise! We have plenty of *adelborsten* for that kind of thing: the *manschap* signed up for the *Nesserak* is one of the best crews I have seen."

"I am pleased to hear it," said I. "For those awful heights up in the topsails scare the *merde* out of me! Frankly, too, my native avoirdupois little suits me to rope-dancing in the yards."

For indeed, England's cakes and ale had rendered me rather robust, and should Sir Godfrey Kneller—*videlicet*, the erstwhile Gottfried Kniller, a Lübecker like me—have stooped to paint my portrait, he might well have flattered me with roguey dimples and double chin, as he did himself, Milords Harley and Bolingbroke, and *tutti quanti*.

"Thou art weighed in the balance, old chap, and found wanting—or should we say, *not* wanting?—too many scruples, what!" he teased inappositely. "Mene, mene, tekel, upharsin! Daniel 5: 26–27, don't you know! You are certainly much fatter than when last we met."

Some people never know when to stop, and Frans Zegers was one.

"A word, Captain Zegers," said Colonel Chavonnes, coming up.

"Of course, sir."

"You sail, I believe, this May 26. Mr Tornator here has applied to me for employment, and Bram van Riebeeck could undoubtedly use a man of his kidney—the Javanese are again getting jiggy [*as always, I do my best to translate*], it seems. Could you undertake to deliver him to the dear G-G [*i.e., the governor-general*] in Batavia?"

"Certainly, sir," Zegers said, clicking his heels with finesse.

"There you are, Mr Tornator! You told me you were available to serve in any capacity, and here is this fine opening in the Indies. Permit me to make some remarks of a historical nature. In 1699, Willem Adrian van der Stel was appointed governor of the VOC station at the Cape of Good Hope. A substantial number of the population subsequently petitioned Amsterdam to protest his abuse of the Illustrious Company's trading monopoly and use of its resources to enhance his own estate. Willem Adriaan was accordingly dismissed in 1707, and Company employees were henceforth prohibited from owning land at the Cape. But many of the signatories of this petition against him were Huguenots, and it is feared, however fancifully, that such former Frenchmen might betray the colony to France. Of course, this is the last thing any Huguenot would do, but appointing a Huguenot governor is the solution hit upon by the Gents XVII, and I am to go out there myself a few months hence in that capacity. Any governor at the Cape must work closely with the administration in the Indies, and I wish to place a man there who knows my mind, and what I think is wanted. I shall instruct you on this in detail in the weeks to come. At Batavia, you will work directly under Governor-General van Riebeeck. You'll find him a very interesting man—a great explorer with a considerable interest in South Africa. He was born at the Cape himself, as it happens, since his own father was the very first Company governor there."

I was filled with joy to learn that I had an official appointment in the Indies.

"It is convenient that you go out with the nominal rank of *adelborst*, but a higher appointment will no doubt soon be forthcoming. In any case, an *adelborst* is whatever his captain, or indeed the governor-general's office, says he is, whether a midshipman, a junior officer in the army, or even a technical expert in some field, such as agriculture. Speaking of which, do you know much about horses?"

"Not much, sir, although I am reckoned a good rider."

"So you are persuaded," said Frans.

"I am persuaded, old mate."

Thus it was that on May 26, 1713, after many an interesting conversation with Colonel Chavonnes, henceforth my spymaster, I went to the recruiting office at the East India House in Amsterdam and made formal application to become an employee of the East India Company. Applicants were taken in batches. "There are so many that men are sometimes crushed to death or have their limbs broken in the scramble to get in," Frans said. And indeed, I saw that some had climbed up to the window above the entrance and hung onto the iron grating until the door was opened, then let go and so were carried in with the press. In a court within, each man in turn was handed a musket and called upon to perform some sergeant's drill, who then made the selection.

In my case, everything had, of course, been arranged in advance, and Captain Zegers was standing right beside me. So for me it was a done deal. Only when the clerk asked my name, I had to think for a moment.

"Isacq. And from Alguer. Let it be that. Write 'Isacq d'Algué,'" I said on inspiration. And in his lovely flowing script the Company pen-pusher carefully entered my new nom de plaisir into his ledger: "Ysack Dalgú, van Holstijn."

You can still see it there today in a ledger at the Dutch National Archives in The Hague.

"Cool name!" said Frans. "I get the 'd'Algué.' But why 'Isacq'"?

"Just a jab at *pater*, who tried to pummel me into a copy of himself—unfair, of course, because the old Procrustes can't counterpunch now—unless from Heaven! But to quote a fellow spirit: 'L'ennui, avec un pseudonyme, c'est qu'il ne peut jamais exprimer tout ce que vous sentez en vous." You'd need to write a book or two for that!"

The Stowaways

L ATER the very same day, to the sound of drums and trumpets—or, to say it in the Dutch, the language I was henceforth to speak, *met het geklank van trommels en trompetten*—I marched with the other recruits to the lighter waiting to carry us to the fleet assembled for the long journey.

Company soldiers were paid 8 or 9 gulden a month. However, being an *adelborst*, I got 10—with two months' salary in advance on signing. I also put my name to a promissory note called a *transportbrief* against a loan of 150 gulden. This was to be repaid by deductions from my pay and served as insurance against shipwreck: for if the ship was lost, all was lost, and in that event, although the Company would stop my salary, neither would I have to pay back the loan.

Normally, until this *transportbrief* debt was paid off, however, a soldier had only his rations and less than a stuiwer and a half a day to live on, from which petty cash he also had to buy his uniform and boots, ribbons to tie his hair, and other kit when replacement was needed. Frans had given me a sea chest, so I had no need to buy one, but I invested some 40 gulden

---

* Romain Gary, *La promesse de l'aube* (Paris: Gallimard, 1960), 22: "The trouble with a pseudonym is that it can never express everything you feel in yourself."

in extra clothing, a hammock, a mattress, a knife, a spoon, a mug, a water bottle, tobacco and pipes, though I did not yet smoke, and a keg of ginger brandy, containing about two and a half gallons, as a specific, with a little metal tube to tap it. I rinsed my throat with a spoonful of this panacea upon arising each day we were at sea, as long as the liquor lasted (which was to about latitude 25° S), and I believe that it preserved both my health and my teeth. Also at Frans's suggestion, I added to these things a supply of gold and silver lace, braid, ribbons, buttons, and pins and needles, all of which, I was assured, could be sold at a very good profit in *de Landen van Overzee*.

No sooner had we set foot on the *Nesserak* than a terrifying change came over my amiable friend Frans. His face set hard and in an icy tone he commenced rapidly to issue commands to all and sundry (myself only excepted), while a set of brutal quartermasters scourged with rope whips they unwound from around their waists any seaman or *adelborst* who delayed for a moment in implementing these orders. Even the master and the boatswain hopped to it. Everything proceeded rapidly, and in a few hours, we were one of an assemblage of ships that were arriving from all directions as the East India fleet got itself together. In the middle distance, I noted a long-boat approaching from the shore, and I stood by the rail observing with interest as it came alongside. A dozen or so ragged little fellows, whose faces seemed curiously pale and drawn for sailors, with cauls pulled down over their brows, came aboard.

"Good, the stowaways are here," said Frans at my back. "Get 'em below, please, why don't you, Jan? Have 'em hang their hammocks in the rear of the canvas wall behind the sick bay on the middle deck. Can you find it? No, of course not. But Mergl will show you." And he grabbed a passing boy by the ear and said: "Show Adelbors Dalgue where the sick bay is, Mergl." And to me: "But the one in the yellow dress goes to my own cabin."

The "stowaways" were waiting in a group with their bundles. Coming up to them with Mergl at my side, I saw that they all appeared to be beardless, and some of them were decidedly plump for boys. And some were clearly farded! I wondered how I should address them. Mergl swiftly resolved this for me.

"Come along, you harlots!" he said, in a deeper voice than I would have expected from one whom I took to be about fourteen. "Come along now, this way!" And to me: "Please, sir, Meneer Adelbors Dalgue, sir, is the sick bay to be the nannyhouse on this voyage?"

"The space behind the sick bay is where they are to go for the moment, I believe. What their further disposition will be, Captain Zegers will decide."

So they were women, presumably whores. I counted a dozen or so misshapen drabs. The thirteenth, who wore a yellow sarsenet mantua under a tattered soldier's cloak, stood out like a tulip in a bunch of turnips, as the expression goes. She was a very fine thing to look at. To my astonishment, even as I took her measure, she came up to me and said in English: "Well, Mr Orion, do you not recognize your Serpentaria?"

I had never looked upon her face, which had been masked with velvet and buckram in our prior encounters, when my own mask had muffled my own nose, and the mal'aria had yet to render it so improbably sensitive. But I instantly knew Zippie *by the vapors of her person*—something between nutmeg and witch hazel, with just a hint of wood sage, impossible to describe: it could no more be told than the hue of a robin's breast or a kingfisher on the wing could be put in words.

"Miss Ardis . . . you are among *them*!"

I felt no horror or contempt, merely pity for the circumstances that must necessarily have reduced her to such a condition.

"But not *of* them. I am she whom you are to deliver to the cabin of Captain François."

"I understand."

"No, you don't," she said. "But he had best explain it to you himself, for your contumely makes me blush."

"I surely did not mean to offend, Madam! Come, Mergl," I said. "Let's disperse these ladies where they must go. Point me first the way to the captain's cabin."

"It's at the stern just back here, sir," he said.

I escorted my whilom love there with as much dignity as I could muster, made her a hasty reverence, then returned to convey the travestied drabs huddled by the starboard rail to their whore's cave behind the sick bay. The surgeon's mate, engaged in honing a blade, looked up with a start, then nodded sagely as though to say, "Them 'stowaways' again!"

When I ascended again to the quarterdeck, the *Nesserak* advanced beneath a bright half moon across a calm sea. The other ships of the spring fleet made a row that stretched far ahead and behind. I was full of rage and wondered why I was so angry.

Frans was strolling to and fro on the quarterdeck with a gratified look on his face. But when I said, "I was already acquainted with Miss Ardis, you know," he frowned.

"How do you come to know her, and by that name?"

"It's how she introduced herself at the Elector's Court in Hannover. What name did she give you?"

"Tijmtje Koekemoer is the name under which I found her in the Spinhuis. She's a German—born Kokemohr, it seems. But she speaks Dutch like a real Amsterdammertje, so I have no idea whether that's true or not. The moment I saw her I loved her. She claims to be from a place called Diepholz in Kursachsen. Ever heard of it?"

"It's quite near Lübbecke. My own folk emigrated from there back in Henry the Lion's day, when the city of Lübeck was founded."

"Perhaps she's a relation of yours!"

"I am beginning to think everyone's a relation of mine. But she told me she was an American."

"Perhaps an American—do they have Kokemohrs there?— but surely no virgin! Damn you, Hans, if you've already thumped that cushion!"

"Désolé, mon ami! But I had no idea when I thumped it that I should one day be so fortunate as to count you my friend. It was, you know, before we ever met aboard the *Troost*."

"My Uncle Braam who's one of the Spinhuis regents said the little Saxon was lucky not to have had her neck stretched and advised that I shun her—a bad lot, he said. I don't know what her crime was in the first place, but she seems to have made a great nuisance of herself in the workhouse—deliberately messed up her spinning and sewing—and the dragon wardresses were quite glad to get rid of her. I had to promise my uncle I'd just keep her for a bit and then peddle her to the Portuguese at São Tiago—they're always wanting blondes, you know—but I'm thinking I might take her on to Batavia with me if she turns out to be handy in the hamacoe. If she cuts up nasty, of course, I can always dump her later at the Cape of Storms. Or in Ceylon."

"So where's São Tiago?"

"Cabo Verde. Portuguese islands where we'll take on food and fresh water. It's our only real stop before we round Africa. After that we follow the Company's 'wagon trail' to the tip of Brazil. But we don't usually make landfall there, just catch the westerlies to speed us back across the Atlantic. It's the best way."

"Frans, since we love each other well, there is something I must tell you. But let me first ask you a question. Have you lain with her yet?"

"Why no, but she has given me every encouragement to think that I may do so soon."

"Then falls upon me the sad duty to tell you this. I swived her myself at Hannover, as she likewise gave me every encouragement to do. But she gave me into the bargain the clap."

"She swore to me that she was pure! Are you quite sure it was she that gave you it?"

"As sure as shit, for she was the first woman I ever fucked, lad that I was, and the *chaudepisse* put in appearance less than a fortnight after. I was so mortified, it was an age before ever I jumped another."

Frans grasped my hands in his and embraced me fondly on both cheeks.

"Dear Hans," said he. "Then I must thank you from the bottom of my heart for telling me this! For I too have had the clap and was cured of it only by having mercury injected into the *pupilla* of my poor yard with a syringe. Pray God I may never have that vile sickness again!"

"If you should," I said knowingly, "don't let the quacks treat you with their damned quicksilver. I myself was completely recovered, I'm glad to say, by freely coating my dick with the fat of a turned-off villain that the Elector's hangman sold me." Wretch that I am, I could not escape this lie, which sprang all unbidden into my throat, as such lies will, as though wanting of its own accord to be vomited up. "The grease must be rendered *alliatum* with a head of garlic, of course. And then one must drink a pint of ginger wine infused with cardamom and cubeb upon rising in the morning and another last thing at night for some weeks. It's not as foul as you might think; slips down awful grateful, in fact, when you get used to it."

"We'd have been wise to have shipped a load of garlic and felon grease then! For damn me if our other 'stowaways' aren't all clapped too! I was obliged to bring 'em you know. Not my idea, but the notion of him who named this vessel—'Meneer *Nesserak*' himself. The Gents XVII want to keep the lads happy in Africa, and there are hardly any spare white women there apart from officers' wives and daughters, so by all means bring some in, even if they are raddled old bags that no one in his right mind would prod with a barge pole. Meanwhile though, what shall we do with the lovely Zipporah or whatever her name is?"

"What is there wiser than kindness? I suppose you must lodge her with the other jades for now and drop her off at Santiago or whatever that place is called."

"To tell the truth I dread telling her this, lying little *levretée* though she be!"

"So have to hand then one of those quartermasters I saw wielding the rope's end to such good effect just after I came aboard."

"Indeed, I have somewhat of an inkling to do so, coward that I am!"

"But pray tell, dear chap, what's a *levretée*?"

"Why, a bitch that has been sarded *en levrette*, of course! Or, to put it in plainer terms, fucked up the arse by a greyhound. I know it's wrong to employ such diction of Zippie, but to tell the truth, I've been wanting to say it ever since I heard it from the captain of the *Meermin*, Coen du Preez—comical swine that he is!"

"Don't you think, Frans, that it's wrong to abuse her?" I said. "After all, we have both loved her, and we must have seen in her something worthy of it. I confess that I even conjectured that I might make her my wife."

He looked at me in surprise.

"But she clapped you! And you have only a minute past advised me to have a quartermaster flog her to the bawdy house!"

"I gave up the idea of marriage to her as soon as I smoked that I had the *chaudepisse*, of course. And I spoke just now in rage, thinking both of that and of you. But the truth is in my heart I wish the girl well. If she has sinned, how much the more have we too sinned in imposing on her in her helpless woman's state?"

"Are you turning parson on me, then? Soon you'll have us down on our knees praying for the jade's salvation."

"I suppose I must have something of the parson in me, being sprung from such a line of 'em. So I say parsonlike, have pity. Don't put her with the whores. For something tells me that she's not one."

"Then must I suffer her in my apartment . . . unfingered?"

"Perhaps I could keep her so with me, if you wish it."

"Your own cabin's a very small one, Hans. Barely a closet! Best I could do for you, the ship's so crowded."

"And I thank you for giving me such room of my own, for in truth I should not wish to lodge with my fellow midshipmen in the common mess. But I think there will be place enough in my little compartment for Zipporah, if that's indeed her name."

"Take care that you do not fare with her as you did before!"

"Have no fear—I am quite resolved to be chaste as a Carthusian. I've learned my lesson after all."

"I warrant it's a lesson many learn quickly and then just as quickly forget! Also, she has yet to agree to be accommodated with you in your cubby."

"I think she will do so rather than go behind the canvas wall down below, where even if she hold aloof, she must hourly be confronted with license and worse."

"No doubt. The men will be hot upon them."

"Let me confabulate with her a little and see what she says."

"Do one thing for me, dear fellow. Do try to smoke whether she's cured of the clap!"

Thus we bandied it to and fro between us, joking licentiously but arguing piously, in our respective Evangelical and Reformed ways (for like most Dutchmen, Frans was a Calvinist) till it was agreed that one of us should wait on the captious minx and discover the plan to her. We drew lots, and it fell to me. Not without trepidation—for in truth the person behind it still strongly addressed my poor heart—I hustled to the oaken door of the captain's cabin at the stern end of the quarterdeck and rapped forcefully upon it.

"Well, if it's not my familiar Hänschen," said she. "I was just stepping out to take the sea breeze at the tafferel. Pray escort me, then!"

And she permitted me to take her arm.

"What's the tafferel?"

"Why my dear lubber, it's the aftermost portion of the poop-rail, of course. What sort of seaman are you that don't know that?"

The Nesserak had a *vuurlantaarn*, or poop-light, hanging astern to mark her for the other ships of the fleet, and we mounted to that, she leading the way.

"A pilot in spite of your bite, Madam," said I. "For I am come to steer you free of the shoal on which you find yourself stranded."

"And what shoal is that, pray?"

"Why it's the captain's hamacoe, a berth you can neither renounce without maddening him, since he believes you to have already committed yourself to it, nor enter into without fatal acclamation—or shall we perhaps call it clapping?—that is sure to surprise him monstrously. In fact, when I hinted to him of such applause, the like of which I have known myself, he swore that he would in that event cheapen you as a whore at Ribera Grande in the Cape Verde Islands, our next port of call. The place was sacked only last year by the famous corsair Jacques Cassard, and the French carried off all their girls, leaving the Diegos horridly short of sluts, however poxy, to keel their pots."

Even by the flickering light of the *vuurlantaarn* I could see that she had turned pale.

"You are very unkind, sir," she said, "to speak to me thus."

"Not nearly as unkind as you were, my dear, to dismiss me with a dysury, which I was only able to cure with the help of the garlicky grease of some poor felon sold me by the Hannover *Henker*"—the white lie clung to my tongue—"and enough ginger wine to make drunk a Jamaican," I said, permitting myself to get somewhat carried away.

"I did not know that you would be clapped," she said. "I did not know then that I had it myself."

"How is that possible?"

"Please, you must believe me! Mr Paisley—he's not really my uncle, you know—raped me in his apartment. I swear I was a virgin before that, pure as the driven snow. I thought it could not count that I had been forced. I *so* didn't want it to count!"

"Did you report this crime to Baron von Görtz?"

"I did. But Paisley had left the electoral court by then and could not be found—it was said that he had gone to Russia— and I had no one to vouch for me. Görtz's footmen put me out on the pavement and told me to get me gone and that I was lucky not to be flogged into the bargain. I was just able to get that serving girl to take a note to you."

"Which you signed under the name of Ardis, asking me to write to you in care of the Grecian Coffeehouse in London. I am told, however, that your name is actually Tijmtje Koekemoer and that you were found by the captain in the Amsterdam Spinhuis, quite a different sort of place!"

"It is true that Ardis is not my name, but a character that Paisley compelled me to assume. Even so, a letter in care of Mr Constantine at Devereux Court would have reached me in the end, for Costa is a friend of mine and knows my aliases. And I did want to see you again. It was only later, after I discovered . . . that I realized that it would all be impossible. But like you, you see, I am cured now!" She almost wailed. "An old *vroedvrouw*—that's a wise woman—doctored me, as she does some of the finest ladies in Holland."

"Very good. But Captain Frans cannot be expected to believe that, and he so orders that you quit his cabin forthwith."

"But what is to become of me on the voyage then? Am I to be put with those horrible drabs again?"

"The captain is not so unkind. He has requested that I take you in. My cabin is very small, but there's room for another hamacoe."

"Oh, Hans," she said, "would you be a saint?"

"I such must be, dear lady, for I can only do this thing if our relations are chaste. You shall henceforth be as a vestal sister to me."

"And our mutual accommodation a nunnery, then—but one that shelters a perpetual fire like any vestal temple, which may perhaps spring up in the weeks ahead?"

"Should any such flame make itself known, let it be quenched forthwith!"

"But why? Have not you and I passed through the same trial, through no fault of our own, and are we not both well again now?"

I did not like to say that I had lost all desire to know her as a female, although feeling a strange, brotherly tenderness for her. So I said: "If we cannot rule over our own carnal forks, we might as well be dead—and so likewise, I think, all crotched creatures born to Original Sin. Reflect on all the sluts and brutes you have seen drawn down to the verge of hell by such lickerish bait."

"But it is great creating Nature itself that bifurcates us," she said. "So how can it be a sin to be so split? Why, surely Our Lord himself was forked!"

"Our Lord surely ascended the Cross a virgin. Let us emulate his chastity as best we can, poor wretches that we are, Fräulein Kokemohr."

"Pray, don't call me that, but rather by my American mother's name that died breeching me, which I prefer."

"And I suppose her sire's name was Ardis?"

"Indeed it was. And her sire's sire who settled in Virginia was a Monsieur Ardois, just as I said."

"So how did you come to be at the Elector's court in Hannover where I found you?"

"You may well ask, and I am happy to tell you. Indeed, it is quickly told," she said.

"I grew up in Ireland, you see, where my father had gone as a captain in King Billy's army, which was mostly Germans and Dutch, as you know, for all the English boast of their victory. He got a pension and a bit of land after King James was defeated. Thereafter we lived in a sort of ruin called Croghan House, from which the Papist owners, named Kinsella, had been expelled.

"Even as a small child, I knew it was a vile, bad place. The street door danced back and forth with all its weight upon the lower, the upper hinge of it being broken, so we were obliged to go out and in at the back door. There was only one chair fit for sitting on, and a great hole in the living-room floor, hazarding a broken leg at every hour. My dad used his great-coat to stop the wind from coming down the chimney, without which we must have died of the cold.

"The old pair of fire tongs was often absent, since it was likewise employed to take meat out of the pot and traveled through the house to that end. The wall of my bed-chamber was full of large chinks, letting in so much wind that it almost blew out the candle. The little table was broken in the joints and in a very tottering condition, and my bed threatened every night to fall under me. Mice made a nest in my dad's tie-wig, and the soles of our shoes were full of holes.

"Mrs Kavanagh, who kept house for us, was a firm believer in the Banshee, or female daemon, which attends on certain ancient Irish families, and, she said, she distinctly heard the Banshee of the Kinsella family wailing in an unpleasant manner beneath the front-facing windows of Croghan on the night we came there. It was no good omen, she said. And so it indeed proved."

"The kitchen was inhabited by savages, and Mrs Kavanagh waged war on a nasty crew of both sexes—arrant thieves as to victuals and drink—to preserve order and cleanliness. The most common necessary utensils were egregiously wanted. Bottles were stopped with bits of wood or tow, instead of corks. The spit was blunted by poking into bogs for firewood and tore our meat to pieces.

"That said, there was scarcely a bit of mutton or beef to be had in the country, and cats passed continually into the cellar and ate what there might be, for which they were sometimes tried, condemned, and executed by the sword at the hand of my brother William, that puppy, who afterwards took up the profession of stand-and-deliver but was hanged at Tyburn before he had got well established in it."

"I am sorry indeed to hear of your brother's misfortune," I said.

"The truth is he was a fool. One day in an old copy of the *Daily Courant* that he got from somewhere or other, he read a letter from a London coxcomb who wrote to the editor: 'It is my misfortune to be six foot and a half high, two full spans between the shoulders, thirteen inches diameter in the calves; and before I was in love, I had a noble stomach, and usually went to bed sober with two bottles. I am not quite six and twenty, and my nose is aquiline, etcetera."

"Despairing for love of a coy Précieuse, the writer desired to know if he might not 'make use of a little force, and put her to the rack and the torture, only to convince her, she has really fine limbs, without spoiling or distorting them.' Why, he asked, should his Platonne 'wish to be a cherubim, when it is flesh and blood that makes her adorable?'

"'Why,' says William, "this bloke's description exactly matches my own, save that I am a few inches shorter, not quite so broad between the shoulders, and confine myself to a single bottle of wine of an evening (or at most a bottle and a half). I am also *bien enjambé*, as the French say, and step out on calves worthy of a first-rate footman, though I should never wish to be one. Then again, I would certainly never 'play the inquisition,' as he puts it, with a lady, and in that sense much his superior. As the poet remarks, an acquaintance with the liberal arts softens men's manners: *Ingenuas didicero fideliter artes emolit mores*, etcetera. All this being the case, why should I too not tease the pretty précieuses at Westminster?'"

"Ah," I said, supposing angrily that she rigmaroled thus to hide falsehood. "A latinist, was he? Alas the more, then, the crime that informed his final declension!"

"Not a very good latinist, as you see. For Ovid writes *didicisse*. I looked it up. William was dissembling, as usual. I do believe he dissembled his way into the grave, for he told such tales at his trial that no one believed him.

"After my father died of a quinsy, Croghan House and its attachments were swiftly claimed by his creditors, the chief of whom turned out to be a cousin of Mr Paisley, whom you met with at Herrenhausen."

"I never actually saw him," I said.

"William and I were put out in the street to starve—I do believe the papist Irish servants would have liked to throw us into the water like so much rubbish. But Pat Paisley took a fancy to me and offered to send me to his uncle, then in London, saying he thought I might be of some service. For, he said, flotsome, jetsome, and lagan, such as you are, you know, belong to His Majesty. Being but an ignorant little girl at the time, I did not smoke what monarch he meant and thought foolishly that I might become a maidservant in a palace. It did not occur to me that there was no king in London at that time but rather a queen."

"The viper clearly misinformed you on more than one count," I could not help remarking. And I impertinently added: "But had you a better grasp of the law it would not have escaped you that such goods of the sea as flotsome, jetsome, and lagan have since the Glorious Revolution been perquisites rather of the Lord High Admiral."

"Pish! There's no need to be so saucy and pragmatical with me!" she said. "Why should a girl have any knowledge of nautical law?"

"So," I said. "Thus it was that you fell into the grasp of the Pretenderists."

"Thus it was," she said.

And in the weeks that followed, we continued to banter our histories back and forth, being in very good humor with each other. Our hamacoes were slung side by side in the narrow space allowed them, and we had to measure our movements very carefully so as not to impede one another.

Frans decreed that for the sake of suitability, it would be best if Zippie should dress as a male, though the *manschap* knew, of course, that she was not. She was given the clothes that had belonged to a little adelborst who had tumbled to his death from the rigging, not being properly instructed in how to handle himself when up in those airy regions.

She always behaved very properly with me, and sought no special treatment by reason of her sex. Only, she begged me, that I would stand watch while she made use of the head in the officers' roundhouse, which we both had access to, and see to it that no man intruded on her there. This I very cheerfully did whenever it was required of me.

When they came on deck, the nannyhouse trulls made no pretense of being other than they were. They had shuffled off their drag and farded their phizzes; several now wore tabby mantuas. But they simply hiked up their skirts to use the common seats of ease, much as any sailor might drop his pants. Some of them had no doubt been born to such ways, and the rest learned them by example. Zippie thought it disgusting, and so did I. But what else, after all, were these hapless females to do? As were we, they were travelers on the *Nesserak* and could not get off until she arrived somewhere.

Cabo Verde

OUR first landfall was at Cape Verde, which we reached almost exactly a month after departing the Texel. By this time, we had need to replenish our stock of fresh food and also to take on water for the long voyage ahead, which was to be uninterrupted until we reached the southernmost tip of Africa. Since the Portuguese, who had held these islands for centuries, were now allies of the United Provinces, they were habituated to such provisioning. Meanwhile, a Portuguese gentleman sight-seer came aboard to examine us, accompanied by a black papist priest, Father Franciscus, who told me that he was the child of aboriginals of the Portuguese territory of Angola, who had come to that island as slaves. Since we had no other language in common, our conversation was entirely in Latin: the good father interpreted the remarks of the Portuguese official to me, while I interpreted those of our captain to him. Brandy and Dutch cheese were served, both of which this priest consumed in astounding quantities, then fell to singing and dancing in the manner, he said, of the land of his ancestors, while his Portuguese companion gazed on with some equanimity, as one to whom such show had grown tedious. I for my part did not know whether to be more amazed at a black man speaking the language of Vergil and Tully so fluently or at a man of the cloth, even a black one, playing the jackanapes in this fashion.

Captain Frans had meanwhile sent gifts of Dutch manufacture to the governor, requesting that we be allowed to seek the provisions we needed among the populace. This agreed, we found ourselves able to trade such commonplace things as hats, sheets, and stockings, of which we had a good stock, for what we most wanted: bullocks, pigs, and goats were cheap, and fat chickens sold for pennies. These animals were then taken aboard the ship and confined in pens that had been prepared for them, while hay and straw in great quantity for their food was put into the hold with the great cannon balls.

I myself traded a packet of pins for a thousand lemons, and in exchange for a bit of braid, the sellers agreeably pressed the juice from them into a large wine jar, on top of which I had them pour a quarter of an inch of olive oil as a seal. This jar I carried to my cabin and took care to secure in a chest, well bundled in straw to preserve it from breakage. I also obtained from the Cape Verdeans a great bag of oranges, as well as some strange fruits called papayas and bananas, which they pressed on me as gifts. These I presented to Zippie, whom Frans had obliged to remain on board. She liked the papayas but thought the bananas insipid; for me it was rather the other way round.

"Lemon juice," I said, when she asked what was in the jar I had so carefully put away. "It's medicine for a sickness called in Dutch the *scheurbuik*, or 'gut ripper,' which commonly afflicts those who voyage into the high and low latitudes. The English name it 'scurvy,' and the Portuguese *escorbuto*. It rends apart not only a man's belly but every other part of him too, causing his teeth to become loose and fall out of his gums and his body to blacken and shrivel up, while he is overcome with a dreadful weakness that almost mimics death and quickly leads to it. Eugalenus writes in his *De Scorbuto morbo liber* that it is God's chastisement of us for our sins, but that seems absurd to me, since the Algerines, who sometimes sail as far as Iceland on their raiding expeditions, ward it off by sucking lemons. They even oblige their slave oarsmen to do so, on whom they depend to row their xebecs and thus wish to keep in good health. Divine retribution could hardly be so handily averted. Here, try one."

I give her a lemon from my bag, and biting into it, she pulled a face.

"I've never tasted something so sour," she said. "I shouldn't wish to drink it."

"I hope nonetheless that you will do so. As they say, strong physic bites bitterest!"

Alas, she stubbornly refused to take it, as I did each morning, but I did obtain sauerkraut for her to eat from a barrel in the galley, which is also one of the best remedies, if not so good as lemon juice, and she did eat that. Our food was otherwise mostly grits (cooked with prunes), dried peas and beans, and salt fish and flesh.

"If I could do anything for you, what should I do?"

"Persuade Frans that I am cured of the clap," she said. "Just think you what it is like for one who had supposed—supposes—herself to be a lady to bear such a blot!"

Bargemen

I HAD told Frans about the advantages of lemon juice, and he had obtained a supply for his own use. But the rest of our crew did not have it, and as we sailed on southwards, they increasingly fell victim to *scorbutus morbus*. Their gums swelled and rotted, their teeth tottered in their mouths, their breath reeked filthily, their bones ached, their skins grew black, and they gradually lost all power of movement. Long-healed wounds broke open and bled, and broken bones rejoined years before again unknitted themselves. It seemed as though the very cement that held the body together was dissolving. The ship's doctor treated the sick furiously with oil of vitriol, but to scant effect. Soon it seemed that scarcely a day passed without a corpse being flung into the waves. No one was well, save perhaps for our captain himself, who strode about the *Nesserak* as firmly as ever, and the younger midshipmen, who seemed to bear up better against the scurvy.

Supplies of food and water steadily diminished. The ship's biscuit was from the start infested with small brown beetles and their grubs, which were bitter, and cold, fat white maggots that the *manschap* ingeniously called *binnenschippers*, or "in-skippers," because they are found inside hardtack. The English sailors' name for them (translated, as usual, from the Dutch) is "bargemen."

Four months out, what water remained had become very foul. You held your mug in one hand, pinched your nose with the other, and then drank carefully through your clenched teeth to keep from swallowing the worms that teemed in it. Somehow you got used to it. Beer and wine had run out, and there was only a faint slosh of brandy left in the bottom of my little keg.

Though she swallowed the sauerkraut I commanded to be served to her, and I got her to take the sunlight and breathe fresh air on the deck every day, poor Zippie was steadily weakening. She was a little thing. Her lungs had never been well since a child. She got drenched in a sudden squall one day, and she died—just like that, as so many die.

The angel Thanatos sometimes comes quietly, unexpectedly, gently, with a faint fluttering of wings, like a bird in the forest. So it was in these remote seas with my Zippie. One moment she was there, the next she was gone, who knows where, leaving behind only the frail remnant of flesh and bone of which she no longer had need, that was no longer her, that the sea would take into itself on the morrow. Like incense smoke floating away above an altar. So quickly we vanish.

No doubt you are surprised at this turn of events—and so was I! There in the midst of the endless southern ocean, where the sky was now lightening toward morning, my thoughts ran on, yes, I am ashamed to say, even to a muttering of "Et in Arcadia ego"—remembering as you may guess Poussin's painting of the shepherds of Arcady discovering their tomb in the shrubbery.

Which I had seen at Chatsworth House in Derbyshire, where I was one time a guest of Billy Cavendish, the second duke.

[*Admit it, you puppy: his lordship did not so much as know you were there!*]

Seeing my misery, the ship's surgeon, Mr Coleridge, a Devonshire man, came to my elbow and drew my attention to a flock, if such be the term, of dolphins, dark gray, with flashes of white beneath their fins, that played silkily in the lee of the ship.

"Look! Are they not beautiful? O happy living things!"

"They are, Sam," I said. And I swore I'd be true to her.

The *Nesserak*'s sibylline name thus proved itself a prophecy, a true oracle: my heart was sawed in pieces. Thus it is that from time to time in the midst of our impertinencies, God lets us glimpse that there is indeed a plan—*must* be a plan, however incomprehensible to us—behind the workings of the world.

So, at least, I foolishly reasoned.

As I leaned back against the varnished taffrail, Proverbs 30:15–16 sprang to mind: "There are three things that are never satisfied, yea, four things say not, It is enough: The grave; and the barren womb; the earth that is not filled with water; and the fire that saith not, It is enough."

But what the hell did that mean? And why did I think of it?

The dawn, I noticed, had just broke. Addressing a wordless prayer to the Erinyes, those vengeful Furies, who, Homer tells us, exact retribution from men who have sworn falsely, I went and poured a bucket of seawater over my head, shook myself like a dog, and felt a bit better. Life went on. Zippie would surely forgive me for making plans.

The Mountain

W E'D long by then passed the tip of Brazil, glimpsed only as a faint line in the distance as we tacked southwest. Somewhere in the midst of that endless sea, with the stars of the Southern Cross blazing us on our way, I lay on the poop deck and gazed at the sky. The loud, slow creaking of the ship's timbers was the only sound. My brain swam in confusion, and I silently reiterated to myself those lines of Matt Prior's:

> Reading ends in melancholy,
> Wine breeds vices and diseases,
> Wealth is but care, and love but folly.
> Only FRIENDSHIP truly pleases:
> My wealth, my books, my flask, my MOLLY,
> Farewell all, if FRIENDSHIP ceases.

Words Matt wrote for Jack Cromwell, whose voice was so high and clear you would have sworn it was a woman's.

When they tipped her small, shrouded form into the waves next morning, like so many others, I looked away, far up at the foretops and further yet to the blue sky way above them; but gaze as I might, I could not help hearing the splash.

Gradually, the pain of this loss eased a little. I myself was well enough in body, but I thought I might be driven mad by the tedium of the voyage. The world seemed to me like a puppet show, and myself a puppet with the rest. I had begun to see things out of the corner of my eye that could not be there. More than once as I lay there I distinctly thought I glimpsed the embroidered slipper, with its upward-curving toe, of the bosun of the *Ghazi*—but had not TF gut-stabbed the Greek dog and shoved him overboard with the tip of his sword two years before?

Then again I closed my eyes and clearly saw my mother's face stooped over a steaming vessel in the kitchen at the parsonage in Grube, or some other kitchen, perhaps, such as that in the house of my brother Thomas Heinrich at Grömitz, where I supposed her now to be. She was turned away from me, and I could not make out her familiar features, but I knew it was her, and I was as unreasonably cheered by this domestic vision as I was dismayed by the slipper of the slave-driving Greek, whose lash had left scars still to be found on my shoulders. Why should I see his foot as I had so often flinched from it on the gangway beside me but not his hateful yellow eyes and fish-gaff nose? Why should I see my mother's blackened kettle and not her dear lineaments? These are questions for Providence and I cannot answer them.

I could hear music too. And it was not the music of the sea but that of a mighty organ, such as Master Buxterhude played in the Marienkirche. The sound swelled above the firmament, as though it descended from the stars; it penetrated everything—I could feel it on my skin, and almost see and taste it. Something moved me to stand up, which I did with difficulty, almost tripping over my own feet, stumbling this way and that, reaching for support to the nearest limb of the ship, as though to a living being, to the tree in some northern forest of which it had once formed part. Once up, starting slowly, I dumbly danced, a wooden sort of Punchinello dance, such as I had seen at Covent Garden. Meanwhile, the spray of the sea too made itself felt, and the taste of its salt, which coated my lips and slipped into my throat. All my five senses seemed to unite into one.

Dawn was breaking. I might write like Homer of the sun's rose-red fingers awakening the wine-dark ocean but that's not how it was for me. I was too little well, too punch-drunk with hunger to take any mental note of that sunrise, perhaps the most important of my life. In short, I can't remember how it was. It just was. And in the remote distance I picked out the blue-mauve bulk of a great flat-topped shape on the horizon.

"The mountain!" I yelled. "I see the mountain!"

"Congratulations!" said Frans behind me. "The first man on a Company ship to spot the *berg* always gets a couple of rijksdaalders as a reward, along with a rehoboam of wine, which last he is expected to share with those of his shipmates still standing. And *everyone* gets a *dop* of brandy. But I think we'll wait until we have dropped anchor and had a bite of fresh food before serving it out. Too many of us are on our last legs."

A few hours later, I saw a covey of watercraft bobbing around us in a deep green sea, from which brown-skinned slaves (as I later discovered them to be) offered a foretaste of the good life to come in the new land: to the famished they held up fresh manchet bread, broiled sheep's heads, roasted fowl called penguins, which we now saw for the first time (and which tasted to me like swan basted with whale oil), pickled and fried fish of many kinds, giant crevice lobsters (*kreeft*) and several kinds of huge periwinkle or sea snail (*alikreukel, perlemoen*), both boiled and eaten with butter, as well as apricots, peaches, onions, and other fruits and green vegetables.

The date was November 8, 1713.

Filled with an indescribable joy, I steadied myself for what I knew must surely be the best meal I would ever eat. And the water! They scooped mugfuls of the lovely fresh clear water from barrels and held them out to us, knowing full well that every man of us would want that first, above all things, and laughing at our measureless appetite, for almost all of us, I think, slavered shamelessly as they swarmed up the ropes bearing these delights.

"Don't eat too much!" shouted our captain. "You'll be sorry if you do!"

He had the quartermasters stand ready to separate the crew from the vendors, but not even their rope's-ends could hold back the mob.

The mountain and the new land loomed ahead. My destiny, I thought, will emerge from this world, shaped by the hand of God, as the form in the rock under the sculptor's chisel. Once I had thought that I might make of myself an Englishman, but now I was content to be nothing and await what I might become. For, although nothing, I knew myself to be, as Godfrey William liked to say, *phenomenon bene fundatum*, which is to say, patient hearer, "a well-founded phenomenon."

So ended the first part of my life, and the rest began.

Wriggling Out of It

I might indeed have wished the novel of these times to have had a better dénouement; but perhaps it is not finished yet. . . . Our Lord God might . . . still add a few volumes to his novel, so it may turn out better in the end. Letting everything fall into a hopeless muddle and then unexpectedly wriggling out of it is one of the novelist's best tricks . . .

　　　　—Gottfried Wilhelm von Leibniz to the novelist Duke Anton Ulrich von Braunschweig und Lüneburg, April 26, 1713

STEPPING off the longboat, I saw before me a village of a few hundred houses, built of brick, mostly one-storeyed, and thatched with reeds. The settlement's main structure was the pentagonal Vauban-inspired Castle, and it was to this that we proceeded, entering through the gateway onto a mustering ground or square, across which paraded a bird of monstrous appearance. I estimated it to stand several feet taller than myself. Since none of us ever having seen an ostrich before, we gazed at it open-mouthed, provoking a hearty round of laughter from the sentries.

An elegantly dressed gentleman approached us and said: "Is there one here named Tornarius?" Although I had last seen him when I was only twelve years old, I recognized by the cut of his jib, so distinctive in that family, one Johannes Blanckenberg, the son of Conrad Gottfried Blanckenberg, *pastor primarius* of St. Nicolai in Berlin, Uncle Augie's spiritual father. Blanckenberg I knew had emigrated around 1700, doubtless on account of some faux pas, to the Cape. He was accompanied today by a young man of more modest appearance.

Since none of my party knew me as Hans Tornator, save only Captain Frans, who had gone to meet with the governor, I went up to Blanckenberg and said quietly, "We last saw each other when I was just a boy, Hans. You should address me now by my VOC name, Isacq d'Algué."

He looked at me impassively and said, "Isacq, old chap! Good to see you! Your Uncle Augie wrote word through my dad that you were coming, and since your wretched tub was so long in getting here, it arrived before you did, three weeks ago, aboard Captain Felkin's *Nightingale*, out of London."

For one coming from that wild, that godforsaken sea, the Company's Garden, to which Blanckenberg now led me was the more wonderful in that it lay in a place so utterly dry and stony, beneath the horrid and frightening mountain. We walked amid delightful arbors beside a rustling streamlet, and looked with delight on apple, pear, cherry, peach, orange, lemon, and pomegranate trees. One may walk everywhere one wishes but picking even the smallest flower or fruit is strictly forbidden, and the garden slaves keep watch and report such thefts, which are rigorously punished. I had plucked a fine Bon-Chrétien pear, and on Blanckenberg's advice, I slipped a stuiwer to a slave that saw me do it to purchase his silence. These slaves are Muslims, brought here from the Indies, but he did not understand my Maghreb Arabic, let alone "la Franque," the Lingua Franca of Algiers. Here at the other end of Africa, master and slave more commonly communicate in pidgin Portuguese.

Admiring the garden, too, was a French Jesuit, Père de Tachard, who had come to the Cape to observe the moons of Jupiter from there and recalculate its longitude. He kindly invited me to see his twelve-foot telescope and the pendulum clocks he had brought with him, which were, he said, of Christiaan Huyghens's design.

Blanckenberg was himself the son of an Evangelical pastor, and like me he had grown up singing in a church choir. He presently brought me to a supper with his friends, after which there was a fine music of voices and instruments, and Blanckenberg sang an arioso composed by Johann Sebastian Bach, the brother of the oboist who had played at that fatal duel at Wismar. They kindly invited me to sing too, and although I protested my poor voice, would brook no refusal. I knew no Bach or Lully, so gave them "Bannisons la mélancholie" instead, which I had learned to sing with Matt Prior and Peter Motteux. Afterwards, I had occasion to tell the company of my acquaintance with GW, in whose philosophy all were most interested but not persuaded that the world could be reduced to perfect infinitesimals and yet turn out for the best.

I had, I began to see, come to a very civil place.

My way was greatly eased by fortunate acquaintance. Johannes Rhenius, an officer of the garrison, and a Holsteiner himself, introduced me to Peter Robberts, who was from Neustadt, a place nearby Grube where I was born. Barend and Willem, the Cape-born sons of Robberts's late brother-in-law, a Lübeck man, as it happened, also welcomed me as their parent's compatriot and asked me to go with them to hunt elephants, rhinoceroses, and hippopotamuses in the Swartveld (but we never had the luck to meet with any of these and had to content ourselves with some springboks, a kind of antelope).

When Maurits Pasques de Chavonnes arrived to assume his post as governor a few months later, he immediately set about overhauling the overall military posture of the colony and put me to work supervising the building of a new sixteen-gun battery commanding the roadstead. Chavonnes's nephew, Dominique Pasques de Chavonnes, now became commander of the Cape garrison and thus my superior.

In 1715, I was appointed messenger of the court at Stellenbosch, about thirty miles east of the Castle, and the following January, I married my lovely Sarie—Sara van Wyk, sweet sixteen, the daughter of Arie van Wyk, that swag-bellied Stellenbosch burgher.

Then came our sons and daughters, whose children will people this wilderness: Johannes Frederik, Johannes Augustus, Sara, Thomas Frederik, Andreas, Anna Cornelia.

> Bannisons, bannisons, bannisons la—
> Bannisons la mélancholie . . .

From the Laubschers' at Oranjezicht, with its view of the Orange bastion of the Castle, I repaired to my bog-house. I had a vivid strong recollection of dear TF saying, as he used to like to say, "I go now to purge my inwards," in the Jack, or the House of Office, whichever term came to his wits at that moment.

Ours was a good clean one, with hardly any scent at all of excrementitious stagnations, serving now as it did only the wife and myself—and sons, if any showed up, that is, which they did seldom enough. Customers employed the pub privy, and slaves, of course, the common green *latrina* that dresses the mountain.

[Ah, well, he is doubtless gone from this vale of tears now, dear TF, like so many others. In any case, I shall not look upon his likes again. That's the worst of being an old man. All your dear friends are dead, or lost forever, and the young ones will not be friends with

you, not even if they would, as some pretend, out of charity I suppose and Christian kindness.]

I did the needful with some dried leaves of *varkoor,* the plant called pig's ear, from the garden, my favored *torchecul,* since it is reputed an excellent preventative of piles, thinking with a grin to myself as broad as Gargantua's, of this passage, which I had read in the English translation by my dear friend Mr Motteux:

> *I wiped me with sage, with fennel, with anet, with marjoram, with roses, with gourd-leaves, with beets, with colewort, with leaves of the vine-tree, with mallows, . . . with lettuce, and with spinach leaves. . . . Then with mercury, with parsley, with nettles, with comfrey. . . . in the sheets, in the coverlet, in the curtains, with a cushion, with arras hangings, with a green carpet, with a table-cloth, with a napkin, with a handkerchief, with a combing-cloth. . . . Yea, but, said Grangousier, which torchecul did you find to be the best? I was coming to it, said Gargantua, and by-and-by shall you hear. . . . I wiped myself with hay, with straw, with thatch-rushes, with flax, with wool, with paper. . . .*
>
> *. . . with a kerchief, with a pillow, with a pantoufle, with a pouch, with a pannier, . . . with a hat. Of hats, note that some are shorn, and others shaggy, some velveted, others covered with taffeties, and others with satin. The best of all these is the shaggy hat. . . .*
>
> *. . . I wiped my tail with a hen, with a cock, with a pullet, with a calf's skin, with a hare, with a pigeon, with a cormorant, with an attorney's bag, with a montero, with a coif, with a falconer's lure. But, to conclude, I say and maintain, that of all torcheculs, arsewisps, bumfodders, tail-napkins, bunghole cleansers, and wipe-breeches, there is none in the world comparable to the neck of a goose, that is well downed, if you hold her head betwixt your legs. . . . And think*

not that the felicity of the heroes and demigods in the Elysian
fields consisteth either in their asphodel, ambrosia, or nectar,
... but in this, according to my judgment, that they wipe their
tails with the neck of a goose, holding her head betwixt
their legs, and such is the opinion of Master John of Scotland,
alias Scotus.

And so came out of the bog-house with a silly smile on my face at the thought, happier than I went in, Rabelais' masterstroke being in my opinion the attribution of this recommendation to Duns Scotus, the *Doctor Subtilis*, who proved by his teaching of haecceity, or quiddity, or "thisness," that everything is what it is and not another thing [*an idea later taken up, says the unborn ghost backstage, by Bishop Butler, Heidegger, and Wittgenstein*].

I used to pay attention to such stuff when I was young and sat at the feet of my master GW.

But now I concern myself only with particular things. Whenever I am troubled by vicious humors about the state of the world and feel my virtue getting the better of me, I just take a strong laxative and relieve myself of it by a purge. All desire to reform mankind disappears with a good cleansing of the viscera. There is no better remedy for that spurious species of godliness.

I should have gone to see Asahel off, though, I thought. He might have liked a friendly face, if at such times you notice any face but that of the executioner raising his cudgel over you as you lie shackled to the wheel in expectation of that first mighty blow, how it smashes down, and after that you surely notice nothing at all but agony, unless fortunate enough to have been wacked unconscious, on the first stage of your passage to the *pays noir*.

No, I can't stand it any more. My stomach has become sensitive, shifted up toward the heart, as they used to say on the old *Nesserak*, unlucky ship that brought me here (reported sunk on its second voyage out from the Texel), but a good enough berth for me and Zippie in those days.

Asahel! What a sentimental fool I've become. I never knew him, and just because by some accident he was the spit and image of the Prince-Elector whose life I once saved—or I *think* I saved, anyhow—calling me back to my young years, where one likes to be called, is no reason to suppose any tie between us.

Walking on the mountain slope one day musing to myself, I found myself confronted again with the black Travancore *tovenaar*. He greeted me courteously.

"Asahel is no more—*capot*," he said.

"It's the law, you know," I said.

"You Europeans and your law govern here now," he said. "You possess many strong things: not only horses and guns, but paper, money, calendars, clocks, tobacco, brandy, computers. Great is their power. But one day their power will end too, as all things end."

"So you say."

"It is now the year 1752, and the Sooterkins, as you call 'em, have been masters here for a hundred years already. God will give 'em three hundred more perhaps, give or take a few. Then they will drown."

"I'm not English," I said. "Call me rather an Unkraut. That's all I have to say for myself. *Ich will nicht mehr in reden und geberden!*"

But how on earth did he know of Sooterkins, my English term for the Dutchmen, which I used with no one here—not even Sara—but myself?

"Drown in what? The sea?"

"In the great ocean of slaves," he said. "Because then everyone will be a slave, even the Sooterkins."

"That will be in the year 2052," I said. "Who can imagine such a thing! Surely the Last Judgment will have come before then, Old Mar!"

"Perhaps then," he said. "Perhaps that is when it will come. Who knows!" He grinned, always a startling thing in an elderly man, especially a black one with few teeth left in his head. "By the way, I am no longer Mar Bartolomeo. I am changing my name and my profession."

"And what is your new name and business?"

"I haven't picked 'em yet," he said. "For now, I have no name, no office. Perhaps I'll call myself Twijfelaar—He who doubts—and set up as a Doubter." I could see the old devil was laughing at me. "Or I'll borrow your own former name and become a 'D——.' Will you give it me? It seems you have no more use for it. Bart D——. It has a ring to it, don't it?"

"Sure," I said. "Take it for you! The more of us the merrier."

Again I wondered: How could he know these things about me? Was I asleep and dreaming this whole conversation?

"But in fact perhaps I'm done with names," Old Mar said. "I'm sick of 'em, to tell the truth, and sick of time too. I'm old. The only time left to me is just enough time to die in."

"Godfrey William—a philosopher I knew long ago—used to say that what we call 'time' is nothing but a way of measuring certain mathematical relations among the things we suppose it to contain. As too is what we call 'space.' Time and space are not real in 'emselves. So we can only know 'em by their contents. And to know their contents we must name and number things."

"That's your great white way," he said. "Naming and numbering, naming and numbering, naming and numbering. Don't you ever tire of it?"

He was right impertinent for a black midget, I thought, but recognizing that the Latin we spoke put us on an equal footing,

I tolerated it. Such is the power of the learned language! Even a murderer, if he knew it, could escape hanging in England (as Ben Jonson once did). *Legit ut clericus*, the London lawyer would tell the judge: He reads like a priest. And the prisoner at the bar would prove it by reading (or perhaps reciting, all the while reverently holding the Good Book upside down) Psalm 50 from the Vulgate: *Miserere mei, Deus, secundum misericordiam tuam*—"Have mercy upon me, O God, after Thy great goodness."

"Why is there something rather than nothing? That is the great question, Godfrey William used to say."

"Why that's easily explained," said the ex Mar. "A child could answer it. Nothing is *no thing*. It doesn't exist. It is nowhere, and in no time at all. So if anything exists, it can only be in the shape of *something*. Doesn't your Aquinas teach that matter cannot exist without form?"

Our philosophizing being soon enough exhausted, he proceeded down the path on his way. Standing there after he had left me, I mused a bit on dying, which must soon be my lot now too. Van Goens was younger than me, I recalled, and a paralytical palsy had brought him to his grave in a fortnight.

In any case, I consoled myself that I had done as well as most and better than many in this *labyrinthus lacrimarum*. My six children all lived and thrived, except the pig-headed Johannes Frederik, the eldest, who had found no better thing to do in the world, alas, than to be a bookkeeper in the slaughterhouse!

Johannes Frederik aside, I am on excellent terms with all of our boys. Johannes Augustus is negotiating to buy a fine farm near Riebeek Kasteel—he'll be a rich man one day. Thomas Frederik's doing well too, and Andreas—he's the finest silversmith there is here at the Cape. And the girls, Sara and Anna Cornelia, should soon make good matches.

Sara will surely marry that ingenious Hessian Jan Bresler, a man I like, who does such fine carpentry work and is both master pyrotechnist and a member of the fire brigade. And our Antje is walking out with a fine Amsterdammer, Casparus van Eerten.

And my surviving brothers and sisters? Thomas Hinrich had three sons at Grömitz, where he was pastor and consistorial assessor, but I shall doubtless never meet them. Our sister Adelheit married the mayor of Neustadt in Holstein and had a couple of daughters—same there. Uncle Augie's son Gotthilf August succeeded him as director of the Franckeschen Foundations in Halle. TF and Ziza had sons, that I know, because someone told me, and there are surely young Thomas Frederiks and Zizas in Alguer and Sassari today—they'll be handsome too if anything like their parents. Dan'l had sons, of course, and so did Peter Motteux, but I know nought of them. Godfrey William had no children—he was never a man for the ladies in that way, though he preferred them as interlocutors, and he did not care to marry, it seems.

It's an odd thing, but the greater you are in the world, the unluckier you are in your offspring. King William had no children from Queen Mary. Queen Anne's issue were all stillborn or died young. The Blackbird's son is a sot, though called the "Bonnie Prince." Great Peter of Russia had the tsarevich Alexei thrashed to death, believing him a traitor. And poor old Lewis Baboon lived to see all his children and grandchildren die of disease—only one poor little *marmot* was left out of the lot—the future King Louis XV, *le bien aimé,* "the well-beloved" as he's called. Marlborough's sons, too, both predeceased him, the first as an infant and then Jack, marquis of Blandford, at fifteen, of the small pox, just when he was getting set to go soldiering in Flanders like his dad.

Feeling distinctly queerish, I went to sit down on a boulder. Suddenly, like a flash of lightning, it came to me, and I *knew* with some pleasure who and what I was: why, *no thing at all!* And with that I toppled forward, and hit the ground with a resounding smack (I heard but did not feel it), thinking at the last, to my distinct amusement . . . *incognito finito!*

[*When Marlborough was expiring of an apoplexy, Sarie, they say your namesake Duchess Sarah had fetched from Nîmes in France a basket of vipers, it being thought a broth of which might save him. The recipe's in a book you'll find on the little shelf in the boggard by the heap of* varkoor *leaves,* Nouvelles expériences sur la vipère . . . et les remèdes exquis que les artistes peuvent tirer du corps de cet animal, *published at Paris,* Chez l'auteur, au faux-bourg Saint Germain, ruë des Boucheries, prés du Petit Marché, et Olivier de Varennes, au Palais, dans la gallerie des prisonniers, au Vase d'or, *MDCLXIX (1669). But let me write it out for you here too:*

Take eight or ten large vipers alive, chop off their heads, skin them and gut them and cut them in pieces about two inches long. Stew them, with their hearts, with white wine, salt, pepper, and mace or nutmeg to taste. Best drunk piping hot.

You can't get Nîmes vipers here, of course, but should I ever have the misfortune to be so palsied, dear heart, do stew some puff adders for me—those fat stippled snakes that bask in the sun on the rocks there by the stream. There are enough of them on the mountain! Have Philander find them for you and get Rosetta to cook them in some of that nice Picpoul de Pinet that Jean-Baptiste sold us.]

* * *

But what fools we all are! As old Epictetus says, all men who are not wise are mad. He was a slave too, you know, Sarie. His name in Greek means something like "More Property." But when he spoke, emperors paid attention. Let's have a bottle on it! Bannisons la mélancholie!

[You've had far too much already as usual, my old treasure, Sarie said. Why don't I get the girl to bring the coffee pot instead?]

My dear husband died peacefully on April 6, 1759, at six o'clock in the afternoon, aged seventy years, three months, and six days. I, Sara d'Algué, daughter of Arie van Wijk and Cornelia Helm of Stellenbosch, have made this book from the stories he told me and papers I found lying around the house. All true, every word, Jannie said. Even those backstage family spirits, he really heard them! But believe what you will.

Kyrie, eleison! Christe eleison!